NEVER KISS A GOAT ON THE LIPS

NEVER KISS A GOAT ON THE LIPS

THE ADVENTURES OF A SUBURBAN HOMESTEADER

BY VIC SUSSMAN

Rodale Press, Emmaus, Pa.

Printed in the United States of America on recycled paper, containing a high percentage of de-inked fiber.

Library of Congress Cataloging in Publication Data

Sussman, Vic S
Never kiss a goat on the lips.

1. Country life—Maryland—Potomac. I. Title.
S521.5.M3S97 975.2'84 80-39485
ISBN 0-87857-346-1 hardcover
ISBN 0-87857-347-X paperback

2 4 6 8 10 9 7 5 3 1 hardcover
2 4 6 8 10 9 7 5 3 1 paperback

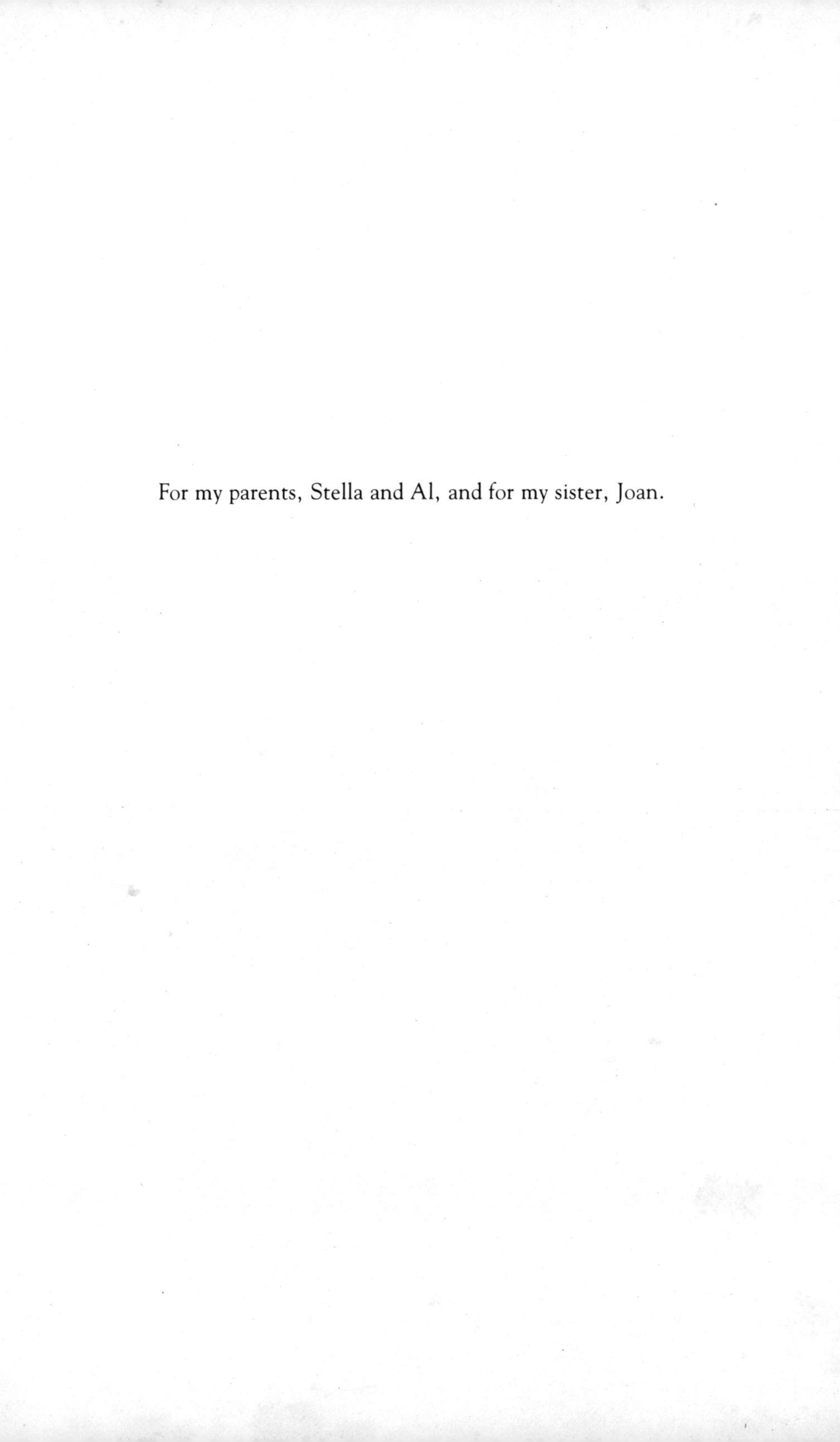

For my parents, Stella and Al, and for my sister, Joan.

Acknowledgments

Writers traditionally drive their families, friends, and editors crazy. Lord knows that's one tradition I've adhered to. So let me offer thanks to some special people:

First and foremost to Betsy Millmann Sussman, for enduring me, for loving me, and for sticking with me through yet another ordeal by verbiage. Thanks also for her contributions of the recipes. (Betsy, are you sure you wanna go through this again? I could always go back to being a disc jockey.)

To Noah and Rachel, our children, who put up with their Dad's erratic moods and strange occupation. I thank them also for not changing the margins on my typewriter or stealing all my paper, pens, clips, and rubber bands.

To Alan M. Pollock, my best friend and coconspirator, who was always there to share the laughter and the tears.

To Patricia Brett-Pollock, who read the manuscript, made suggestions, and tasted my wine. (Not fruity enough, eh?)

To many people at Rodale Press, but especially Roger B. Yepsen, Jr., for his continuing friendship and encouragement; Shirley Schuck, who read my rough copy, gave me pep talks and dinner, and believed in me from the start; and finally, to my editor and friend, Marcy Posner. Words can't possibly express my gratitude to her for her patience, humor, and considerable skill in guiding me from first draft to finished book.

We were sleeping in the goat barn because goats can't talk. If they could, they would say, when appropriate, "Pardon me, I'm having contractions about five minutes apart now and I think birth is imminent. Please ready yourself." Goats have a lot of natural dignity. That's the way they'd talk if they could.

But they can't, so the newcomer to goats has to estimate when a doe is going to kid. The gestation period is 143 to 155 days. A calendar is a big help. You put an X on the supposed day of conception and continue X-ing out days until you get to 155. But it's hard to know the actual day of conception, so the spread of days is only approximate. You stay watchful and anxious from the 143rd day to the 155th day at least. And you don't bring the calendar into the barn because one of the goats will eat it.

Why worry about the actual birth? Goats have been kidding for thousands of years on rocky hillsides without human midwifery. They have also been stepping on their newborn kids or rolling over on them or dropping them in the middle of a freezing night. So you stay close to your animals to avoid finding tiny carcasses instead of healthy kids.

Not long out of the city and being new to goats, and to rural living besides, my wife Betsy and I decided the only way to be there at birth was to sleep in the barn. I say "barn," but the building was actually a large shed. The only place to lay out two sleeping bags was in with the goats.

We bedded down on the 145th day of Annie's pregnancy. The 143rd and 144th days were nerve-racking for us. We checked constantly for the signs our Basic Goat Book told us to look for: restlessness, lack of appetite, a desire to be alone. The goat book was exactly right, except that Betsy and I had all the signs, not Annie. I think we expected her to kid exactly by the numbers. But trains don't run on time and neither do goats.

We only had two goats then. Besides mild-mannered, doe-eyed Annie, there was Rosemary, a belligerent yearling whose hobby was butting small children across the yard. We'd bought Rosie from a suburban family only a few months before. Neighborhood children had apparently teased her regularly, which encouraged her in turn to spend her days plotting the destruction of all children and unwary adults.

I should point out that I was never enthusiastic about getting goats. That was Betsy's idea and goats remain her domain. I use the milk, of course, hypocrite that I am, but I find goat management and upkeep an enormous amount of work and responsibility. Books on homesteading and small-scale farming make goat keeping seem so idyllic. I suspected the truth on the day we met Rosemary and she tried to butt Betsy through a barn wall.

But on that evening of the 145th day, all was quiet. Both Rosie and Annie were bedded down, chewing their cuds. They got up to investigate when Betsy and I unrolled our sleeping bags. They sniffed the bags and stared questioningly into our eyes. I believed then as I do now that goats regard humans as largely unpredictable and thoroughly droll characters. Credit goats with intelligence and sensitivity for having lived with humans for centuries, accepting our antics with patience and bemusement.

Annie and Rosemary settled back down again, nestling deep into their straw bedding, again chewing their cuds and watching us as we also nestled down for the night. Betsy was soon asleep but I remained awake, thinking. I ran my eyes over the 2-by-4-foot studs of the goat shed, looked up at the ceiling, and congratulated myself again on the good job we had done. Building this shed had been our first major construction project beyond hanging up pictures and putting up shelves.

We were only 20 miles from downtown Washington, but already we were light years away from our urban lives of the previous year. I dozed off finally, satisfied, thinking again how the rich odor of hay and straw has always intoxicated me. City born and bred, I still wonder why the smell of hay and manure can tug at me, suggesting undecipherable secrets and promises.

I don't know how long I slept before the sound of rain awakened me. I moved slightly in the bag and realized my feet were wet. Damn! The roof leaks. Betsy and I had shingled it not more than a month ago. Were we that amateurish, I wondered, to have made the roof a sieve? Then I saw where the leak was coming from. It wasn't raining. It wasn't the roof. Rosemary was in a half-squat at the end of my sleeping bag. And she was peeing all over my feet.

Goats always get a faraway look in their eyes when they squat. The urine pours out of them like water from a bathtub faucet, but they remain a study in nonchalance. Rosemary's indifference made me all the madder as I helplessly watched the last drops of urine spattering onto the sleeping bag and me.

I lay there for a while not really knowing what to do. Sometimes when you're wet or cold you stay still, stupidly hoping that somehow it will all go away and you'll be magically dry and warm again. So I lay there for a moment letting the details, and the urine, sink in. Rosemary, supremely indifferent to me and the world at large, ambled back to the smooth impression she'd made in the straw and lay down with a grunt and a groan of comfort.

Nothing personal, of course. She had to go and my feet simply happened to be on the spot she'd picked out. Drowning victims are supposed to see their entire lives pass by in a flash as the waves envelop them. There wasn't enough of Rosemary's pee to engulf me, though it was already puddling at my heels, but still my life unrolled like a ball of twine. All of my 30-odd years—and this was one of the oddest—were compressed into a few seconds as I lay there soaking.

I have a college education, I thought. A master's degree. My wife, sleeping dry and warm next to me, also earned a degree and comes from a good family. Both of us come from good families. Both of us are intelligent, capable, and sophisticated. Then why, I wondered, am I lying here being peed on by a big brown goat? What unknown forces in the cosmos have converged to bring me to this soggy point? The existential implications of those questions were too much for me.

"Hey!" I shook Betsy awake. "Hey! Wake up!" I gave her a good shot on the arm. She got me into this.

"W-wha? Mfff? Who?" Betsy is a lovely woman with a lot of natural poise, but when she wakes up it's like watching Sleepy of the Seven Dwarfs tumble out. Her eyes get big, she sniffs deep breaths through her nose, and she stays disoriented for a few seconds. I'm normally very gentle with her, but I don't get peed on by a goat every night.

"Rosemary just peed on me," I said.

"You're kidding," Betsy said, still only half awake.

"You're not kidding?" She reached down and touched the end of my sleeping bag. "Oh my."

"Gee," I said, "one of the things I really love about you is your ability to brilliantly reduce a complex situation to a few pithy words."

"You should know. You're the one who got pithed on."

"Very funny, isn't it?" I shouted in anger and laughter, pushing at her as she giggled. "Do you realize that 20 miles from here people in the White House and Pentagon are struggling with life-and-death problems? And here we are, the products of millions of years of evolution, children of technology, sleeping in a goat shed in a pool of pee. Can you explain that to me?"

"Well," she said, "maybe we're just lucky."

Betsy was right, of course. We have been extraordinarily fortunate. We moved in 1969 to two acres of semirural land in Washington's Maryland suburbs. We had few practical skills when we stepped into our old house, but that was the point: we meant to learn whatever was necessary to move us toward self-reliance. Caught up as others were in the back-to-the-land movement of the late 1960's, we read the *Whole Earth Catalog, Green Revolution, Organic Gardening,* and books like *Living the Good Life* by Helen and Scott Nearing. And we ached to get back to the earth, to get compost under our nails, to become self-sufficient and level-headed like the Nearings.

But we couldn't go "back" to the land because we'd never been there in the first place. So much for the romantic ache. And we had no country skills unless you count Betsy's expertise with horses. Yet even this had been gained through years of riding and competition in the show-ring, not behind a team of draft horses on a farm.

I was surely a most unlikely candidate to be a suburban homesteader or a homesteader of any kind. Born in New York City, I grew up playing stickball and hooky. When I was 13, my family moved to Arlington, Virginia, where I struggled with adolescence and the transition to what was then a quiet, conservative suburb of Washington.

Although Arlington was close to woodlands and rural areas (now swallowed by suburbia), my major interests were anything but rural. With a driver's license at 15, I was interested mainly in girls, driving around town, and—from 16 on—working as a disc jockey and writer in a succession of radio stations.

My sights were on New York and Hollywood. I had planned since the age of six, due to a prolonged exposure to Milton Berle, to be a comedian. And all my interests pointed me toward a thoroughly urban life. I altered some of my ideas after several years of college, however, and decided there might be more to life than living out of suitcases, doing endless one-night stands, and trying to pry "yaks" out of a semidrunken audience. Yet still, the city beckoned.

Betsy was no better suited to a rural life. If her family had had their way, the closest she would have come to the country would have been a singles' weekend in the Catskills. Like most families in the United States, hers valued money, material goods, and status. They assumed Betsy would grow into normal womanhood with a taste for expensive jewelry, fine clothing, and a color-coordinated living room.

But unlike me, Betsy never developed a liking for urban life. She grew up in a small New Jersey town about 20 miles from New York City. And her loves, right from the start, were horses, riding, and being outdoors. All through her childhood she got up every morning before school and rode miles through the woods, summer and winter. She did the same thing after school. As she matured, her family tried to push her in the "right" direction to no avail. Horses, they said, were all right for children but there were more important things for adults to think about. Think of the future, Betsy was told. Come to your senses. Get married. A doctor, a lawyer, an orthodontist from Short Hills. A CPA from Massapequa, for God's sake!

Betsy thought instead about woods and fields and barns. "You've had the best things in life," her mother scolded, "and you've somehow turned into a country bumpkin!" Betsy's family still hopes she will come to her senses and one day move into a Tudor house with a circular drive and a stained glass foyer.

I think about that sometimes when I see her out in the goat shed helping a doe give birth to a set of kids, her arms and hands smeared with mucus and afterbirth. I think of it when I see her beside me on crisp October days splitting firewood for the stove. I think of her deliverance from Danish Modern and Wedgwood and Miami Beach when I see her walking across a meadow with our children, Noah and Rachel, watching them run ahead to pick wild flowers and chase butterflies.

"This is where I belong," Betsy's smile says. "This is how I always wanted it to be." And I wonder about that. How both of us, against the tide of our backgrounds, wound up smelling of wood smoke and apple cider.

Our need to be outdoors, near open spaces and wildlife, caused us trouble when we lived in the city, because we compensated for this need by keeping pets in an apartment building that didn't allow them.

We bought a white rabbit, ostensibly as a "nature study" for Betsy's first grade class. But Lora, as we named her (the spelling is the first graders') spent weekends and all vacations with us. And, of course, we fell in love with her. She was a dear creature; intelligent, affectionate, and housebroken. She used a cat's litter box, so we let her run loose in the apartment.

Now this apartment building—Walnut Park, near Georgetown—wasn't an easy place for us to live in, but it was our first place together after getting married. And it was posh compared with the cramped apartments we'd lived in as students. The "no pets" rule was hard on us, but no worse than the way we were regarded by many of the tenants and the resident manager.

This was the mid-sixties—you remember them—and to the geriatric clique that ruled Walnut Park, any male with hair over his ears was a hippie, any young woman in dungarees the same.

We shared the elevator with unsmiling blue-haired ladies who wore white gloves when they shopped at a Georgetown supermarket; with retired State Department officials, slender, pale men, as brittle as bone china tea cups; and with pensioned-off elderly widows who smelled of Pine-Sol and Jean Naté.

Once we rode with a woman and her husband, she an overweight matron in a blue suit styled by Omar the Tentmaker; he a washed-out bureaucrat in a seersucker suit, his rep tie flecked with tiny bits of dried gravy. The four of us stood silently as the elevator doors closed. Trapped. Tense. I could hear myself swallow. The couple stood next to us, staring straight ahead, doing their elevator yoga.

Then the doors slid open and they walked out, the woman saying in a purposely loud voice, "This building is letting *anyone* move in these days!"

"I'm too young to be a pariah," I said to Betsy.

We laughed about the incident, but the hostility in Walnut Park was palpable. We needed something to insulate us from the cold shoulders, the concrete, the muted voices filtering through the steel-reinforced walls. Lora the Rabbit filled that void. She became our secret connection to the natural world.

Keeping her could get us evicted, we knew, but we needed some way to touch the earth. House plants and sprouting alfalfa seeds weren't enough. Besides, Lora was a perfect apartment pet. Clean, small, house-broken. And she never barked.

But one day the resident manager, Mrs. Inlander, stopped me in the carpeted lobby. She was a frumpy little woman. "Mr. Sussman," she whined in a nasal voice, "do you have a white rabbit in your apartment?"

My stomach tightened, but I was prepared for this. I showed no reaction. "Why, whatever do you mean?" I said, maple syrup dripping. Good start, I thought. "Whatever" was a class word.

"The woman who lives above you says she can see a white rabbit in your apartment."

The apartment above us angled out and the tenants were able, if they chose, to peer down into our living room.

"She's *peeping* into my apartment, Mrs. Inlander?"

"Not *peeping*. . . I . . . ah . . . "

"A peeping Tom in Walnut Park? And she sees white rabbits?"

"No, wait a minute now. . . " she was rattled, "she saw *one* white rabbit . . . in . . . your. . . . "

"A *big* white rabbit? Does it have a name?"

"This isn't funny, Mr. Sussman. . . . "

"I'm not laughing, Mrs. Inlander," but only because I'm biting the inside of my mouth, I thought.

"We have strict rules against pets in this . . . "

"Did you ever see Jimmy Stewart in *Harvey*? Elwood P. Dowd was the character, I remember. He drank a lot. Does the woman up-stairs . . . ?"

"Not anymore . . . oh . . . I mean, wait."

"First come the bunnies, then the bats and snakes. Ever see Ray Milland in *Lost Weekend*? There's one scene with these bats . . . "

"She *saw* a white rabbit, Mr. Sussman, in *your* living room!"

"I'm sure she did, Mrs. Inlander. Does she use binoculars? A lot of peeping Toms do."

Mrs. Inlander suddenly developed a coughing fit, much to the delight of Benjamin, the Nigerian desk clerk who was listening to our exchange and biting the inside of *his* mouth, from the look he shot me. "Can I get you a glass of water?" I offered solicitously.

"No . . . I . . . arrgh . . . " she choked through a dry throat.

"Well now, look," I said, "let's take this up another time. When you're feeling better. We can sit down in your office," and here I paused a delicate second before firing the *coup de grâce*, "*with the police* and. . . ."

The matter never came up again. Mrs. Inlander averted her eyes whenever our paths crossed. Or she coughed a lot. Betsy and I kept the blinds closed from then on because Lora was only the beginning.

Snuggles, another white rabbit, came next. The mother of one of Betsy's students brought him into school one day. "We can't keep him any more," she told Betsy, "and since you already have a rabbit here I knew you wouldn't mind." Snuggles went into a separate cage next to Lora's.

Every Monday morning we'd stuff the two bunnies into separate canvas shopping bags and sneak them down to Betsy's car for the ride to school. On Friday evenings we'd sneak them back to the apartment. We used the elevator, always entering an empty car and praying no one would get on until we got out.

But once an elderly couple got on at the second floor. They smiled politely as they walked in, then turned and faced the doors. Betsy and I stood in the rear of the car holding our shopping bags (we had several towels stuffed into the bags to keep the rabbits from popping up). Suddenly, Snuggles sneezed! A muffled "ker-chew!" straight out of a Beatrix Potter story. Then again, rapid fire, "ker-chew! ker-chew!"

The woman turned and looked at Betsy. "God bless you," she said sweetly.

"Thank you," said Betsy, sniffing for effect.

"Ker-chew!" said the shopping bag. The woman looked shocked, started to say something to her husband, who was absorbed in watching the lighted floor numbers flashing on and off, but was interrupted when the elevator stopped at our floor. We mumbled "excuse us" and hurriedly walked past them.

"Ker-chew!" said Snuggles.

"You'd better do something about that cold, Dear," I said to Betsy, as I looked over my shoulder at the woman, and caught her confused glance as the doors slid shut. Then we exploded in laughter.

Sometimes I think this kind of silliness runs in my family.

Once, during one of my mother's visits to us in Maryland, she decided to buy a puppy. "How will you get it back to Florida?" I asked.

"I'll take it back on the plane."

"Will they let you bring a puppy on board?"

The answer was no, according to several calls to airlines. The puppy would have to go in a crate and be shipped as luggage. "The hell they say," Mom laughed angrily. I agreed with her. The airlines have a terrible record of handling animals. The situation has been cleaned up somewhat, but animal welfare groups, not airlines, initiated the reforms.

But years ago, when Mom cradled the puppy in her arms, animals faced dangerous journeys in the unheated cargo holds of airliners.

"Don't worry about it," Mom said at the airport. "I'll sneak it on board."

"I wish you wouldn't do this," I said weakly, but I had no other ideas. "If they catch you they'll put you off the plane."

"In mid air?"

"If they get mad enough, who knows?"

Mom told me the rest of the story over the phone. She got on the plane carrying the puppy in a large handbag. She sat with her hand in the bag the entire two-hour flight to Miami, stroking the puppy to stop it from whimpering. Whatever sounds it made were inaudible over the engine noise, but a flight steward did note with suspicion my mother's hand movements in the bag.

Finally, halfway through the flight, he could contain himself no longer. "Madam," he sniffed, "do you have an animal in that bag?" My mother must have been subconsciously prepared for this moment of truth, though she's always been lightning fast with a comeback.

"Young man," she said in an icy tone loud enough for everyone to hear, "it might interest you to know that I have a palsied hand. I keep my hand in this handbag so I won't be embarrassed by its uncontrollable trembling."

"I——I . . . uh, er, I'm . . . " the steward stammered, probably wishing there were bomb bay doors that might open under him.

"I hope," Mom hissed, twisting the knife, "that you're proud of yourself!"

The rest of the flight was uneventful. But when the plane landed in Miami, Mom couldn't resist a parting shot. As the passengers disembarked (as people on airplanes do, rather than simply get off), the flight attendants and stewards stood by the doorway smiling and saying, "Hope to see you soon," while the passengers said, "Thanks for a nice flight."

Mom moved down the aisle, her hand still in the bag patting the puppy, who by now was getting feisty. As Mom neared the doorway she spotted the steward, though he tried to look past her and her trembling hand. Her timing must have been perfect. Just as she got to the doorway and the steward and flight attendants looked straight at her, she pulled the puppy out of the bag, held it up, gave everyone a big grin, and said, "Wooof!"

Well, at least my mother was content with only a puppy. We, however, found our secret menagerie growing into an apartment-sized game preserve. A few months after we added Snuggles the Rabbit to our family, we welcomed Iggy the Iguana. Iggy, a prehistoric-looking green lizard, was another first grade nature study who ended up living with us, housed in a tiny tropical world—a ten-gallon aquarium on our coffee table. He ate live mealworms and bits of fruit. The perfect house guest.

Then came another iguana named Godzilla, given to us by a friend who was moving overseas. Godzilla lived in a ten-gallon tank next to Iggy's.

Then came the two tanks of tropical fish. Two 30-gallon aquariums on a wrought iron stand, complete with fluorescent lights, bubbling aerators, colored sand, live plants, and a little fake deep sea diver. And of course, lots of tropical fish. Nobody gave us these. We bought them ourselves. Having living things around made the apartment more livable, we told each other.

The only thing we worried about was that Mrs. Inlander, who had a passkey and a legal right to enter our apartment with good cause, might just do that on a whim—especially if she ever figured out how I bamboozled her about the white rabbit her friend saw.

Poor Mrs. Inlander, I thought. She'd probably die of a coughing fit right in our living room, our annex of the National Zoo.

Some people just don't appreciate nature, I guess. Mrs. Inlander even complained when we fed the birds in winter, the smallest of our concessions to the natural world.

At first we only scattered seed on the windowsill. Then Betsy, ever the compassionate soul, put out slices of oranges and apples. "Birds need a varied diet, too," she said. So she added bread scraps, dabs of peanut butter, and sunflower seeds.

And the birds came—pigeons, starlings, sparrows—all of them squawking and cooing and peeping, jostling for position in a ruffle of feathers.

"Mrs. Sussman?" (Mrs. Inlander on the phone.)

"Yes?" said Betsy, holding her breath. What was it this time—rabbits again? Lizards?

"We've had some complaints from the tenant on the floor below you. It seems, ah, his balcony is littered with birdseed and rotten apples . . . and ah . . . bird-doo. Do you think, perhaps. . . "

The birds went hungry that winter.

We moved out in the spring.

Our next stop was a rented house in Cleveland Park, one of Washington's oldest, moneyed sections, probably the most beautiful community in the city. Rambling Victorian houses line the quiet streets, their big windows and gingerbread molding shielded by ancient oaks and maples that tower protectively over the sidewalks and wooded backyards. Crows call from the treetops. Squirrels dart along the railings of front porches. A few blocks away, flocks of turkey vultures circle high over the National Zoo, waiting to share in feeding time.

Finding a place in Cleveland Park we could afford was great luck, we thought. But renting a three bedroom house for just the two of us, after so many years of apartment living, was even more phenomenal. We tried not to be impressed with our good fortune, to be blasé. But the magic of Cleveland Park was overwhelming, even for two basically antiestablishment types like us. Our neighbors were congressmen and syndicated columnists and the unnamed "high government officials" who pop up in *Washington Post* headlines every morning. We've arrived, we thought. Young professionals in Cleveland Park. In the city, but a place apart. The best of all possible worlds. But we really didn't believe it.

Something was wrong. Perhaps it was the ferment of social consciousness of the 1960's, but we found ourselves increasingly uncomfortable about the pattern our lives were settling into. I had recently left broadcasting after more than a decade of working at a series of radio and TV jobs. I'd been a disc jockey, newsman, advertising copywriter, and producer of news and educational radio programs. I'd won some awards and had a chance for the kind of success I always thought I wanted. But something nagged at me. Snippets of philosophy courses were invading my thoughts as I fell into twilight sleep in the comfort of our Cleveland Park sanctuary. Like Scrooge, I was assaulted by ghostly voices:

"The unexamined life is not worth living."

"What? Who said that?"

"Socrates."

"Aww, what do you know? I just put a down payment on a stereo."

"It is physically impossible for a well-educated, intellectual, or brave man to make money the chief object of his thoughts."

"Who's that?"

"John Ruskin."

"Well, leave me alone. I'm saving up for a sports car."

"The superior man understands what is right; the inferior man understands what will sell."

"Confucius, right?"

"Yes."

"Go away."

But my ghostly visitors were right. I hated the nine-to-five treadmill. I despised my easy acceptance of mediocrity and lumpishness in exchange for job security and a big disposable income. As a teenage DJ I had hustled junky vacuum cleaners on the air and delighted in the jammed phone lines when the "suckers" called in for those "free home demonstrations with no obligation." Now, in my late twenties, I was beginning to feel uneasy working for a radio station merely because it played cigarette commercials. I was developing a conscience—the worst thing that can happen to you in commercial broadcasting.

I had worked in noncommercial radio, too, "educational" broadcasting, now called "public radio." I enjoyed the freedom from hucksterism and the chance for more creative control, but I was bothered by the cautiousness, the sedateness. My salary came from government and university money. I could make waves, but only in a small pool.

I was becoming a Marginal Man. I didn't fit in. And I kept seeing my life stretched out before me, its limits marked off by paycheck stubs and cash register receipts and hours of TV watching. Fortunately the chance to try something new came with a phone call from a friend. "How'd you like to teach English to college freshmen?"

"I wouldn't," I said.

But the grant money was running out on a radio production job I had, and no attractive prospects were in sight. So I took the job, "temporarily," and, to my amazement, promptly fell in love with teaching. The classroom gave me some of what I'd been looking for: I could explore ideas, continue my own education informally, serve a useful function in society, and still use all my creative urges as a performer. Satisfaction made up for the lower salary.

At the same time I became a teacher, Betsy stopped being one. She quit her job at the elementary school where she'd been teaching first and second grades for four years. Betsy loved working with children, but she found it harder every day to put up with the bureaucracy of school administration. The same lock-step to mediocrity that deviled me ate away at her. And something else bothered her: the constant awareness that she wasn't the person she wanted to be. She'd abandoned the idea of working with horses when she entered college. Her family convinced her to be practical and to go to school.

We didn't realize it all at once, but we were like two people trying to remember the words to a half-forgotten song. We were looking for something, but what was it? So we lived on in Cleveland Park, took long walks to the zoo, shopped in Georgetown (another kind of zoo), went to the movies, and watched TV to "pass the time." Betsy got a dog, took it to obedience school, read books, took the dog for walks, and got bored.

One night we were sleeping when a loud thud on the roof almost tossed us from the bed. "What the hell?" I muttered as I sat up, peering into the darkness. Bonk! There it was again. Kids are throwing rocks at the house! I jumped out of bed and looked out the window. Nobody. Chonk! Clonk! Two more missiles hit the roof right over my head. My adrenalin pumped and I growled profane incantations as I pulled my clothes on. I was going to catch those rotten kids and break every bone in their . . . Kla-bam! WHUUMP!

The street was empty. Not a sound. Were we being attacked by vandals armed with a catapult? I looked up at the house and saw Betsy nervously peering from the bedroom window. "What is it?" she mouthed silently. "I don't know," I pantomimed, shrugging my shoulders. Then WHA-BLONK! Something hit again. Betsy pulled back from the window and stared up at the ceiling. I ran to the side of the house where the thing seemed to hit the roof. There I found our mystery bombardier. And I felt like a jerk for my misplaced anger and macho belligerence. A black walnut tree was in full fruit. The nuts were ripening and falling on the roof.

"That says something about me, doesn't it?" I said to Betsy.

"Doesn't what?"

"The fact that I automatically assumed we were under attack. I was ready to kill somebody. If I had a gun I might have shot the paper boy."

"WHUMP!" The tree answered.

"How else should you have reacted?"

"I don't know. But it's instructive that my basic response under stress is to revert to Attila the Hun. Maybe it's the city and all the crime."

"There's crime everywhere."

"BUNK! BUNKETY-BUNKETY-Bunk-bunk-thunk."

"That one rolled down the side into the gutter."

"You know," I said, "now that I know what it is, I sort of like the sound."

"The tree?"

"It's like a concert. Like a John Cage composition. Everything has become so predictable in our lives. But this tree is just letting go in its own rhythm, acting in accordance with its true nature."

"Oh Lord," Betsy moaned, "you've been reading too much Thoreau."

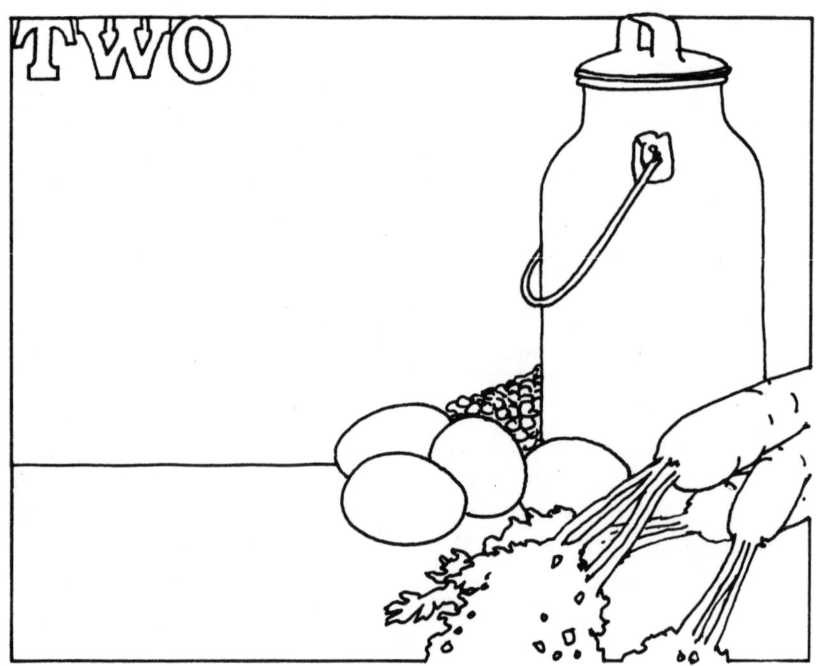

I don't know whether you can read too much Thoreau, but I was certainly dreaming about The Simple Life. Ahhh, pack up your troubles in your old kit bag and head for the country. Toss out a few seeds, buy a wood stove, get a goat, some pigs and chickens, and relax in the hammock. Let the world go to hell with itself.

Says who?

Well, America's bookstores, for one. They're bursting with glorious how-to books: *How to Live Like Royalty on No Money; How to Raise Beef*

Cattle and Become Financially Independent After the Coming Crash; How to Build an Energy-Efficient-Underground-Solar-Powered-Hydroponic-Dome Home.

And newspapers and magazines! They're filled with glowing accounts of how simple simplicity really is: "You Can Raise a Year's Supply of Food on Your Windowsill"; "How to Deliver Your Baby at Home with Recycled Materials"; "Making Methane in Your Apartment: Goodbye Electric Bills!"—and my favorite—"Stockbroker's Daughter Finds Peace in North Woods."

That one, or a variation, shows up regularly in the *New York Times.* The Stockbroker's Daughter gives up her fashionable apartment in Manhattan, sells her Ferrari, her collection of pre-Columbian art, and—pausing only to throw a copy of *Walden* in her L. L. Bean haversack—she buys a run-down farm in northern Maine, puts in a French intensive biodynamic garden, builds a greenhouse enclosing a fish pond (the pump runs off electricity generated by the wind charger she installed herself), bakes stone-ground whole wheat bread in her solar oven, starts a worker-owned tofu factory with unemployed Penobscot Indian youth, meditates two hours a day, jogs, spins her own wool, makes a fortune digging ginseng, cures her cold sores holistically, and really, really, she says, "mellows out."

And that was only her first week in the woods.

Now, this isn't to say that stockbrokers' daughters or sons or anybody's children don't go off and find peace and simplicity in The Country—wherever that is. But the rule, rather than the exception, is that a lot of people have been terribly misled by all the hype about how easy it is to switch from conspicuous consumption to The Good Life.

The truth is that the so-called simple life is quite complex, while modern urban life, supposedly complicated, is really simple. After all, the simplest way to get something done is to have someone else do it. Doing it yourself *seems* simple, and it might be if the task itself is simple—mowing the lawn, painting a table, hanging a picture. But what if the job is complicated? Your car needs a new water pump. Your air conditioner dies. Your pocket calculator picks up reruns of The Gong Show. Faced with a problem beyond your capability, the simplest course may be to have someone else do the job.

Now extend this thinking to basic needs: food, shelter, clothing, energy. The really simple way to have these needs met is to buy them as goods and services. So while the popular notion is that the urbanite leads a terribly complicated existence, the reverse is true—at least on the surface. What can be simpler than living in a house or apartment, with heating and cooling automatically maintained, buying what you need from local shops, and making use of every service you can afford?

All you have to do is push buttons, make phone calls, and scratch out some checks every month. And you've got loads of free time to do what you like, including getting a second job to pay for even more goods and services. *That's* a simple life, no?

Now look at the so-called simple life based on self-reliance. You want food? First, find some land for a garden, a house, maybe a barn. Next, come up with the cash or mortgage money. Then find some more money to pay for the seeds, tools, fertilizer, and soil conditioners. But you can't buy experience. If you've never raised your own food before you'll find the procedure terribly complicated—a dizzying overlay of seeding schedules, plant physiology, soil chemistry, and local climatological variables. Then comes harvesting, canning, and freezing.

The first-time gardener or farmer—even the second- or third-timer—has an enormous amount to learn and keep in control. And I didn't even mention the problems of caring for livestock. Self-reliance is based on knowledge and experience (usually painful) and everything seems to happen at once.

Pick out any other homestead or self-sufficiency task and the picture is the same. You want to heat with wood? Going to cut your own? Chain saw or bucksaw? One is expensive, the other slow and physically demanding. Then the wood must be hauled out of the forest. Tractor or horse? Then comes splitting and stacking.

This is the simple life? Easier than setting and then forgetting a thermostat?

What we think of as the traditional simple life—the bucolic pursuits of country folk—are really complicated, involving skills, long-term experience, muscle power, intuitive wisdom, and money. The "complicated" life in city and suburb takes mostly money.

But something else is going on here. Look again at that profile of modern, industrialized life. The simplicity is only *apparent.* Its basis is really an extraordinarily complex mixture of forces and intangibles. The heating and cooling in your house or apartment is automatically maintained *only* if there is fuel available. The corner supermarket is stocked with food *only* if production and delivery schedules are maintained. The checks you write are good *only* so long as your job remains stable. What seems like a simple life is really a set of systems within systems, each dependent on the other, all built on the maintenance of an unshakable status quo.

Unshakable? Bad weather hits the Salinas Valley in California and food prices jump up 3,000 miles away. Labor disputes cause a truckers' strike in the Midwest and deliveries of commodities are disrupted in a dozen cities. A coal miners' strike means higher electric bills. A holy man in the Middle East raises an eyebrow and we're all waiting in gasoline lines again.

But look again at the complexities of the self-reliant life. All that work you have to do—food production and preservation, woodcutting, livestock tending, and a dozen do-it-yourself projects—are largely built on a simple foundation: your health and your willingness to do the work. You need some cash, of course, but what you spend is often put toward basic needs that pay you back directly—gasoline for the chain saw, seeds for the garden, tools for the workshop.

There is another payback, too, one that directly affects your health and willingness to do the hard work: the personal satisfaction and security that comes from looking into your root cellar or out at a woodpile or solar collector and knowing you'll be warm in winter; the pleasure and security that comes from eating your own food; the rich feeling that comes with the acquisition of a new skill or the honing of an old one.

You don't have to be a homesteader to accomplish this. Plenty of urbanites have put in gardens, reduced their use of gasoline and electricity, and streamlined their lives. But it isn't easy, not when you've grown up, as most Americans have, with the notion that unlimited resources are our birthright. Forming a new social ethic—that each of us has a moral obligation to use less—is difficult, especially when the dominant social ethic seems to be based on consumption.

That's what the Stockbroker's Daughter never tells us—that the labor, responsibilities, and skills needed to care for yourself are complex, demanding, and sometimes the lack of them is frustrating to the point of tears. The trouble starts with the word "simple."

Simple living means *direct* living, confronting the basics, wrestling with the fundamentals. Simple doesn't always mean *easy.* Nor does it mean inexpensive. And there are some days, when you add up the risks of chimney fires, hernias, blisters, chain saw accidents, livestock diseases, snap frosts, the explosive growth of weeds, voracious insects, and all the slings and arrows of self-reliance, when "simple" may not even mean *better.* How hard it is to congratulate yourself for your rugged independence when you get the veterinarian's bill (your chickens have asthma) and the lumber bill (the goat shed will pay for itself in 75 years) and the orthodontist's bill for your kid's braces (that's something the *Mother Earth News* didn't tell you how to do).

The key to making simplicity work in one's life depends on

balance. Some people may wish to hone their lives down to the stark simplicity of a monk's cell. This is certainly possible, and I know several people moving in this direction. Their plan is to have only the absolute basics, as few possessions as possible, while living on a minimal income. If this works for them, it will be because they've achieved an equilibrium between their actual needs, their resources, and their desire to be free of social encumbrances like job stress and excess bills.

But most people, I think, would prefer a little more than a few sticks of furniture and a bowl of bean sprouts. Yet where do you draw the line? I still use electricity. I drive a car (though much less than I used to). I own power tools. Even our grain mill, purchased so we could enjoy the simple pleasure of grinding our own wheat, is powered by electricity. Would my life be simpler if we disconnected from the power company, sold the car, and ground our wheat by hand? Would we have accomplished anything meaningful? What makes sense?

One friend said to me, "You haven't really simplified your life. You've complicated it in a different direction, one that's more meaningful and manageable for you." Another friend of mine "simplified" his life by trading in his Mercedes sports car for a diesel Cadillac. Is a simple life even possible? I think about this when our children, Noah and Rachel, are playing with their radio-controlled Artoo Detoo and the little flashing, beeping, blooping robot whirrs along, bumping into the wood stove or Betsy's spinning wheel or a stack of my books on living the simple life. And how do we simplify our *interior* world? Saint Jerome renounced the material world for the desert, only to find himself assailed by desires and visions of things he thought he'd left behind. (Radio-controlled toys hadn't been invented yet, so he was safe from incessant bleep-bloops and dead batteries, anyway.)

Perhaps the best we can do, for a start, is to sort out the problems in our lives, discarding some and adapting to others as we go. Then, instead of striving for mythical problem-free lives, we might work for a set of goals that are manageable and human-sized.

Look at simplicity in practical terms: most of us can't generate our own electricity, but we can use less of it. My family's electric consumption has dropped sharply over the last ten years. Just lowering the setting on our hot-water heater from 140 to 120 degrees F. saved over $40 the first year. Insulating the tank saved a little more. (Ideally, I'd like to convert to a solar hot-water system, but our old house's design makes it hard to retrofit. Also, I don't have the several thousand dollars it would cost for the conversion.)

We've saved in other ways: Betsy no longer uses the electric clothes dryer. She prefers, she says, our solar-powered clothesline and the drying-rack we set up near the wood stove. The stove has also helped us cut down on the use of electricity by freeing us from a furnace blower. Not only do we save on electricity that would have powered the fan, but we also vacuum less often because the blower isn't depositing dust all over the place. And relying on the wood stove means we don't have a need for an electric humidifier. We don't have a dishwasher, garbage disposal, or TV, and own only a few appliances.

We don't use air conditioning—an act of heroism, considering Washington's summer weather—relying instead on a low-wattage ceiling fan and a carefully scheduled routine of opening the house up at night to capture the cooler air and shuttering it against the heat by day. Even if we could afford air conditioning, we couldn't use it. Moving constantly back and forth between artificially chilled air and hot outside work would soon knock us out.

Food is another area where simple changes can make a big difference. Even a small garden—10-by-20 feet—can produce hundreds of dollars worth of wholesome food if properly managed. Our 4,850-square-foot garden means we have a tiny food bill through most of the summer and a smaller one in winter. Gardening isn't necessarily easy, as I've said, but the problems are right up front, human-sized, manageable, and certainly easier to deal with than the vagaries of inflation. That's one thing about a garden: higher prices only make the garden and the skills you develop more valuable.

The way we eat is also open to change. Adopting a simpler diet—vegetarianism in our case—can have a positive impact on both our food budget and our personal health. Not eating meat, fowl, or fish while relying on grains, fruits, vegetables, seeds, and nuts means we're not paying for waste or fabricated food. We use milk (from our goats) and eggs (bartered for from a friend) but not in large amounts.

Here again, while we can't directly affect inflationary food prices, we can attack the problem from a different angle by eating a simpler diet based on whole foods we grow ourselves or buy in bulk. It doesn't make sense to curse the high price of food while wheeling a supermarket cart filled with nonfood: expensive cartons of soft drinks, sugar- and fat-filled baked goods, and all manner of overpriced, nutritionally worthless snacks, chips, dips, whips, and precooked meals.

Making such a change isn't easy at first, especially if you're used to a traditional American diet based on fat and sugar. You'll have to read a lot of cookbooks, experiment in the kitchen, and perhaps argue with your family, but the dividends for your health and bank account might be enormous.

A simpler diet costs less and—according to a mountain of medical data—preserves or improves your health. Vegetarian and low-fat diets in general, when based on fruits, grains, and vegetables, and coupled with regular exercise and good health habits (no smoking, moderate alcohol use), are linked to optimum health. *Preventive* medicine is the cheapest medical care of all.

Similar changes can be made in other areas. We don't spend a lot of money on clothing, for example. The children do fine in "handy downs," as our son Noah had once called them, or items from secondhand clothing stores. Betsy and I shop there and in surplus stores. When we do buy new clothing it's usually something practical—jeans, wool or heavy cotton shirts, work boots, and well-made outerwear.

Living this way, I realize, would be hard for some people. What do you do if you're compelled to dress a certain way for your job? I have no answer for this. I'm a free-lance writer, a teacher before that, so I haven't worn a coat and tie since 1969. But I think it's a shame people have to spend cash merely to maintain social conventions. I wonder how much our country could save on electricity for air conditioning by simply letting men go without coats and ties in the summer? A United States Congressman stood up to argue for that some years ago but the Speaker of the House ruled him out of order and criticized him for appearing before that august body in his shirt-sleeves. Andy Jackson must have whirled in his grave.

My arguments for a simpler life should not, however, be confused with a wish for a return to the good old days. They never existed. Otto L. Bettmann, founder of the Bettmann Archive, gives us a realistic picture of America from the late 1860's to the early 1900's in his fascinating book, *The Good Old Days— They Were Terrible.*

"Our times," Bettmann says, "have overrated and unduly overplayed the fun aspects of the past. What we have forgotten are the hunger of the unemployed, crime, corruption, the despair of the aged, the insane and the crippled."

Who would trade modern medical care for that of the late 1800's when surgeons routinely operated while dressed in street clothes, their hands unwashed, sutures clamped between their teeth?

Who would long to live a rural life in the good old days when even so simple a task (to us) as doing the laundry was back-breaking toil involving kettles of boiling water set outside and a log trough for a scrubbing board? "The mountains of farm-filthy wash," says Bettmann, "had to be reduced piece by piece . . . hours of beating, rinsing, and wringing."

Go back to those halcyon days on the farm, a sip of cool well water to slake your thirst? "The well," says Bettmann, "was dug close to the farm house . . . exposed to all sorts of noxious matter seeping through the ground. Slush from the kitchen, festering matter from privies, and seepage from animal wastes . . . filled the air with a vile odor."

Those arcadian days also offered the exploitation of children as cheap, expendable labor, the maltreatment of the mentally ill, the lack of hygiene and consumer protection laws in the food industry—milk was often so watered that "a water shortage would put the milkman out of business"—and the filthy air and streets of city and suburb—"The atmosphere was so polluted at times as to produce nausea."

Obviously, what we're after is a blend of our *perceptions* of the good in the good old days and the genuine improvements modern technology offers. Our search should be for a middle ground between primitiveness (a relative term, I grant you) on one hand, and unbridled technology on the other: an *appropriate* technology.

That term was popularized by the late E. F. Schumacher and others and its theory and practice are constantly being refined by a variety of economists, planners, and thinkers struggling to determine how the world should best use its energy and industry. Such theorizing is crucial to our survival, but my concern is more basic: how do I, how does my family, arrive at a personal, practical, appropriate technology?

It's all very well to beat the drum, proclaiming that the United States is an energy glutton, that its population, 6 percent of the world, uses 30 percent of the world's resources; that it's become addicted to high capitalization, high-tech "solutions" to self-created problems (using nuclear energy to heat water to make electricity so people can heat water), and that there must soon be an end, one can hope a creative one, to our wasteful practices. And it's fine to suggest, as I have, that there are numerous ways in our homes and habits to conserve energy and move toward self-reliance—if not self-respect. But the larger question remains unanswered. If there are no hard-and-fast rules for the "right" thing to do, how can I develop a philosophy, a personal concept of appropriate technology? Put it another way: what do I teach my children?

In valuing the past, how far back do we go? In accepting the present or the promise of the future, how much technology is enough, how much excessive? If the concept of appropriate technology is a middle ground, how do I get there?

We begin, I think, with some basic questions. Who am I? What are my needs, both mundane and spiritual? What are my goals? What is my responsibility to the local and global community?

To these questions we add the concept of *tools,* those devices, philosophies, procedures, and processes that are extensions of human intelligence and control. We arrive at a single question: which tools, using the word in its broadest sense, will enhance my humanness, help me grow, and encourage my active participation in life?

Here it might help to distinguish between tools and machines, so-called labor-saving devices. A wood stove is a tool. An automatic furnace is a machine. The stove is nothing without my involvement. I tend the coals, keep the woodbin full, and daily, through the medium of the stove, invest a simple task with meaning. But the furnace? It clicks on and off mindlessly, automatically. I am needed only once a month to pay the bill.

A tool then, invites our participation, enhances our power without subtracting from our humanity. Tools, says Ivan Illich (*Tools for Conviviality,* Harper & Row, 1973), should be "convivial."

> Tools are intrinsic to social relationships. An individual relates himself in action to his society through the use of tools that he actively masters, or by which he is passively acted upon. To the degree that he masters his tools, he can invest the world with his meaning; to the degree that he is mastered by his tools, the shape of the tool determines his own self-image. Convivial tools are those which give each person who uses them the greatest opportunity to enrich the environment with the fruits of his or her vision.

Again, this is *not* an argument for an exclusive use of hand tools or a rejection of technology. The search is for appropriateness, not "smallness" for its own sake. Environmentalist Amory Lovins said in an interview with *Mother Earth News* in 1977: "It's just as silly . . . to try to run a smelter with wind machines as it is to heat houses with fast breeder reactors. The object is to crack nuts with nutcrackers and to drive pilings with triphammers, not the reverse."

And how do we decide which are the nutcrackers and which are the trip-hammers in our daily lives? Do we *need* dishwashers, TVs, stereos, cassette recorders, blow dryers, hot combs, electric toothbrushes, electric knives, electric blankets, electric coffee makers? Is our perception of the cosmos deepened by a disposable flashlight?

The questions leading to a personal concept of appropriate

technology have no easy answers. The resolution can come only through an almost daily analysis of our responsibilities and needs. This isn't as dreary as it sounds. Trying to live a simpler, more direct life means *thinking* and *acting,* not merely reacting. We have an opportunity to control more of our lives than if we just let machines take over. Socrates would have approved: this is surely an *examined* life.

As George Nash says in *Old Houses* (Prentice-Hall, 1980):

> The house is a tool for living. We rebuild ourselves as much as we rebuild walls and roofs. The tools we use to accomplish this task should be selected and maintained with the same care we give to grow our gardens. There are those who find their meditations disturbed by the speed and noise of power tools, purists who eschew the smoke and roar of the chain saw for the flash and clean bite of the ax and the song of the crosscut saw. A tool is only a tool. There is a dance for chain saws as well as the hand ax . . . it is the spirit in which it is used that invites judgment.

More than ten years have passed since Rosemary Goat baptized me into the faith of homesteading. Rosie has mellowed with time, though she'll still butt a child across the yard if the opportunity appears. And Betsy and I have progressed, as we hoped, away from our push-button pasts to lives more centered on self-reliance. As for finding a blend between tradition and appropriate technology, we've learned that's a *process,* not a destination you can travel to and settle down in. And while getting there may be half the fun, the process certainly raises as many interesting questions as it answers.

Most of the questions we had a decade ago centered around finding a place to homestead. (I didn't realize then that you don't have to leave the city to simplify your life or even to produce much of your own food. City lots can, with some planning, be transformed into places of wonder with compact gardens and efficient shelters.) We were greenhorns eager to find "a nice old house in the country." But we also knew we didn't have the skills or background to jump feet first into rural living. The solution, we decided, was to find a semirural area halfway between the suburbs and the *real country*.

So, like innocent babes with shining faces and a slender bank account, we started house hunting in Maryland, driving away from Washington and Cleveland Park, heading northwest. In 1969, you could still drive 10 or 15 miles outside the city and really be in the boonies. And the land in Maryland was beautiful.

Rolling meadows merged with wooded valleys. Sharply etched streams zigzagged their silvery threads through dense stands of red oak, tulip poplar, and box elder. There were horses everywhere, grazing quietly on hillsides, their heads lowered, rounding their backs into graceful curves that matched the smooth contours of the land. Thirty minutes from downtown Washington, yet a world away. Flocks of turkey vultures wheeled in graceful circles overhead, their huge wings outstretched, motionless, sailing like black kites. Chubby woodchucks sat rocking on their haunches along the narrow roads, munching on greenery like children nibbling at a salad. Houses were scattered across the countryside, a mix of split-levels, ramblers, mansions, old farmhouses weathered gray, shacks, and abandoned frames looking skeletal against the horizon. Suburbia and the city seemed a long way off. Real estate prices outside the city were comparatively low in 1969, as were interest rates, so we had a chance to find a reasonably priced place and a small tract of land.

But we didn't want just any house. We wanted an *old house.* Ah, the charm, the character of an old house. They don't build them that way anymore, right? Some people have crazy dreams, I guess. They want to climb Mount Everest or sail a balloon around the world. But other people, like us, need a *real* challenge. They have the nuttiest dream of all: they want to find an old house and fix it up.

From whence came this fevered dream? I had never built anything more ambitious than a window box in a fifth grade woodworking class. It took me weeks of sawing, sanding, and nailing to construct that slightly trapezoidal box, which, when planted with marigolds, promptly fell apart, the strain of the blossoms opening being too much for it.

Yet here I had this overwhelming vision of finding an old house and restoring it with only my two hands, a hammer, and a checkbook. I even had fantasies about meeting an elderly couple who desperately wanted to sell their Victorian mansion—the one with the stained glass and hand-pegged floors—but only to someone like me, who, they could tell, "appreciated the finer things in life."

And I had other dreams. A garden that would supply all our food. A well filled with sweet, unchlorinated water. A horse for Betsy. Long walks in the meadows. Bib overalls. And if it didn't work out I could always pop into the city to see a movie, to touch base with what I still considered "civilization."

Now, faced with such fantasies, such distortions of reality, what I really needed was a cold shower and a long rest in subdued light. Instead I got a real estate agent. A dream merchant. Buying a house, of course, is the biggest expense most people, including us, ever encounter. You don't buy a house the way you buy a sticky bun ("Don't bother to wrap it, I'll eat it here."). You should put a lot of deep thought into carefully selecting an agent who will understand your needs and limitations. So Betsy and I put a tight leash on our enthusiasm and went about the selection process in a methodical manner:

"How about this one?" I asked, breaking open the phone book at random.

"Fine," said Betsy.

Deep thought doesn't hurt a bit.

We explained what we were looking for to the agent. She listened carefully, occasionally twisting a large diamond ring she wore on her left index finger or picking invisible motes off her tweed jacket. I painted her a lovely picture of a homestead nestled in the Maryland hills, a picture-perfect garden, a plume of white smoke curling up from a brick chimney, apple trees in blossom, a gentle all-season stream meandering past the front door. When I was finished, she sat silently. I thought I could hear a small boy calling, "Shane, Shane, come back!" Finally, she spoke.

"I have *just* the place you're looking for!"

"Really?" I said.

"Yes," she said. "It's a *farmette.*"

I'm going to throw up, I thought.

Off to the Maryland hills we drove with the agent. "This is a *darling* place," she gushed as she drove, her gold bracelets clinking against the steering wheel. What a wonderful way to start out, I thought. Looking for the Great American Homestead while being chauffeured about in a massive Cadillac, our tour guide a refugee from Bloomingdales, our objective a farmette.

"Isn't this *lovely?*" the agent squealed. We had pulled into the driveway of a huge white farmhouse, actually a former farmhouse. The farm had long since been chopped up into small tracts. The white house looming in front of us must have been the main house once. Now it looked like a beached whale, cut off from the open space it once dominated. It was a familiar story. Pressure from developers was already decimating the old farms, slicing them into sellable pieces, tidbits for the maw of suburban sprawl. But who was I to complain? Betsy and I, young professionals, back-to-the-landers, were part of the reason it was profitable to subdivide the old places.

"Isn't this a *smashing* living room?" the agent squeaked, waving her bejeweled hands in half circles.

"It *is* big," said Betsy, in awe. They don't build them like this anymore, I thought. It had 12-foot ceilings, a fireplace big enough to roast an ox, and huge windows.

"How much heating oil did it need last year?" I asked, my only pragmatic question of the day.

"Oh. Um." said our agent. "I don't have those figures with me, but I can get them if you like. Now let's look at the bedrooms."

I found out later the house burned about $2,500 worth of oil in a mild winter. That was in 1969, in the good old days of cheap energy. We would have been chopping up the furniture to keep warm. And the bedrooms were no smaller than the smashing living room.

"How *spacious*!" the agent said, standing in a master bedroom that measured 20-by-26 feet.

"Yes," I said, "we could start a little bowling alley . . . "

"Ha ha," said the agent, rattling her bracelets.

". . . to help pay for the heating oil."

So it went. We drove out with other agents to other places—mini-farms, gentlemen's farms, mini-estates, ranchettes, country classics, and several more farmettes. Nobody seemed to be selling plain old houses anymore. And real estate advertisements were no help to us at all. They're written in a kind of code, I discovered. It's hard enough to find an old house when your fantasies are bubbling like a rich stew, and the artful language in the newspaper advertisements certainly doesn't make the search any easier:

"Completely restored!" (The kitchen sink works.)

"One of a kind view!" (The lights from the paper mill next door are lovely at night.)

"Recreation area next door!" (The driveway is a teenage hangout.)

"Historically authentic!" (No electricity, polluted well, and the outhouse fell over again.)

"Handyman's special!" (Some usable lumber may be found in the rubble once the ashes cool.)

Next comes dealing with real estate agents. Here I don't mean to suggest that all agents are devious, criminal or callous. Most, like the majority of people, are honest. The trouble is you can't tell the players without a program. Or a lie detector.

I learned this the hard way. It's easy to forget that the agent is just that—an agent. You spend a lot of time riding around looking at houses with an agent. In the confines of a car you soon start chatting, swapping pictures of the kids, expanding on your personal philosophies, and singing old Fats Domino songs. Soon you get to laughin' and scratchin' and before you know it, you're the best of pals.

Wrong.

Take this simple quiz I've developed.

Real estate agents represent:

A. The buyer
B. The seller
C. God and country

The correct answer is D—themselves. What? You didn't see a D above? Congratulations. You've just learned, as I did, two important rules about buying real estate, especially old houses in need of repair:

1. Nothing is as it appears.
2. Make sure *everything* is in writing.

I've also learned that you have to put your dreams on ice for a while. Practice being a flint-hard house-hunter, cool and dispassionate. And when you finally find the house of your dreams don't whimper, tap dance, shout *Hallelujah* or break into a chorus of "Over the Rainbow." I had one friend who went off looking for her fantasy of the perfect house and actually saw it, just as the real estate agent rounded a curve on a country road.

"That's it! That's it!" my friend wailed, bursting into tears of joy right on the spot. The agent, driving with one hand so he could figure out his commission on the fingers of the other hand, started crying too, when he realized he'd just earned enough to bring his mother over from

Liverpool. My friend didn't get the best deal in the world, as you can imagine, having confessed her willingness to die rather than lose that house.

I was determined not to blow my cool. I practiced biting my lip, holding an impassive stare, and mumbling key hard-bargainer phrases:

"Isn't that a termite?"

"This needs work."

"Are those water stains?"

"What's that strange odor?"

A few months later an agent called and told us he had a house we might be interested in. It was in Potomac, Maryland, about 20 miles from Washington. I laughed when he said "Potomac," because even then Potomac was known as a wealthy area with lots of estates. It didn't seem like the kind of place to find a homestead.

We drove out with the agent and found a homely little place, a 1½-story colonial (a catch-all word real estate agents use to avoid saying "nondescript") made of concrete blocks. "It has character," we whispered to each other as we wandered through the house. ("Character" is a word house-seekers use to avoid saying "cruddy.")

But the land the house sat on really moved us, tugged at our dreams. The two acres were in the midst of open meadows on all sides. Huge trees, catalpas, and a silver maple towered over the house itself. Other trees—Chinese chestnut, black walnut, sour cherry, and pear—were scattered across the rectangular tract. The house was set back from the road, sitting on a knoll that overlooked a spring-fed pond on the farm to the west. The nearest other house was almost a quarter-mile away.

I was already fantasizing. The garden can go here. The barn can go there. My workshop can go . . . Stop it! I scolded myself. I dug my nails into my palms. The agent led us upstairs into a pine-paneled loftlike room with a cathedral ceiling and a view of the pond and the fields.

"What do you think?" asked Betsy.

"I think this is crazy," I replied, whispering so the agent couldn't hear. "This place has no closets, a tiny kitchen, and *one* bedroom. I paced it off. It's 8-by-10 feet. Monks meditate in cells bigger than that."

"Well, you always said you wanted an old place to fix up. This is old all right."

"Beautiful view of the pond," the agent chimed in.

"Yes," I said.

"Lovely fields, too," the agent said.

"Yeah," I said.

"But it's all on borrowed time," Betsy said, ruining the poor man's sales pitch. "It won't be long before all this gets cut up into lots and houses pop up all over."

"Five or ten years," I added.

"Well . . . " said the agent.

"We're going to have to think about this," I said to Betsy. "This is a big decision and we shouldn't jump in without some deep thought."

"Right," she said.

"Of course," said the agent.

We stood silently, looking at the pond. There were horses across the field, grazing on the rim of an egg-shaped hill, silhouetted against the blue sky.

"Nice horses," I said to Betsy.

"Nice pond," she said.

"Betsy," I said, filled with deep thoughts.

"Yes?"

"Let's buy it."

"Okay."

I know, I know. What we did was foolish, impetuous. Chalk it up to youthful innocence. (I was only 30 then.) We should have hired a professional housing inspector. We certainly didn't know enough about houses to make an intelligent inspection ourselves. Like most people buying their first house, we counted closets, opened and closed doors, looked in the bathroom and kitchen, and mentally rearranged furniture. Given our dreamy state, even if we had hired a competent inspector we probably would have disregarded or taken lightly whatever damning evidence he presented. We were going to fix the old place up anyway, right?

Needless to say, I'd never buy another house in such a cavalier manner, certainly not an old house. Old houses may be a joy forever, but as I've discovered and rediscovered for a decade, they are also old houses forever. And their fixing up takes just about as long. This sage advice I'm offering falls into the "if-I-only-knew-then-what-I-know-now" department. Betsy and I weren't just building castles in the air. We were planning on moving right in.

We went to the closing a few months later, a numbing time of contractural procedures, legalese, and a flurry of papers to be signed. The previous owner wasn't even there. He and his wife had already moved to Oregon, leaving the details of settlement to his cousin, another real estate agent. None of these details mattered to us. All we cared about was hugging the old house to our bosoms. Don't bother me with trivialities like deeds and titles and mortgages.

I know, I know. We should have had an attorney with us, someone clearheaded, as ferocious as a wolverine, with an encyclopedic grasp of real estate law, and undying loyalty to our cause. As it was, we just dutifully signed whatever was shoved in front of us. We were fortunate that everything was on the up-and-up. Looking back, I realize our naiveté could have had us signing ourselves into indentured slavery. With the last signature, we turned over a check that had enough zeros to make me shudder, smiled, stood up, shook hands, and received the house keys and deed. We were homeowners!

That's when I was sorry the previous owner wasn't there. I'd had this fantasy—it goes with the typical old house fantasy—that the former owner would come up after the closing and take me gently by the elbow. He'd look deep into my eyes, his own eyes misting over, and he'd say, haltingly, "You'll take good care of the old gal, won't you?" That would be the tip-off that I'd bought a gem.

It didn't happen quite that way. As Betsy and I left the office, we heard the former owner's cousin calling Oregon to break the news of settlement. Far be it from me to eavesdrop, but I did catch a few key words and phrases as we stood in the hallway. The cousin said hello, then laughed. He *whooped,* actually. The sound made the house keys feel like dead weight in my pocket. The conversation was garbled but I did hear the words "sucker," "free at last," and "we pulled it off."

"I think," I said to Betsy, "that we may have more fixing up to do than we planned on."

Most old houses operate under occult laws. Like a recruit who collapses into a round-shouldered slump when the drill sergeant leaves, some old places have a way of just letting go once the deed has been transferred. First to go, we learned, is usually the plumbing. That's because, unlike the previous owners, we were reckless enough to flush the toilets and turn on the water.

Our plumbing education began one particularly frigid winter night. Betsy shook me awake.

"Wha——?" I said, drunk with sleep.

"I hear water running," she said.

"I know," I said. "I left the kitchen faucet running a little so the pipes wouldn't freeze."

"No," Betsy said, "I hear *a lot* of water running." I cocked my head and listened. She was right. The sound came from down the hallway, a fizzing, gushing, spattering, rushing noise. We jumped out of bed and ran to the kitchen.

Water, water, everywhere! I flipped on the kitchen light and was startled to see water spurting out of the ceiling light fixture. I flipped the switch off again, thankful I hadn't been electrocuted. Everything was awash. The dogs' food bowls were floating on three inches of water, bumping against the kitchen table like driftwood. Water gushed out of the kitchen cabinets with such force it rattled the dishes inside. Every seam in the ceiling and walls oozed or squirted water.

"What happened?" Betsy shouted over the hissing.

"The upstairs bathroom," I shouted back. "Pipes burst!"

You're supposed to have a cool head at times like this. I had that all right and equally cool feet, turning blue from the icy water. Turn off the main valve! I knew enough to do that. But where was the main valve? I had been so busy dreaming about fixing up the old place that I never bothered to ask about so minor a detail.

It took ten frantic minutes of searching and several hundred gallons of water before I finally found the valve under the house in a freezing crawl space. I was still in my pajamas, of course, the only way to work. Another ten minutes of struggling with the rusty valve, ice water dribbling through the floorboards onto my neck, a pint of penetrating oil, a pipe wrench, a ball peen hammer, gritted teeth, and a catalog of creatively filthy words was all it took to shut it down.

I crawled out of the crawl space and limped into the kitchen. Betsy had already started to sweep the four inches of water out the back door. I looked at the kitchen clock, its face spattered with droplets. It was 2:30 in the morning.

Then we started to laugh.

Betsy and I caught each other's eye and just laughed uncontrollably. We had both been thinking the same thing: we were fixing up an old house!

"Well, anyway," Betsy said as she swept a wavelet of water past her bare feet, "it beats living in an apartment."

Up to that point, I knew nothing about plumbing except how to change faucet washers. But when I inspected the damage in the upstairs bathroom, I realized I was either going to have to learn the more complex aspects of pipe repair in a hurry or I was going to have to take out a second mortgage and hire a plumber.

"How bad is it?" Betsy asked when I came downstairs.

"The pipes burst in eleven places," I said.

"Oh no."

"Yes. And I'm never going in those places again."

I laughed to keep from crying. The damage was awful. And the worst of it was that I'd have to rip the bathroom floor out to get to all the burst pipes. Call a carpenter? Call a plumber? Why, that would have violated the first principle of old house restoration: thou shalt do it thyself. And besides, if thou is I, thou couldn't afford what a professional would charge.

So I learned a crucial truth about self-reliance and homesteading: it's not money or dreams that will sustain you, but practical knowledge about the basic systems you depend on. Funny, isn't it? We Americans pride ourselves on the importance of a good education and getting a good job. But our educational and social systems conspire to keep us specialized to the point of ignorance.

When I was in high school I wanted to take woodworking and auto mechanics because I thought they were invaluable skills. I wanted to take print shop too, because I thought an aspiring writer ought to understand how words get into print. But I was barred from these "blue collar" classes. "You're college bound," a guidance counselor told me. "You have to stick with the academic program." They probably wouldn't have let me take plumbing, either.

I've gotten even with our society's stupid pattern of specialization, however. When that first array of pipes burst, I bought tools and books, and asked a lot of questions at the plumbing supply store. And I've done the same thing over and over again during the past decade, acquiring the basics of new skills by reading, working, and asking questions. Our house has "helped" by constantly coming up with new problems, one right after the other.

I repaired the bathroom pipes. Few projects have given me more satisfaction. I wasn't a skilled plumber by any means, but I had a grasp of the basics. Good thing. Two weeks later the pipes in the kitchen burst in the cold. Back in the crawl space at the main valve once again, I discovered an awful truth, awful truths being the stuff of old houses. The pipes leading to the kitchen sink had been installed first, with the kitchen floor then laid over them. That's what's called "building for the ages."

Old houses give you lots of creative choices. I could have fixed the pipes by working in the crawl space, but a scant 18-inch clearance would have meant working on my back with hot solder up my nose. Or I could have ripped up the kitchen floor and refitted the pipes from above. (At least I was an experienced floor-ripper.) Or I could have taken the easy way out and hired a midget plumber.

I thought this was a great idea, but the most diminutive plumber I could find was five feet tall, overweight, and claustrophobic.

The new kitchen floor is lovely.

Crawl spaces, I'm told, are peculiar to houses in the southern

United States—an excellent reason to house-hunt in the north and west. Under my house, in hand-dug channels and dusty, cramped niches are jammed the oil burner, water-storage tank, hot-water tank, and a random crisscross of pipes, wires, and ducts. This part of the house was obviously designed by the architectural firm of Sleepy, Sneezy, Dopey, and Doc.

Basements are an improvement over crawl spaces because you can stand up in them, play Ping-Pong, and store boxes of stuff you don't need. But basements have their own problems, like dampness and flooding.

If you buy an old house, check the basement troubles *before* you sign the contract, if possible. Look for water stains, tidal pools, or revealing graffiti: "High water mark 1930" scrawled on the wall should make you suspicious. Mushrooms, salamanders, and salmon fighting their way up the basement steps are also signs of trouble.

Welcome to the wonderful world of sump pumps.

An old house can also introduce you to being your own electrician, a trickier task than plumbing or carpentry, one that a lot of people are afraid to tackle. Plumbers rarely drown on the job, but even experienced electricians get zapped. Doing your own wiring isn't difficult, as I've learned, and you can save hundreds or thousands of dollars in labor costs.

I went about learning the fundamentals of electrical wiring the same way I confronted plumbing and all the other skills I've tried to acquire: I start with books, the library being my first stop. I ask a lot of questions of experienced workers. Then I buy tools and plunge in. With plumbing you sometimes literally plunge in if the leak is big enough, but with electricity you go more slowly.

And you always turn the power off at the main switch before you begin. And you slavishly follow the dictates of the National Electrical Code, a set of minimum standards worked out by the trade and electrical industry. (The Code is available at bookstores and libraries.)

If you plan on doing major remodeling in an old place—ripping out walls and ceilings—that's the time to consider total or partial rewiring. Inspect all electrical components as if your life and property depended on them. Look for frayed or rotted insulation, corroded or poorly made splices, cracked receptacles, improper grounding, mouse-eaten cables, or "short-cuts" and other code violations. I know the list well, having found everything in my own home.

And when you do get to ripping out walls, you're going to make another discovery, as I did. Normal frame house construction has studs on 16- or 24-inch centers. But old places, because they've had a succession of owners and tenants, each with their own dreams and eccentricities, may have lumber in odd configurations.

I learned this when I tried to install an insulated metal chimney for our new wood stove. I measured the living room ceiling carefully, locating two studs on 16-inch centers. But when I cut the hole I found a third stud permanently fixed between the two others. Nor was this an ordinary pine or spruce 2-by-4. This was a rough-cut oak stud whose half-century of slow curing had left it with the density of granite.

It took an hour, five saber saw blades, a hatchet, and two chisels to carve out an opening for the chimney. We used the remains of the errant stud as kindling in the stove's first fire. Poetic justice.

But lumber isn't the only thing to go awry in old houses. In remodeling the bathroom we decided to change a window into a doorway, normally a simple procedure of cutting and reframing. But when we started chipping at the wall we struck water—a three-inch black steel pipe ran horizontally under the window frame.

Tracing it back told us why the bathroom sink always drained so sluggishly. Water usually has a hard time flowing uphill or sideways. Yet now we had another problem—a big hole in the wall with a pipe three feet up, and across where the doorway was supposed to be.

A lot of things flashed through my mind, the least of which was the prospect of going back in the crawl space to wrestle with the drain. Why couldn't we just leave the pipe across the door? Why be slaves to convention? We could make it a conversation piece, a chinning bar for Noah and Rachel, a low towel rack. We'd get used to stepping over it just as we got used to lots of bizarre things in the old place.

No use. Betsy voted down my brilliant ideas. The pipe was duly rerouted and we watched the water drain rapidly away with more of our dollars. Still, I wonder about the previous plumber or homeowner who first installed this novel horizontal drain. Was his grasp of basic physics faulty or did he just have a weird sense of humor?

Lord knows that's the most important asset we've relied on (besides money) living in an old house: a sense of the absurd. How better to keep your sanity than by laughing and enjoying the ride?

You might not laugh at the time—when the water's rising, when the floor caves in, when random bits of wood, metal, and pipe wheeze and crumble with age. And the humor certainly wears thin as the years go by. You may find yourself muttering, as I've been known to do, "I've paid my dues, I've paid my dues," every time some new calamity occurs.

But Betsy's right. Things could have been worse. We could have ended up in an immaculate house with lots of time on our uncalloused hands. Besides, fixing up an old place *was* what we always wanted to do, wasn't it?

We've renovated the old place and renovated ourselves in the process. Behind our patina of dust and grime are the people we wanted to become—reservoirs of practical skills and unique experiences. Betsy and I have done more than simply survive the chaos and confusion of a creaky old manse, we've transcended it, becoming home-grown plumbers, electricians, carpenters, masons, and whatever else circumstances have forced us to become.

But not everyone was as thrilled with our decision to seek The Good Life as we were. Least of all, Betsy's family. Now it may seem that I'm picking on her family, but it's just that they're more visible and vocal than my family. Or probably anybody else's.

Soon after we moved into our stately digs, Betsy's grandmother (who regards herself as just below the Dowager Queen in social status) came to visit. To inspect, really. She took the grand tour of the house, excluding the crawl space and attic. All the while, as she moved through the house, she repeated, "Well, I'm pleasantly surprised."

When she first said this, Betsy and I were pleased, as though for once our choice had been accepted by her family. But after a while we realized that was *all* Grandma was saying, over and over: "Well, I'm pleasantly surprised." We found out later that she'd been programmed as neatly as the Manchurian Candidate by Betsy's Aunt Annette. "Bessie," Annette told her all the way down from New Jersey, "if you can't say anything nice, just say 'I'm pleasantly surprised.' " So Grandma did. Over and over again.

Other of Betsy's family members were more direct. Her Uncle Solly also took that trip with Grandma. He stepped outside our house with Betsy and said, "You know, Darling, when I first saw your house I wanted to cry. To think you gave up all you had for . . . " and here he pointed to the house as though it was a slum, ". . . *this*." He gave the word "this" a little twist, like a knife gutting a fish. The painful truth is that even after a decade, Betsy's family still regards us through a glass darkly.

Grandma left still repeating "I'm pleasantly surprised" like a broken record. I wonder if they had to deprogram her somewhere along the New Jersey Turnpike?

FOUR

What makes a kid born and raised in the city want to live in the woods? How about Straight Arrow Skill Cards? Remember them? The Nabisco Company—the makers of Shredded Wheat—used Straight Arrow as a promotional device in the early 1950's. What? You don't even remember Straight Arrow? He was a comic book character, an Indian, dedicated to eradicating evil. Evil won, I guess, because Straight Arrow hasn't been heard from since.

He had no superhuman abilities like Superman, no magic word like

Captain Marvel, and no mutations like Aqua Man or The Torch or Plastic Man. What Straight Arrow had was Indian skills! He could build a fire without a match, make a bow and arrows from scratch, sniff the wind and predict the weather, tame a wild horse by mumbling secret Indian stuff to it, or live in the woods with only a knife and a piece of flint.

During those halcyon days, the Nabisco folks made all these tidbits of knowledge available to us kids by printing up Straight Arrow Skill Cards and using them as the dividers in the Shredded Wheat boxes. I think there were 3 cards to a box. The entire series of cards amounted to about 50, so you had to eat a lot of Shredded Wheat. And, of course, you got a lot of duplicate cards, which meant you had to buy even more Shredded Wheat and swap cards with your friends.

This presented two problems: my mother objected to the amount of Shredded Wheat I implored her to buy. Nobody in the family would eat it but me. Mom and Dad said it tasted like dried grass. "So what are we going to do with five boxes of the stuff?" my mother asked. The dog didn't like it either.

The other problem came in trading duplicate cards to my friends, not many of whom were interested in survival skills. They didn't see the value of learning how to track a moose in New York City or knowing how to tell north by locating the Big Dipper. They relied on street signs.

It took great fortitude and lots of Shredded Wheat to assemble all the Straight Arrows Survival Skill Cards, but I did it. And I read every one and dreamed of the day when I could discover a bear's den or send smoke signals. I had to wait all winter and spring to get to do these things, until it came time for summer camp.

If there's one reason I have always felt a call to wander through woods and fields it's because of summer camp. Every summer, from when I was 6 until I was 13, my parents sent me to camp in the Catskill Mountains, near the New York, New Jersey, and Pennsylvania borders. Almost all these years were spent at interracial or YMCA camps, either all-boy or co-ed, so my sex education, however inaccurate, increased along with my survival skills.

Eight weeks out of each year I spent hiking, swimming in lakes and icy streams, canoeing, whittling, camping out, climbing trees, making forts, playing Capture the Flag, making lanyards and copper ashtrays and leatherette wallets and plaster figurines, and writing postcards home.

Hi Mom and Dad,

I am having lots of fun. My councellor is neat. He used to be a soldier. Today he showed us how to kill a sentry without making a sound. The food stinks. I have impetigo. Send more cookies.

Love,
Your son

And it was in summer camp that I had my first taste of wild foods. I learned how to forage for wild blueberries, strawberries, blackberries, and raspberries. I learned how to make pine-needle and sassafras tea and how to find the delicious Indian cucumber. Such encounters sealed my pact with the wild.

Years after these childhood experiences, when I was an adult living in Washington, the memory of Indian cucumbers suddenly leaped into my mind. I had been walking along the Potomac River just outside Georgetown. My life revolved totally around the city then, but I still came to the river and the green spaces nearby. There were days when I just had too much pavement under my feet. But why, after almost 20 years since I'd seen one, the thought of Indian cucumbers should pop into my mind I didn't know.

They're not a true cucumber, of course, but a small forest plant with a succulent tuberous root. Finding them meant tracking through cool woods, searching beneath the shadows of white birches. The green leaves of the Indian cucumber are subtle, almost nondescript; there's no hint of the treat that lies an inch or two beneath the dirt.

What a discovery they were for me! To feast on those crisp and juicy roots while sitting in the woods—a revelation for a city kid.

As I remembered this, walking along the river, the whine of traffic on Canal Road muffled by the trees, I abruptly turned into the woods, determined to find an Indian cucumber. I walked around for several minutes, searching in all the likely spots, when I was struck by a shattering realization. I couldn't find an Indian cucumber if my life depended on it because I couldn't remember what they looked like! Oh, I had a vague image of a tiny green plant in my mind, but I had forgotten the details. I remembered Indian cucumbers through a haze, like the face of some childhood friend. Too many years had passed since they had been part of my life.

A sense of loss stayed with me for a long time after that, troubling my thoughts. I ruminated on the direction my life had taken—toward the city and away from whatever it was that Indian cucumbers symbolized.

Not long after that I bought a copy of Euell Gibbons' guide to wild foods, *Stalking the Wild Asparagus.* I wasn't sure if what had vanished from my life could ever be rediscovered and even wondered if I should make the effort.

Then I found lamb's-quarters growing in the blanket-sized front yard of the house in Cleveland Park. I was astounded when I recognized it from the drawing in Gibbons' book. This was a weed I had seen all my life. It had grown luxuriantly in the empty lots near LaGuardia Airport where I played as a child. Lamb's-quarters grew out of the cracks in the city alleyways beyond my house, flourishing in tiny depressions of dirt.

Yet until I read Gibbons' description, I hadn't known that it was edible—delicious, said Gibbons—much less that it had a name.

Betsy and I harvested the small patch in the front yard and ate it with dinner. Amazing. Wild food in the city.

Euell Gibbons led us to more: the pungent taste of steamed plantain, a ubiquitous weed that pushes up through the sidewalk (though we picked ours from a more sheltered spot); and that scourge of the lawn-lover, dandelion greens, the queen of wild foods.

After a few weeks of urban foraging, just walking through the city became a new experience. Where before I saw only a meaningless jumble of plants and trees, now I saw specifics—plants with names and uses and individual characteristics. Familiar faces.

Not surprisingly, these experiences added momentum to our discussions about self-reliance and leaving the city. And a paragraph in *Stalking the Wild Asparagus* told me exactly what Indian cucumbers had meant to me:

> Man simply must feel that he is more than a mere mechanical part in this intricately interdependent industrial system. We enjoy the comfort and plenty which this highly organized production and distribution has brought us, but don't we sometimes feel that we are living a secondhand sort of existence, and that we are in danger of losing all contact with the origins of life and the nature which nourishes it?

We continued our foraging after we left the city, studying other wild-food field guides, always adding to our knowledge. Our goal was never to live solely on wild foods, but to have them as an integral part of our lives—as a means of communion with the earth.

Unfortunately, not everyone shared our enthusiasm. Some of our friends curled their lips (involuntarily, I think) when we described our adventures with "edible weeds." "Weeds." What an awful word. What does it make you think of? Crabgrass, weed killer, poison ivy.

Ralph Waldo Emerson said "a weed is a plant for which we haven't yet found a use." His friend, Henry Thoreau, spoke lovingly of purslane, a wild food I know well. But neither of these gentlemen knew Betsy's grandmother, the defender of conventional behavior.

"Why can't you go to the supermarket like everybody else?" she asked over the phone. I tried to explain about secondhand existences and the danger of losing contact with the origins of life. "You'll poison yourself!" she warned.

Maybe we had a bad connection. I tried explaining that we weren't simply wandering around popping strange fruits and berries into our mouths willy-nilly, that we were using excellent field guides and making positive identifications before we sampled anything. And we weren't fooling around with wild mushrooms at all. (Too many dead "experts.")

"Listen, Grandma," I said, "would you have trouble telling a head of cabbage from a head of lettuce?"

"No."

"Right. Well, it's no different with wild foods. You learn to tell them apart just as you distinguish between types of produce in the supermarket—by sight, touch, and smell." There was a pause while my eloquent, reasoned argument sank in. She saw my point, I knew. Any day now we'd have her over for a mess of dandelion greens and . . .

"You let the *children* eat this stuff, too?"

"Of course."

"*Oy gevolt*!" she wailed, lapsing into a string of Yiddish incantations that were either a prayer or a curse—the latter on my head.

Yet teaching the children about wild foods has been one of our great pleasures. Theirs too, we think. But we wanted Noah and Rachel to understand that the natural world is a mixture of benefits and dangers—not absolute good or evil.

The primary rule we made was "you eat no plants, wild or in the garden, without checking with Mom or Dad." Lest we forget, even cultivated plants harbor dangers. Unknowing children and adults have been poisoned by tomato leaves, rhubarb roots, and green-skinned potatoes.

Secondly, we introduced only one or two wild foods to them each season. Noah's first discovery at the age of two was wild violet blossoms—delicious flowers. He loved going out alone with a small basket, gathering several cupsful that Betsy would add to our salad. We always praised his efforts, congratulating him on his help in feeding the family.

Rachel, at the same age, learned how to pull the pistil out of honeysuckle blossoms so she could sip the drop of nectar trapped at its base. She'd stand absorbed in this task, a jungle of honeysuckle vines overhead, sipping at the nectar like the insects that swarmed around her.

As the seasons passed we saw the benefits of this teaching. Both children could soon recognize a wide variety of plants and trees, the dangerous as well as the tasty. They know what poison ivy is, the difference between oak and maple trees, and how to dig up wild onions. And they've learned other things in the process; about insects and birds, the way plants grow, the chemistry of the earth, and a bit of history—how the Indians and our ancestors relied on the same wild plants we were using.

For them, the natural world was thoroughly natural.

Our favorite wild foods are the blackberries and raspberries that grow thickly along the borders of our two acres. Picking them is a chore. The thorns seem to have a life of their own, thrusting out in painful jabs at our thighs and arms. But the sweetness of the berries is a powerful anesthetic.

Several mulberry bushes—actually trees—dot our land. We compete each spring with scolding catbirds for the plump berries. Noah and Rachel can reach only the lowest limbs, but they do well gathering the fallen fruit. Their fingers and bare feet stay mulberry-colored for weeks afterwards. We eat the berries every day in season, out of hand and in cereal and fruit salads. In good berry years, Betsy will make mulberry jam for the winter.

Our favorite wild green is still lamb's-quarters, which grows abundantly everywhere on our land. It grows abundantly on almost everybody's land, in fact, from Pennsylvania to California. Even in Hawaii. (Another local name for it, as uncomplimentary as lamb's-quarters is enigmatic, is pigweed.)

We harvest this in large amounts, using scissors to snip young plants off just below their tops. The plants grow back rapidly and we often get a second harvest from the same patch. So good tasting and nutritious is this dark green wildling that we no longer bother to grow its domesticated relative, spinach. (Lamb's-quarters, a member of the Goosefoot family—Chenopodia—is also related to beets.)

We eat the greens lightly steamed and usually freeze a dozen or so quarts for the winter.

Purslane is another delight, growing luxuriantly throughout the gardens. A little too luxuriantly, in fact. One year I left the purslane to itself and almost lost a garden in the process.

Originally from India, where it's been eaten for 2,000 years, purslane is a thick-stemmed succulent with small, fleshy leaves. We eat it fresh in salads, enjoying its tart taste. We also steam it and freeze it for the winter, using it in vegetable soups. We've even made pickles from the thick stems.

Early spring brings us pokeweed—or "poke sallet" as it's called in the South. Mature pokeweed grows in clumps well over six feet tall. The stems are as thick as your wrist; the root about six inches in diameter.

In the fall, the pokeberries appear, beautiful purple-black berries that a variety of birds feed on. At this stage, however, the plant is only nice to look at. Mature poke—leaves, stems, root, and berry seeds—is poisonous. We use only the first shoots in the spring. Gathered when no more than a foot or so long, these shoots are a premier wild food—especially after a greenless winter.

We cook them in two waters. The first pot of water, containing a bitter flavor, is tossed out. The second simmering produces tender stalks that look and taste much like asparagus. We've had a lot of good-tasting asparagus casseroles made only with pokeweed.

We've also enjoyed day lily blossoms dipped in batter and fried, elderberry jam, milkweed shoots, wild watercress, wineberries, wild onion soup, mustard, and more—though we've only flirted, I think, with the wealth of wild foods available.

I've yet to taste the fruit of the mayapple, an umbrella-shaped plant that looks like it might shelter an elf from the rain. In spring, I see hundreds of the plants in low, woody spots. But in the fall, when the fruit is supposed to ripen, I always go hungry. I wonder who beats me to the yellow, egg-shaped fruit every time—forest animals or other wild food enthusiasts?

Other wild foods I hope to try soon are paw-paws (the trees grow wild along the Potomac River); bread made with acorn meal; arrowhead tubers (a favorite food of the Indians); cattail sprouts and cattail pollen flour. The list grows every year. Most of all, I'd still like to find Indian cucumbers. They don't seem to grow in our area, but now, once again, I know what they look like. That is its own satisfaction.

Yet even after all this time and all our success with wild foods, Grandma still doesn't like hearing about it:

"You're so poor," she asks, "you have to eat *weeds?*"

Almost everyone who visits us and sees the goats gets a faraway look and says something like, "Gee, I'd like to have a goat someday." I've heard this murmured by so many dreamy people over the years that now I automatically snap back like a police interrogator, "Why? Why do you want a goat?" I'd twist a lampshade and shine a bright light in their faces if I thought it would squeeze the truth out.

But the answer is always the same. They turn to me with eyes lit by an inner glow and they mumble, lovestruck, "Gee, I don't know." I've heard this sort of thing from telephone men who came to repair a wire and paused to say, "I always wanted to have a little place and a few goats." I've heard suburban matrons who can't bear to sift through the kitty litter whisper dreamily about mucking out the barn and milking twice a day. And even United Parcel Service men drop off their packages, then lean on the goat fence and recite soliloquies about growing up on a farm and their old dad.

Sometimes I think I hear Kate Smith singing "God Bless America" in the background. Goats do that to some people.

For us it all started with a glass of goat's milk. We were living in Washington, in the Cleveland Park house, and beginning to talk about homesteading and self-reliance. We were also rapidly changing our diet over to natural foods. We'd become vegetarians, sworn off junk foods, sugar, and salt, and we were eating more grains, vegetables, and fruits.

Then, Paula, a friend who worked in a natural foods store, suggested that since we were lacto-ovo vegetarians, we might be interested in fresh goat's milk. "Right from the goat," she said. "No hormones, antibiotics, pasteurization, or homogenizing."

"Goat's milk," I said, making a face. "Yuk."

"Why yuk?"

"Because it tastes funny," I said, regretting the words even as I said them. Betsy caught me.

"Why, you've never even *tasted* goat's milk, you clod!"

Shamed, I admitted I hadn't. I was turning up my nose because I believed the propaganda I'd always heard—that goat's milk tasted bad, that goats ate tin cans, that they smelled, that they'd butt your keester over a fence if you gave them a target.

"You're hung up on cartoon goats," Paula said. "Maybe it's time you got to see some real ones."

Paula sent us off to Vienna, Virginia—a suburb about 15 miles from Washington—to meet Bob and Mary Clarke, proprietors of Cherry Hill Farm. The Clarkes—in their mid-twenties—weren't professional farmers. Bob worked for the telephone company and Mary cared for their two daughters at home. The Clarkes were homesteaders—the first we'd met.

Their five-acre farm was across from a housing development and only minutes from a busy highway. But once we pulled into Cherry Hill's driveway, I was in a different world. The Clarkes were doing most of the things Betsy and I only dreamed about. They gardened, put up food for the winter, kept chickens, and—of course—raised goats.

Betsy saw the goats and got that faraway look.

Cue Kate Smith.

Not that I was immune to their charms, either. All my misconceptions evaporated as I watched them wandering about their enclosure. They seemed like bright animals, alert and curious. And there was something else I didn't fully realize at the time: goats are compact and manageable. At least, they give that impression. Unlike a herd of cows, goats seem more on a human scale.

Goats also happen to be humanity's first domesticated animals (along with sheep). Is it possible that goats trigger something in our collective unconscious? Many times, while sitting with the goats on a mild spring evening, watching them graze, hearing the quiet chewing and the shuffle of their hooves, I get this feeling of being—well—*Semitic.* And when I was immersed in the beauty of *The Odyssey,* discussing it for weeks with college students, I'd sit with the goats and feel thoroughly Greek. Goats do that to some people.

The Clarkes kept Nubians, a lop-eared, Roman-nosed breed originally from Africa. "How many do you have?" I asked.

"Fifty," answered Bob. "We do a lot of showing at county fairs. And we sell the kids to other breeders. These are all purebloods, so they bring a good price."

We stood leaning on the fence, watching the animals mill around. Several came up to us, nuzzled our fingers and leaned in to have their heads scratched.

"They don't smell," I said, surprised at my discovery.

"No," said Bob, "the does don't at all. The bucks do, though—that's where the reputation comes from. We keep our bucks separate. That's why you don't smell anything. Besides, the stink would get into the milk."

"So that's why people think goat's milk tastes funny?" I asked.

"Yes," said Mary, who joined us at the fence, "milk picks up odors, especially that buck stink. But if you keep your place clean, most folks won't be able to tell the difference between fresh goat's milk and fresh cow's milk. They just think they can because of stories they've heard."

"I know about all those stories," I said, a little embarrassed at my closed mind.

"Did you know the bucks urinate on themselves? On their heads and front legs?" Bob laughed.

"What?" I said.

"That, along with their musk glands, is what makes them stink. But it's important to them. It's a territorial thing and a sex attractant."

"I'll stick with after-shave lotion," I said.

Betsy had been silent all this time, in a daze, leaning against the fence, one foot on the lower rail, her arm wrapped around a fence post. She hadn't taken her eyes off the goats. "Where are *you*?" I teased.

"Huh? Oh," she smiled, "they're beautiful animals, aren't they?"

"Smart, too," said Bob. "Let me show you something." He explained that all 50 goats had names—Biblical names for convenience—and would come when called.

"Bathsheba! Hey, Bathsheba!" Bob called. I was amazed to see one goat snap its head up and come walking out of the herd toward Bob. None of the other goats moved or paid any attention to his call.

"Somebody figured out," Bob said, "I don't know how, that goats have an IQ of about 70, measured on a human scale."

"Gee," I said, "with an IQ that high, they could probably run for office."

"Might not be a bad thing," Mary laughed. "They'd eat up all the red tape!"

We visited the Clarkes regularly after that, driving out from the city each weekend to buy fresh milk. And every time we visited, Betsy asked more questions about goats, their habits, and requirements. Mary Clarke became Betsy's "goat lady," a font of information on goats' health, breeding, housing, and feeding.

By the time we moved out of the city, Betsy was ready. "I want to have goats," she announced.

"I know that," I said, struggling with a box of books, "but can you at least wait until we get unpacked and moved in?"

"What time will that be?"

We started out with two goats: Annie, a mild-mannered liquid-eyed two-year-old, and Sybil, a bumptious kid of eight months. (Annie had been one of Mary Clarke's favorites. We were touched when Mary offered her to us as our first goat.) We housed both animals in a small shed near the garden, about 200 feet from the house (too far, we soon learned). We hauled in straw bedding and built a wire fence to keep them from wandering.

Betsy quickly got into the rhythm of doing the goat chores, something she still loves to do. Neither goat was milking yet. Annie was pregnant and Sybil hadn't been bred yet, but there was still plenty to do for them. Water had to be hauled from the house twice daily, the stall had to be cleaned regularly, and they had to be fed twice a day.

Both of us loved just to wander down to the barn to sit with "the girls," as we called them. Sybil loved company. She was full of spunk, always skittering around on two legs, leaping into the air, and pouncing onto our shoulders when we sat on the ground. Annie regarded all this foolishness with a dignified air, the same way she regarded us. "She won't really be your goat," Mary warned, "until she kids for you." Annie, being so aloof, would only go so far as to let us stroke her head. Then she'd close her eyes and moan in pleasure.

Then, one awful morning a few months later, we learned a hard lesson about keeping livestock—especially in the suburbs. Betsy had left the house early to teach a riding lesson. I was to bring the goats water and feed. But when I got within 50 feet of their pen, I realized something was wrong.

Annie stood off to one side. She was strangely still, not chewing her cud. Sybil was lying on the ground, stretched full length. That, in itself, didn't surprise me. She often relaxed that way, especially when the sun was warm, as it was that morning.

"Sybil?" I called, as I neared the gate. "Sybil?"

She was dead. I knelt and saw the puncture marks in her throat. Tiny traces of dried blood flecked her black coat, already gone dull. I rushed over to Annie, afraid she might have been wounded in the attack. She was unmarked, but she stood very still.

Her big eyes locked on mine. Then she peered around me, looking at Sybil. I burst into tears then, sobbing in anguish and fury, enraged at the dog that did this, hating myself for my stupidity in erecting such a rotten fence. I saw how easy I'd made it for the dog. The fence—the first I'd ever built—sagged badly. There were six-inch gaps between the bottom strand and the ground. I couldn't have made it easier if I'd left the gate open.

"It's my fault too," Betsy said later. "Maybe if I hadn't been so impatient . . . " We took Annie back to the Clarkes and began building a new goat shed closer to the house, one with a dogproof fence. Losing Sybil was a terrible way to learn an essential lesson about tending livestock: of all the things that assail goats, sheep, and cows, nothing brings so much disaster as dogs. And the problem is at its worst in the suburbs because a lot of people have the idea they should give their dogs "freedom." So they open the back door and let them run loose.

Not far from Washington, in one of those communities like ours where the suburbs are rapidly disturbing the countryside, a small sheep farm sits only a mile from a new "community" of expensive colonials. The trouble started shortly after people began moving into these houses. First, it was only a single dead sheep. Hard to bear, but these things happen.

Then two sheep dead in a week. Then two a night. All of them, like Sybil, killed and mutilated, but not eaten.

So the farm owners and some friends parked their cars and pickups on the edge of the pasture one night. And they waited. Soon, they heard a far-off sound, at first only a rustling, hurrying sound coming across the field. Then they heard jingling, like loose coins. They waited until the pack got close, then they flashed on their headlights.

A dozen dogs, some of them already tearing after a stray sheep, milled about in the harsh light. Their tongues lolled out of their mouths and they were frisky, their rabies tags and ID tags jingling as they scurried about, unafraid of the people who walked toward them with guns.

The dogs' owners got the phone calls that night, their phone numbers read from the ID tags by flashlight. There were tears and outrage and threats of lawsuits. "My dog wouldn't do this!" A woman screamed, her dead poodle lying in the middle of the pasture with the dead German shepherds, retrievers, and silly mutts who never so much as chewed on the furniture. But Ma'am, she was told, he did. And he'd keep doing it over and over again once he'd gotten that taste of blood and the excitement of running with the pack.

Now we house our goats (we have four) in a shed Betsy and I built right outside the back door. The fence around their yard is six-foot-high woven wire, pegged to the ground in places with steel tent pegs, and topped with barbed wire to discourage dogs eager enough to try a leap into the yard.

We haven't had too much trouble over the years, with the fence and our ability to see the goat yard from a kitchen window. But once in a while we'll get a couple of neighborhood mutts racing around, barking and snarling at the goats through the fence. We'll go to their owners and tell them what happened and ask that they keep the dogs penned or tied up. And we'll get a long explanation about how it "wouldn't be fair" to the dogs to do that, to restrict them, and how, anyway, their dogs wouldn't hurt a fly.

And that's why, vegetarians or not, we remember Sybil and keep a loaded shotgun near the back door.

We were trimming the goats' hooves one day—one of those jobs the glowing articles in homesteading magazines ("Goats: The Fun Animal") never tell you about. A hoof is like a fingernail. It grows and has to be trimmed regularly. Goats in the wild, on those rocky hillsides in Greece, wear their hooves down naturally. Good for them. But our local farm supply shop is fresh out of Grecian hillsides, so we have to trim the goats' hooves about every month to keep the hooves from growing too long, or growing deformed and throwing the animal's footing off.

"I hate this job," I said to Betsy through gritted teeth. I was holding on to one of Rosemary's hind legs, angling the hoof up so Betsy could work it down with a rasp. Rosemary, a staid old lady built like a water tank, doesn't like having her hooves trimmed—in fact, likes very little besides eating and sleeping. She was showing her displeasure by bawling and fighting me every inch. I finally pinned her against the shed wall and Betsy rasped away. I was feeling pretty raspy myself at that point.

"That's *another* thing I hate," I snapped. "The stink that comes out of those hooves is overwhelming!"

"I thought that's what you came to the country for," Betsy said, "manure and all that."

"This *isn't* the country," I roared, "and that stench of rotted hoof and putrid manure isn't exactly the earthy air I had in mind!"

Ah. Conversations over a goat's rump. But it all came out then. The pressure had been building for a long time. "I *like* goats," I said, almost shouting again, "I *like* animals. But I *hate taking care of the damn things!* I hate all the things you enjoy about it, in fact—the chores, the routine, the doctoring, the responsibility! Look," I said, dropping one of Rosie's feet and grabbing another before she could get away. "I'm a gardener. I know that now. A vegetable gardener. Vegetables I understand. A carrot gets sick, I don't have to call a vet. A cabbage drops dead, we don't hold a wake. And if I don't get down to the garden for a day or so, there's no tragedy. That's what *I* like about homesteading, about this goddamn simple life—the garden, the compost pile, *the dirt!*"

"Okay," said Betsy, quietly, not looking up from her hoof trimming.

"What?" I said, still feeling defensive and certainly expecting some shouting back.

"I said okay. I understand. It's not your thing. So I'll take care of the animals and you take care of the garden."

That one conversation over Rosemary's uncooperative body did a lot for our marriage and even more for our ideas about homesteading. Tension builds up when people assume that the responsibilities of a self-reliant life are always to be shared joyously. Far better to divide the work as much as possible according to personal preferences. Having Betsy handle the animals and me the garden, has worked. I know I can call on Betsy when I need garden help, and she can shout for me if a goat problem needs two more hands.

Ten years have passed since we first looked over the Clarkes' fence. Betsy still feels the same way about goats, and I still think goat keeping is a lot of hard, expensive work. I cringe whenever somebody gets that dreamy look, goes limp hanging on the goat-yard gate, and murmurs, "Someday . . . ." Let me give all you would-be goatmongers a rundown on what it takes to come up with those several quarts of milk each day:

First, goats need good housing. This needn't be palatial. A tight lean-to or shed built facing away from prevailing winds and deep enough to offer protection from driving rain and snow will suffice. Allow 12 square feet of space per animal.

The floor should be earth with good drainage, bedded heavily with straw. The stall must be cleaned every day or so. Or you can build a deep litter by adding fresh straw to cover the droppings and wet spots. Doing it this way means you'll clean the shed out less frequently, but spend more time and energy on the job.

Cleaning regularly in summer will help cut down on the fly problem. In the fall, however, let the litter build up gradually and deeply for insulation. If you bed deeply enough, the decaying manure and litter will produce some bottom-heat.

Another thing we've learned the hard way is that your goat shed or barn needs a separate feed and milk room, one *securely* closed off from the goats' quarters. Goats are smart and strong. If they can get into a feed room, they will. Then they'll wreck the joint and eat themselves to death in the process.

And try to design a separate entrance so you can carry in feed, hay, and other supplies without walking through the goat yard. Goats are superior muggers. They will rip apart a bale of hay, tear open the corner of a sack of grain, or dump a bucket as you carry it in.

Next comes fencing. Aside from dogs, goats are their own worst enemies. Dogs may try to leap over or dig under a fence, but a goat will wreck a fence from the inside out. They do this quite innocently. They love to scratch, rubbing themselves on everything: trees, posts, buildings, fences, even your leg, if it's handy. And because they weigh over 100 pounds, they stretch wire fencing, bow it out, and snap the strands where they're stapled to the fence posts. The fence soon lifts off the ground and you lose sleep wondering whether dogs can get in and the goats out.

And woe to you if your goat-yard fence is bordered by honeysuckle, wild rose, or any other plants goats love. They will stand on the fencing, force their heads through any holes, and bully their way under to eat those leaves on the other side.

Barbed wire is no solution. You'll end up doing almost as much damage to your animals as a dog would. Sharp wire points and pendulous udders aren't a good combination, anyway. The best fencing for goats is made of stone walls at least six feet high. Unfortunately, walls cost a fortune to have built and more time than you've got to build them yourself.

Next best is a stockade-type fence, preferably of the type that surrounded Fort Apache. But itchy caprines can even overwhelm a fort. They eat wood. So whatever lumber you use around them should be free of preservatives.

The most practical fencing for goats, then, is electrical wire (or a combination of wood, or woven wire, and electrical strands). Charged wire is an excellent inexpensive goat and dog repellent. The biggest outlay is for the charging unit. The fencing is nothing more than single strands of thin wire attached to plastic or ceramic insulators. Fence posts for electrical wire can be lightweight rods of wood or fiberglass.

Electrical fencing is humane and effective. I know, having backed into one on several occasions. (The goats never heard language like *that* before.) The electricity comes in pulses, one every fifth of a second or so, though few creatures will stay close enough for more than one belt.

Lay the fence out with one strand 6 inches off the ground, with the others 12 to 18 inches apart, up to a height of four feet. Some may argue that a smaller fence will do. But wire is cheaper than goats.

Electrical fences are not without some problems, however, a power failure or short circuit being the most obvious. Without power, the strands of an electrical enclosure won't hold a chicken. So you must check the fence regularly. You do this with a little neon tester sold in farm stores (or wherever they sell chargers). And you must keep the grass and weeds clipped wherever they might touch a strand. A single weed stalk, particularly in rainy weather, can short out your entire fence.

(My own plan for a dog-and-goat-proof fence includes that six-foot stone wall, ground glass along the top, and gun slits. Once I got that up and paid for, I'd add the land mines, electronic listening devices, and private security forces. You only have to lose a goat once to get a little protective.)

Most goats only need one zap to persuade them to avoid an electrical fence. Watching them discover this is funny, though you may think me cruel for laughing at another creature's discomfit. Just think of all the times the goats laughed at *my* expense.

My first use of an electrical fence was only temporarily effective, anyway. I installed several strands of hot wire after the goats had rubbed a new woven-wire fence into a ball of scrap metal. I locked the girls up while I worked—they'll nibble on the hammer while you're nailing—and when they came out they naturally made for the fence and some good down-to-earth scratching.

Annie was first up, approaching the fence with her eye on a tasty patch of grass just outside the yard. A fence-wrecker of Olympian proportions, Annie marched up, ready to poke her head right through the wire. She leaned forward until the wire zapped her full on the nose. Then she bellowed and ran screaming into the shed, racing around inside like the devil was on her heels. Panting in terror, she peered around the corner of the door, trying to find whatever or whoever bit her.

Seeing no one, she came out again on tiptoes, determined to reach the grass patch, but still wary. "BAAAW!" Another jolt and another mad run around the yard. Annie's screaming this time was more in embarrassment than pain, but the other goats, victims of mob psychology, joined the wild dance until they were all out of breath. A light went on in Annie's eyes. The fence! She'd figured it out. After that no goat dared get too close to the fence. I figured my troubles were over.

Not quite. The particular fence charger I was using was an old model given to me by a friend. It clicked loudly every time the circuit closed and transmitted an electric pulse to the fence. After several weeks I realized the goats had gotten the message. So, ever the energy miser, I turned the charger off one morning, hoping to save a few cents' worth of power.

I came out that afternoon to find the girls leaning against the fence like slatterns, poking their big blockheads through the wires, and, as a final show of contempt for me and technology, Annie was chewing on one of the insulators with a mischievous twinkle in her eye.

The girls had figured out that no clicking sound meant no zapping. Before I could get the charger back on they had torn the wire down and balled it up under their feet.

Goats are full of surprises like that, but even more surprising are the strange ideas people still have about these animals. I wish I had a dollar for every time someone asked me, straight-faced, "Do your goats *really* eat tin cans?" And how often have I heard or read that goats are virtually self-caring, that all you have to do is "just turn them out and let them graze"?

There is some truth to all of this, but it must be sorted out. Goats won't eat anything or everything, though to say so often becomes a self-fulfilling prophecy. Some people simply let their goats fend for themselves, or go hungry. A hungry animal will, of necessity, eat a wider range of stuff than normal, but that's the point: it's *not* normal. Nor is it beneficial. And as for goats eating tin cans: they eat the paper labels. Maybe that's how the crazy idea got started.

I guess this naiveté about goats comes from the distance separating our sophisticated society from animals and the natural world in general. The closest most people ever get to farm animals, after all, is when they're eating them.

I remember when we drove our pickup truck, with two of our goats in the back, into Bethesda, Maryland, a congested suburb. We were on our way to Dave Zeiler, our veterinarian. Every time we stopped for a light we saw necks craning and faces smiling. One man rolled down his car window and yelled, "Are those goats?"

"Yes," Betsy said.

"See," he said to a woman sitting next to him, "I told you so."

We got stopped and were asked questions so many times on the way down to the vet that I began to lose patience. When a gangly teenage boy gawked, made a face that rearranged his pimples, and asked with a laugh, "What are *those?*" I'd had enough. I leveled my best cold stare at him and said in a somber voice, "They're Tasmanian War Dogs. Don't get too close. Dangerous when they get excited."

He took a step back on the sidewalk, started to laugh again but looked at my serious face and pondered. He looked at the goats tethered in the back of the truck, then at me. "No kidding?"

"I wouldn't joke about these dogs, boy, they'll take your leg off."

Then, just as the light changed and we pulled away, one of the goats leaned out and said, "*Maaaaaa!*" The boy jumped back three feet.

Another time we had two baby Nubians in the back of our car. We pulled into a supermarket parking lot to do some shopping. Betsy got out just as a woman and her young daughter walked by.

"Look at those cute little dogs, Mother," the girl said, pointing at the kids, who were staring out of a side window.

"Oh," said the mother, casually, "those are Bedlington terriers. Aren't they cute?"

"Maaaa!" said the terriers.

Yet another naive notion about goats (and cows) is that they somehow "give" milk, the way a tree gives apples. Goats and cows aren't milk machines that can be tapped endlessly (though today's agribusinesses treat them that way), but mammals who only produce milk as food for their young. We've confronted many would-be goat keepers who have been amazed by the fact that goats must be bred and give birth every year or so to produce milk. A lot of people go away disappointed when they discover they can't just buy a "milker," a goat that just naturally gives milk as a permanent condition.

Another thing to remember is that once you've got your goat milking, it's *you* who has to *do* the milking every day. Let's not wax romantic about milking. I like doing it myself, but anything you have to do twice a day, *every* day, can get to you after a while. Goats never take a day off and neither can the goat herder.

And having milked, what are you going to do with all that milk? Depending on the animal, you'll get up to a gallon of milk or more each day. That's at least 21 quarts a week. This means you'd better plan on using a lot of milk or get a bigger refrigerator. Or find some customers to buy your surplus. Or buy a pig or calf to drink up the excess.

See how it expands, this simple life? A moment ago you dreamed of having a peaceful doe who'd deliver milk with a gentle grace. Now you've got baby goats, payments to make on a new refrigerator, a mean pig quartered in the garage until you find time to build a pen, Hare Krishnas pulling into your driveway wanting to buy a quart of goat's milk, and a visit from the health department wanting to know if you're the party illegally selling unpasteurized milk.

That's another thing—it's illegal in most places to sell so-called "raw" milk unless it's sold as pet food. We never sell our milk for human consumption. We do, however, have a lot of folks with very hungry pets. One woman buys a gallon of milk from us each week. We always warn her—"You better not let us catch you drinking any of that stuff or we'll turn you in, y'hear?" She says she feeds it to her canary. Biggest bird you ever saw.

If nothing will deter you from keeping goats, then recognize the difference between keeping them as pets and keeping them as productive dairy animals. As pets, they can do well in the warm months with nothing more than lots of good pasture, mixed brush, and ample water. In winter they'll need daily rations of grain and hay.

If your goats are going to be milkers, however, kidding annually while remaining healthy, they're going to need extra-special care. Producing babies and milk puts a lot of stress on an animal, as any human mother will confirm. And because dairy animals have their lactation extended far beyond the normal weaning period, they need the best of nutrition and husbandry.

In warm weather, Betsy has her goats out browsing every day. Goats will graze on grass, but their favorite foods are weeds and brush. They love bark and tender twigs (goats can destroy a fruit tree in minutes), honeysuckle, wild rose, blackberry bushes, most green leaves, and poison ivy. They wade into dense growths of the latter, stuffing themselves the way children dive into ice cream.

Folk wisdom says that if you drink milk from goats who eat a lot of poison ivy you'll be immunized against the rash. I'm always skeptical about such rustic advice, but this particular information seems to have some validity. Both Betsy and I were extremely allergic to poison ivy. We share childhood memories of being bedridden for days with huge weeping blisters on our hands and faces, our eyes swollen shut.

Yet, though poison ivy grows everywhere on our land in tropical lushness, neither of us has had a serious case in a decade, nor have the children. Part of this may be due to our increased ability to recognize and avoid the stuff, but we can't avoid it entirely. Poison-ivy oil gets on the dogs' and cats' fur, and we're always brushing against unseen plants when we're outdoors.

The cases of poison ivy we get now are always limited in intensity and duration. Of course, there was that time Betsy got a severe rash on her face. But that was because she hugs and kisses her goats with abandon. Never kiss a goat on the lips, I always say, especially after they've been snacking on poison ivy.

Browsing is a goat's natural behavior. Wandering around munching on a variety of plants gives goats a chance to ingest all kinds of trace minerals and nutritive factors that may be unknown to science. Given enough goats, this browsing can keep your place nicely trimmed back. We know of an army base where a herd of over 60 goats is used exclusively for brush and grass control. The army figured out that it was cheaper to maintain goats than to use tractors and manpower. And unlike engines, which give off sparks and heat, goats are entirely safe trimming around ammunition dumps.

But browsing alone isn't enough to fully maintain a pregnant or milking goat, not if you're trying to create optimum health. And once winter comes, the brush disappears. So a grain ration is a necessity.

Betsy feeds a variety of grain mixtures: corn, oats, barley, and some commercially mixed sweetfeeds (grains and molasses). Milking goats need a regular grain ration of 14 percent protein, and Betsy supplements this with bran, beet pulp, vitamin and mineral supplements, chopped vegetables and fruits. Goat heaven.

Goats also need hay, milkers needing the best quality—high-protein alfalfa, clover, or lespedeza. Good leguminous hay can cost $2.50 a bale. Our four goats eat a bale a week in winter, less in warm weather when they're browsing. There are cheaper hays—timothy and orchard grass, or you can feed bagged, pelletized hay, available in feed stores.

If all this sounds complicated and expensive—not the idyllic notion of having no-care goats that provide you with endless gallons of milk and wheels of cheese—*it is.*

And as long as I'm debunking myths, let me knock off another one:

the myth of the hardy beast. Along with their reputation for having cast-iron stomachs, goats have also been acclaimed as almost indestructibly sound animals. But goats *do* get sick, sometimes with baffling ailments that will drive your veterinarian back to his or her graduate school notes.

We had a problem with a goat named Lucinda, a doe out of Annie, who was the herd runt. Not that she was physically small, but she *acted* like a runt. The other goats picked on her, butted her around for the hell of it, made sure she was always last in line at feeding, and once even shoved her out into the rain. She stood outside the shed screaming her head off. Goats *hate* rain. A few drops make them dance around like marionettes.

Lucinda didn't help matters by being a whiner, a professional victim of imagined slights. She complained constantly, maa-ing and moaning and sometimes baw-ing at the top of her considerable voice. In time, we all—goats and humans alike—began to dislike her.

But we feared for her safety. The other goats were getting increasingly rougher, slamming her into the walls and butting her savagely. We worried about broken bones and internal injuries. She had already developed a limp that ate up a lot of time and money in X rays and veterinary consultations. And the diagnosis? Psychosomatic.

"What do we do now," I asked Betsy, "take her to a psychotherapist?"

"I don't think anyone would let her get on the couch."

"Great. We can't separate her from the others, we can't sell her or give her away—that's a cop-out—so what do we do?"

"Well," Betsy said, "if Lucinda is at the bottom of the heap, why don't we add another goat to the herd and change the social structure?"

"Spoken like a true social meddler," I said, "but what if the new goat picks on Lucinda?"

"We'll get a younger goat, one that Lucinda can pick on," Betsy said brightly.

"Have you ever thought of going into public relations?" I said. I thought getting another goat was a dumb idea.

We called Bob and Mary Clarke and they agreed the experiment was worth trying. They offered to loan us a goat. I still thought this was a loony idea and doubly so when Betsy brought home Edwina, an eight-month-old black doe who was also a virtuoso screamer.

"Wonderful," I grumbled, "now we're going to have *two* neurotic goats to deal with."

"We shall see," Betsy said, sagely, the old goat lady dispensing her mystic knowledge.

For several weeks Lucinda continued to limp, whine, and get

rejected and butted by the other goats. All except Edwina. Edwina just screamed a lot for no good reason and ran around in panic. Double trouble.

Then the situation began to change in subtle ways. What happened was fascinating to watch. Edwina never actually replaced Lucinda as herd runt. The goats never bullied her with quite the nastiness they meted out to Lucinda. Nor did Lucinda push Edwina around much. Yet, as Betsy had suggested, just adding Edwina did something to the social structure of our small herd.

Lucinda suddenly began gaining weight. She lost her limp. And she grew, not just in girth, but in stature. She held her head higher, had a different look in her eyes, and stopped whining. Her manner suddenly seemed to say, "Nobody's going to kick sand in *my* face any more!"

Within a few months she became a big, muscular, aggressive doe that nobody picked on. Edwina went back to the Clarkes after we added several kids to our herd. Eventually, Lucinda became the queen goat, the one given a wide berth. Everybody jumped if Lucinda so much as flicked her tail.

Besides emotional problems, goats can also catch colds, have allergies, develop tapeworms, eczema, arthritis, and a variety of other ailments designed to confound the goat herder and enrich the veterinarian. And let's add to this what goats can do to themselves. I've already suggested the importance of having a feed room secure against the battering of curious goats. Bitter experience speaking here, friends.

Before we knew much about goats, we trusted a piece of rope tied in a bowknot to hold shut the door between the goats' stall and the feed room. The girls must have chuckled in expectation as one of them wiggled a prehensile upper lip and slipped the knot.

We were in the kitchen when we heard the commotion, the rattling of feedbin lids, the ripping of paper bags, the baa-ing and thudding of goat bodies as they fought over the spilled grain as humans might riot over a broken bag of silver dollars.

We ran to the feed room, chased them out, and barred the door with a goatproof 2-by-4. The damage from a few minutes of goat mischief was amazing. A tornado couldn't have scattered as much grain and torn paper. And they had compounded the mess by scattering their droppings, stepping in them, and smearing manure all over. At times like this you wonder why you're not buying milk in a container, just like everyone else.

Then we realized the worst: Rosemary had eaten faster than we had run. Now if humans or dogs overeat, they can throw up. But goats can't. Their rumen (the first of their four stomach chambers) becomes impacted and filled with gas—a potentially fatal condition aptly named "bloat."

After a few frantic phone calls to our veterinarian and to the enduring Mary Clarke, we began administering the cure, in this case, almost as bad as the ailment.

To free the animal's system and dispel the gas takes simple but drastic measures. First, we had to mix up a solution of mineral oil and soapsuds, an awful brew. Second, we had to force this noxious potion down Rosemary's throat. If this sounds easy, consider that Rosemary has the solidity of a sumo wrestler. Forcing her to do anything, even removing her hoof from atop your foot, is almost impossible.

Squirting that vile concoction down her throat with an oven-baster took every ounce of energy both of us had. And, of course, we were facing the probability that Rosemary was going to die no matter what we did.

Forcing liquid down an animal's throat is called "drenching." I suspect the term got its name from the condition of the drenchers rather than the drenchee. And you can't make a mistake in the process. If you squirt the liquid down the wrong way—into the windpipe—the animal may develop fatal pneumonia.

So we wrestled, cursed, squirted, and got drenched with oil and soap and sweat and dirt. Our feet were nearly crushed by cloven hooves. The fact that we were trying to save Rosemary's life didn't matter one bit to her. Death before dishonor.

After the drenching, we tied a stick, fashioned like a rough bit, across the back of Rosemary's mouth. This was to get her to chew constantly, because chewing stimulates the gut so the gas bubbles break up and pass from either the mouth or the rectum.

Once that was in place—no easy matter—we had to leave Rosemary chained to the fence, to chew and chew and chew. We checked her constantly, consoling her and apologizing for what must have struck her as insane behavior. And we patted her ample stomach, checking to see if her bloated sides had decreased in girth.

Ben Franklin cursed flatulence as "a vortex in the bowels," but never was it more welcome. Rosemary's bloat subsided after two hours of steady chewing on the stick. We removed the bit, alternately condemning Rosemary for her stupidity and congratulating her on her survival. All we got in return was a withering look from a tired, oily, dirty, humiliated goat who—given the opportunity—would have broken into the feed room that night and gorged herself all over again.

Sometimes a sick animal demands more than drenching, drugs, or a veterinarian's visit. I said earlier that Mary Clarke became Betsy's guide to goat husbandry. But one night I realized that Betsy herself had really become a "goat lady," possessed of intuitive knowledge and wisdom.

I was sleeping soundly when I was awakened by a strange sound. I lay there, staring into the darkness, wondering if the sound was part of a dream. Convinced it was, I fell back asleep.

"Waaaa!" There it was again, muffled and distant, coming from down the hallway. I reached over to Betsy, sleeping next to me. Gone. Her covers were rumpled into a pile.

I got out of bed and padded down the hall to the living room. There, in our old and tattered easy chair, was Betsy and a baby goat, both sound asleep, breathing in unison, snuggled into a wool blanket Betsy had pulled around them.

The kid was Emmy, born two weeks before and sickly since a few days after birth. Betsy had been running her back and forth to our veterinarian to little avail. Dave tried all manner of things, called every goat specialist he could think of, and cursed himself for his ignorance. Nothing helped. Emmy didn't get any sicker but she didn't get well, either. For a newborn with low resistance, that usually means a slow exit to death.

But Betsy doesn't give up easily. She had awakened in the middle of the night, thought about Emmy out in the barn, thought about the cool spring weather that had moved in, damp and chilling, and did the only thing she could think of. I've seen her do this many times—sit up all night with a sick creature, stroking it and gently encouraging it. An Earth Mother with a bedside manner.

Emmy's head was pressed against Betsy's chest, those spindly goat legs splayed out in four directions. Betsy was deeply asleep, snoring lightly, her head tilted back at an uncomfortable angle, her arms wrapped around the kid, holding it close to her body.

I laughed to myself as I watched her. Betsy came from a family so attuned to "what other people think" that her grandfather would rarely leave the house without a coat and tie on. And here sat his granddaughter, nestled down in a broken chair with a sick baby goat, not caring about anything but life and survival. Standing there, I remembered how that chair got broken. Once I was sitting in it and Betsy walked by. I grabbed her and pulled her into my lap. She laughed as she fell into my arms. I hugged and kissed her just as the springs gave way with a loud snap! The chair collapsed onto its wooden feet and we laughed all the way down.

The collapsed chair, sitting so low to the ground, made Betsy and Emmy look that much more snuggled. Goats in the house? In the living room? Her family would have been aghast. But Emmy got well after that night. Her health improved and she blossomed into a sturdy little animal. Goat ladies, I discovered, can sometimes overcome the limitations of veterinary medicine with nothing more than love and an old chair.

I teased Betsy the next morning. "I remember your mother's living room and your grandmother's and *my* grandmother's—formal parlors that no one but company could enter."

"I remember too," Betsy laughed. "The lampshades still wrapped in cellophane . . . "

". . . the spotless wall-to-wall carpeting, the doilies on the back of the couch, the porcelain figurines on the side tables . . . "

". . . the baby grand piano nobody knew how to play . . . "

". . . and here we are, in the wealthiest town in the wealthiest county in the U.S.A., with broken-down chairs, pumpkins curing by the wood stove, and baby goats using the living room as a clinic."

"It all goes back to my Chicken Grandma," Betsy said. "Something must have skipped a generation."

Chicken Grandma, as the family calls her, was Betsy's grandfather's mother. She was one of those sturdy women who, with her family, left Europe at the turn of the century for a new life in America. They settled in New Brunswick, New Jersey—a far cry from her farm in Lithuania—but Chicken Grandma never lost touch with her roots.

"She raised children, chickens, ducks, and geese," Betsy said. "That's how she got the nickname. She used to carry chicks and eggs in her apron pockets, to keep them warm. And her home was always just that—a home. Never a showplace. Even if you just dropped by, you got a glass of wine and some food. You had to *visit.* "

Betsy never really knew her Chicken Grandma. Her knowledge comes from family stories. "I met her only once," Betsy said. "She was in her eighties or nineties then, bedridden and dying of consumption. But what I remember was a wiry, bright woman with love in her voice. That memory and the stories about her really stayed with me. All the time my mother and grandmother were hassling me about 'the finer things in life', I was thinking about being outdoors and working with animals. Chicken Grandma would have understood."

And she would have too, especially if she saw Betsy at kidding time.

We don't sleep in the goat shed anymore when a birth is imminent, but all of us—the children included—feel a special kind of tension as a doe nears the due date. Betsy checks regularly for signs of an impending delivery. The pregnant goat may begin "talking" to Betsy, "maa-ing" softly, or rubbing against Betsy's leg. Sometimes the doe will go off to a corner of the shed and dig out a body-sized hole. That's her nest. The digging is a sure sign that birth is coming soon, though exactly *when* is a mystery up until the last minutes.

This is a time when we don't go too far from home. Betsy gets up several times during the night to check the doe. If it looks like labor is coming on, she'll bring out a lawn chair and a book. Then she'll sit, waiting.

We like to be there right at the birth—and we haven't missed one in a decade. Sometimes a doe will need help delivering. Breech births aren't uncommon among goats, nor is it unusual for a kid to come through with a leg bent the wrong way. Betsy likes to be there to act as midwife. And even when the delivery is normal, there's always the chance that the mother will accidentally step or roll on one of the kids.

Our tension increases as the due date arrives and, sometimes, passes. Calculating the actual date is difficult unless you actually witness the buck and doe mating. And that's no easy trick, given the speed with which a buck performs his duties. So Betsy plays a waiting game. She gathers her equipment—iodine to put on the ends of the umbilical cord (we don't cut the cord, though), and plenty of clean towels to rub and wrap the kids with. If night falls before the kids come, we rig up spotlights in the shed.

When the doe finally goes into the final stages of labor, a peculiar quiet settles over the goat shed. We lock the other goats out of the barn to keep confusion to a minimum. But once the pregnant doe begins her final contractions, the other goats get very quiet. They can't see into the shed. They have no way of knowing exactly what's going on, but they *know.* All during the last moments of labor they stand quietly in the yard, their heads lowered, eyes half shut, chewing their cuds. Waiting. Only when the first kid is born do they become animated again and resume their browsing. They seem to sense the seriousness of the moment.

The birth of goat kids is no less significant for us. All the wonder of Earth's renewal is played out in the shed. The doe bellows and heaves; a sac appears, shiny, slippery, filled with birth fluids. We can see the kid through the membranes, a murky image, looking like an astronaut sealed in a translucent capsule.

Betsy lays her hands on the doe's haunches and murmurs encouragement, "Push now! Sophie, push again! Atta girl, a little more!" One final push and the sac pours out like a heap of wet rags sliding onto the straw bedding. Betsy quickly pulls the membranes away from the tiny face. This is always an anxious moment.

Is it alive? The kid is wet, limp, unmoving. A little pile of entwined legs and wet fur. Suddenly, a tiny sneeze! "Few! Ka-few!" The kid tosses its head, opens its eyes for the first time, shakes, and sneezes again.

Betsy calls this "the sneeze of life." The sound is like a miniature Bronx cheer. How appropriate, I always think, that goats, of all animals, should announce their arrival in the world with a rude noise.

But this is only the first kid born. We wait now for the second. Single kids—singletons—are uncommon. Two kids are more likely, triplets not unusual. Only the doe knows how many she's got. We feel the doe's sides—"palpate," Betsy says with a professional air—but all we can do is wait. Often we've had two kids born within minutes of each other, then a half hour passing with no more. That's it, we figure. But then the doe stands, grunts, and another bundle of wet wash slides out with a plop.

The wonder of baby goats is that like all herd animals, they develop so rapidly. Betsy rubs them vigorously to dry them and stimulate circulation. They lie in the straw, sneezing and wobbling, but within 15 minutes they're standing and walking haltingly on knob-kneed matchstick legs.

Their eyes are bright and their lips are pulled back into comical grins. And they find their voices in the first minutes after birth. They maa softly, plaintively at first. How strange the sound of their own voices must sound to them. Within an hour they're bleating loudly and trying to nurse on our fingers.

If it seems like we're taking the responsibility from the mother doe in doing all this, you're right. Many does pay no attention to their kids at first. Some, I suspect, don't even know they've given birth. In a natural setting this may work fine. Some kids will die and some will survive. But we prefer to save all of them, if we can.

We take the kids away from the mother immediately after birth. This may sound cruel, separating the doe from her newborns, but there's no fuss at all. The does never scream at having their kids carried off, nor do the kids protest.

What happens is interesting. The doe forms a mother-kid relationship with *Betsy*, regarding her as her offspring. That's what Mary Clarke meant when she said Annie would never really be ours until she kidded for us. It's true. The doe talks to Betsy, screams when she walks away, and even cleans her carefully by licking her arms and face. Betsy milks the doe soon after the birth, and the doe—from what I can see—naturally accepts this as her baby nursing. The intensity of this bonding wanes after some weeks, but the doe always regards Betsy as someone special after that.

A similar phenomenon occurs with the kids. They don't scream for their doe-mother because we are feeding them. We raise them in the house—the shed would be better, but it lacks a separate kidding pen. We keep them in a large kennel crate until they outgrow it, but by that time they're big enough to go in with the mature goats. We bottle-feed them using their mother's milk, warmed and fed through a lamb nipple stretched over the neck of a Perrier water bottle. (How middle class can you get?)

Aside from around-the-clock feeding the first few weeks, we also have to guard against colds, chills, pneumonia, coccidiosis (a protozoan parasite), and malnutrition. Sometimes the kids have to be coaxed to eat properly.

All this creates a certain amount of confusion in the house, what with two children, cats, dogs, and a constant stream of visitors who come to see the baby goats. The kids stay in their crate—unless we've got them out running around—or, if it's warm, on the back porch. But most of the time they're running around the living room with Noah and Rachel, who—as you can imagine—love having such frisky playmates.

Noah was about 18 months old when he saw his first set of baby goats being born, a powerful scene even for an adult. A goat's birth isn't like seeing puppies or kittens being born. Newborn goats are almost the size of a human infant, and their dramatic entrance is always accompanied by the doe's bellowing.

Rosemary was in her final stages of labor as Noah toddled around the goat shed, poking into the grainbins and eating a little sweetfeed as he played. We had talked about what was going to happen, but trying to explain the mysteries of birth to an 18-month-old is like discussing astrophysics.

Betsy was sitting with Rosemary, comforting her as the time neared. Suddenly, Rosie's contractions reached their peak. She yelled, "Maaaaawww!" gave a hearty push, and a baby's head popped out of her vagina.

Noah was standing next to me and jumped in fear when Rosie screamed. I knelt down and explained that the doe's bleating was okay, that goats did that when they had babies. I put my arm around him as I explained.

"Is Rosemary sick?" he asked.

"No," I said, "having a baby is hard work. She yells that way because she's pushing the kid out."

"C'mon, Rosie," encouraged Betsy, wiping the membrane away from the emerging kid's face. "Push! Push!" Rosie obeyed, gave another mighty heave, and out slid a sopping wet kid.

Noah watched, fascinated, no longer afraid now that he understood what the commotion was all about. The tension and yelling and Rosemary's strange contortions were all balanced by Betsy's happy shouts and enthusiasm. Two more kids followed the first one and Noah quickly joined the postnatal activities. He helped rub the kids down with a rough towel, Betsy let him put some iodine on the umbilical cords, and he got to help with the first feeding.

The days and weeks after the birth found Noah still excited about the event and the active role he'd played. He told everyone, "Rosemary had babies and they came right out of her pajama!"

But goats die too, and this is much harder to explain to a child than birth. Goats have strong, individual personalities. When they die, it's like losing a friend or a family member. And, oh—the questions the children ask: Why do things die? What *is* dying? Will I die? Will you die?

One of our goats once had a spontaneous abortion of four fetal kids. They were fully formed but dead when they came out. Noah was about two years old then, playing in the yard with a friend. He saw the dead babies and was thoroughly fascinated. Maybe a little frightened, too.

This was a hot day and I wanted to get the kids buried as soon as I could, so off we all went on a funeral—me, a shovel, Noah, and his little friend. As I look back, maybe I should have waited and done the burying alone, but it's hard to make the right decision when a goat is aborting and the children are clamoring with questions and Betsy is on the phone with Mary Clarke.

Noah watched me dig the hole. "Why are you digging a hole, Daddy?"

"To bury the kids, Noah."

"Why you wanna do that, Dad?"

"Because they're dead." I gently placed the bodies into the hole and began raking dirt over them.

"Why are you throwing dirt on them?"

"Well . . . " Lord, some things we adults take for granted sure sound dumb when you have to explain them.

"Why can't we keep them?"

"I couldn't let you keep a dead animal, Noah."

"Why not? Maybe they'll come alive again."

"No, they're dead for good."

"For ever and always?"

"Yes."

But don't you know, the next morning at breakfast Noah got into my lap and asked, "Daddy?"

"What?"

"Would you dig those babies back up again so I could look at them once more?"

Noah is older now and his interest in goats always wanes as the kids mature. He loves playing with the kids and feeding them, but once they become goats, losing their friskiness and small size, he moves on to other interests.

Not Rachel. There we have another goat lady or Chicken Grandma in the making. Like Noah, she saw her first goats born when she was 18 months old. (Just a coincidence; we didn't plan it that way.) Her comment on the birth—one she repeated for weeks—"Momma say 'poosh-poosh', anna babies come out!" Perhaps it's Rachel's strong identification with Betsy, but her enthusiasm for the goats, for *all* animals, in fact, never falters. She loves the babies *and* the grown-ups.

But Rachel has a special relationship with the adult goats. She treats them like other children. And why not? She's been playing with them ever since she could toddle around the goat yard. I can't tell exactly what they think of her, but they seem to enjoy the attention.

Rachel orders them here and there, pulling them by their collars and chatting incessantly. The goats are docile—far more than they would be with Betsy or me. They indulge Rachel. Sometimes we'll look out a kitchen window and see the goats all lying down in the sun, with Rachel sitting amidst them, lost in deep conversation. And one day I went out and watched Rachel—she was two years old—leading all the goats around, shoving them into a definite order, scolding them when they didn't move fast enough. When she got them all lined up in a row, she stood in front of them and piped, "Okay, everybody—now let's all clap our hands and *sing!*"

Sometimes Rachel's love of animals produces curious problems. We had a goat boarding with us once, a buck named Hawkeye. Betsy had borrowed him to breed the does—easier than bringing all the girls to Hawkeye. Now bucks stink, as I've pointed out, though it's not the scent so much as the strength of the odor that gets to you. Imagine a stink powerful enough to knock you down.

But Rachel is an equal opportunity animal lover. She either didn't notice that Hawkeye stank, or she didn't care. He was just another goat to play with, and she pulled him around the yard like a toy cart. Most bucks are aggressive and stubborn, but Hawkeye loved all that affection and did whatever Rachel asked. He was rewarded with pats, hugs, and kisses. He just stood there, soaking it in. Unfortunately, Rachel soaked something in too—Hawkeye's overwhelming fragrance.

I had to go on some errands one morning and Rachel asked to come along. "You'd leave your friend Hawkeye for me?" I teased her, "I'm honored." Off we went to the post office. Rachel held onto my trouser leg as I counted out some stamp money. But then I had this feeling I was being watched. I looked up to see several postal workers and customers eyeing me suspiciously, though they turned away when I looked in their direction.

Then I looked down at Rachel, clinging to my leg. Sweet Rachel. Tiny, innocent, reeking. Well, Americans are funny about ah . . . personal problems, so I knew nobody was going to say anything to me. And I couldn't really explain it to them. I certainly couldn't tell them the truth—that it wasn't me but my little daughter who stank like the Black Hole of Calcutta.

As we turned to leave, another man pushed through the door, a Good Ol' Boy from up-county, one of those characters that's disappearing as the suburbs absorb farmland. "Gaw damn!" he bellowed, a cross between Chill Wills and Lyndon Johnson, "who in hell's been messing with a billy goat?"

"It's my daughter," I said as Rachel and I walked past him. "They're in love."

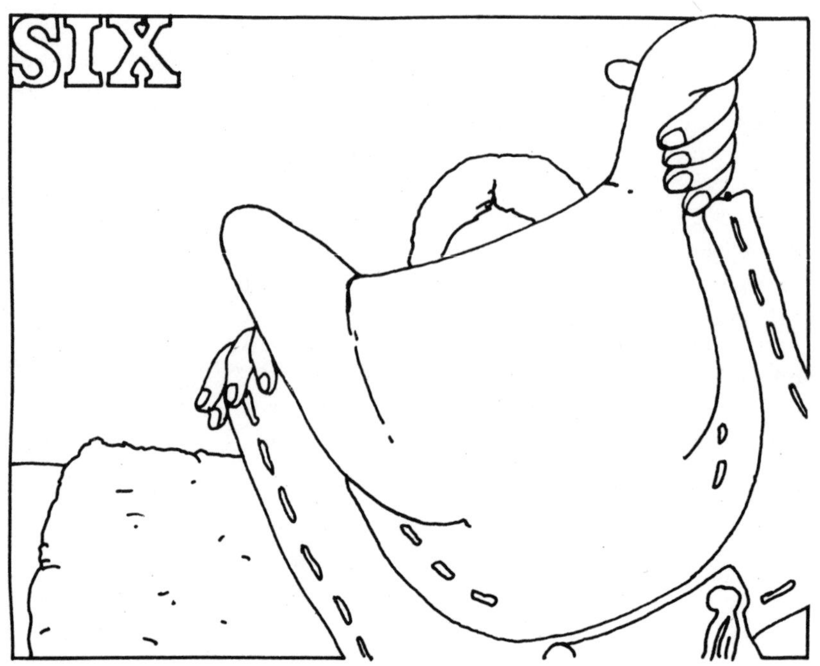

Two acres is plenty of land on which to homestead. You can raise more than enough vegetables and fruit for a family of four there and find ample room for chickens and other small livestock if you desire.

But two acres isn't enough to wander about on, to hike on, or lose yourself in thought on. So we were fortunate to buy two acres in the midst of hundreds of other acres of open land. Much of this land, as we learned shortly after moving in, belonged to a neighbor, Nathan Major, a securities broker whose passion was horses.

The Major farm consisted of roughly 500 acres, mostly rolling hills, some patches of trees, and a pond that sat directly across from our house. Nathan and I used to joke that I had the best part of the pond—if not of all his land—while he got to pay the mortgage.

There was more open land behind us, about 100 acres of open fields. The nearest house to us was almost a quarter-mile across a meadow, so we lived in splendid isolation.

After we moved in I found Betsy looking out the upstairs window, lost in thought. She was looking at the horses, Major's horses, feeding in the field across from the house.

"I know what you're thinking," I said.

"Yes."

"Why don't you call over there and introduce yourself and see if they need anyone to exercise their horses?"

"Oh, I bet they get calls like that all the time."

"Not from people who ride as well as you do."

The farm was a working horse farm populated by polo ponies, hunters, and steeplechase horses. Nathan quickly realized that Betsy was more than just an "exercise girl" and soon had her involved in training horses. Betsy didn't need much encouragement. This was something she had always wanted to do, to be on her own working with horses.

I remember one February, a particularly cold month when early morning temperatures never got out of the teens, when I'd look across the field and see Betsy riding a steeplechase horse, racing across a meadow white with hoarfrost, horse hooves pounding like muffled drumbeats, horse and rider a single organism.

One year Nathan had more than 50 horses turned out, not all his, some were boarders, but still they had to be fed and cared for. Betsy had by this time become the unofficial barn manager, a position she held for almost two years and one she refused to accept money for.

"I'm doing what I like, what I want to do," she told Nathan when he offered to put her on salary. Then to me she said, "If I take money for it then I'll just be an employee. It won't be the same. I'm not selling anything."

Though Betsy was always around horses as a kid, there were certain things she wasn't allowed to do. No mucking out the barn. Dirty work. Not for a girl. You'll get calluses.

So Betsy made up for lost time and mucked out barns like crazy, sometimes doing 25 and 30 stalls a day. She never looked better. The hard work gave her a glow (and muscles) and she was radiantly happy.

I liked being around the horses, too, though I never shared Betsy's interest in or commitment to them. I especially liked seeing them grazing in the fields. Even in the midst of the suburbs, a herd of horses strung out across a meadow can convey, for me, a sense of peace, of primeval simplicity and order.

Nathan's back field held about 30 horses, all of them turned out for the winter. They were fed and watered, but like their wild kin, they lived unsheltered from wind, rain, and snow. I spent many winters watching them adapt to this life in the open, and it taught me a lot.

The land was rolling hills, and I discovered, as the horses had, that though uniform in appearance, the land was really a series of microclimates. Often on a freezing day with the wind slicing out of the northwest, the horses would gather together in a dell or valley, protected against the wind, warmed by their collective body heat.

Sometimes these microclimates were startling in their temperature differentials. Once I walked around the lower part of a hillside into a tiny glen. No horses were there, four inches of snow covered the ground, and the air temperature was in the 20's. But as I stepped all the way into the glen it became almost balmy. The wind howled around but never penetrated the sheltered cove. I felt as though I'd stepped into another world. I've never looked at a woods or meadow since and seen it as a single entity. Now I know that what I see is a matrix of zones and special places and secrets waiting to be discovered.

I didn't realize this all at once, of course. At first I thought leaving horses out unsheltered all winter was cruel (as it might well be in a harsher climate). But I saw the animals thrive. Their coats grew long and shaggy and they seemed to relish being unsaddled, away from humans and the constraints of the barn and its stalls, free to run the hills and wander as they pleased. They were obviously hardier and healthier than they would have been cooped up in a too warm stable.

The horses had to be fed every day, though, a job Betsy and I took special pleasure in doing. We'd load Nathan's old rusted-out farm truck with hay and grain and rumble out across the field, hearing the crusted snow crunching under the bald tires. The horses would see us coming and begin walking toward us. They'd start running, slowly at first, then picking up speed, thundering, the entire herd turning and pulling together, their manes tossing, great noble heads bobbing, the vapor from their breath making a haze of steam as they raced toward us, whinnying in expectation.

Were we only 20 miles from downtown Washington? No, this was Montana, Wyoming, a John Wayne movie, not suburban Potomac. Horses suddenly surrounded us, nickering and snorting and pushing each other to get closer to the hay we tossed over the side of the truck.

And when we poured the grain into tubs in the field the horses milled around us like centaurs, their great bodies pressed close to us, respectful of our puny frames, but eager to get their share of oats. Often I felt a ripple of fear as I stood inside that crowd of eager horses. But at the same time, I felt no fear at all but a strange sense of peace and harmony. Perhaps I could feel a kinship with a herd that I never felt with a single horse. Perhaps I enjoyed the touch of danger from those tons of energy and power that swirled around me.

I loved it. And when we were done haying and putting out the grain we'd clamber back into the truck, our noses running from the cold and exertion. And I'd look over at Betsy and we knew this was all we ever wanted, to be outdoors, at work, feeling life within and without, with just a hint of danger in the air to make that life all the more precious.

But this wasn't Montana or Wyoming, and if John Wayne were to come riding over the hills he would be in a car. This was the suburbs, and the land we were on was on borrowed time. Nathan never made any bones about that. His farm was an investment. He put his money in land, sure that its value would increase in time. When it appreciated enough he would sell it and the dells and springs and pond we loved would sprout houses. Perhaps this knowledge sharpened our pleasure while saddening us. We could never allow ourselves to become complacent about our good fortune in having a farm without paying for it. We knew the land wouldn't stay as it was for long.

I felt this impending loss most in winter when I walked Nathan's fields at night. I run every day for exercise, sometimes across the farm, but more frequently along the Potomac River, two miles from our house. But sometimes, after a winter storm, the snow would be too deep to run through, or the road to the river would be snowed in. Then I'd exercise by hiking across the meadows, trudging through the powder, sweating lightly, feeling my heart pound. Many of these hikes were at night, not by design, but because the short winter day turned to dusk before I could get outdoors. The snow reflected all the light I needed for my solitary rambles. And my regular tours gave me an internal map of every woodchuck hole, dell, rock outcropping, and briar tangle on the farm.

One night was especially magical. A full moon hung in a cold blue sky, the stars only pinpricks of frozen light. The snow was several days old and a thaw had caused it to glaze. Walking was almost impossible in my heavy insulated boots. (The ice would have cut leather boots to shreds.) I didn't walk as much as I crunched, lifting one foot after another to break through the crust, trudging slowly across the white meadow.

The moonlight was pale white. The snow and ice cover blue and vast, each undulation of hill and dell coated with frost, shimmering in the moonlight. Then the wind kicked up and I heard the trees near the pond rattle their brittle frozen branches, tapping against each other like dry leaves blowing down the hallway of an abandoned house.

Then I heard a strange and beautiful sound. The wind was blowing tiny bits of ice across the glazed snow. Some were the size of pebbles, others no more than ice dust. The wind blew these bits and they hummed and tinkled and whined as they flew across the field, making an eerie sound like wires humming, like celestial music, like the tale a crystal goblet might tell. I stood there transfixed, listening.

On the road I could see cars crawling along. The wind was blowing snow across the road, swirling it into a haze. Cars slowed and stopped, their headlights a sickly yellow cutting across the fields. I heard tires whine against the ice. A horn blared angrily.

I turned away from the road, from the headlights slashing through the night, and I walked on listening to the electric whistling *screeeee!* as the ice crystals raced around me.

The pond on Nathan's land was most special to us. Though it lay across the road, it was visible from the upstairs living room, from the land in front of our house, and from anywhere we walked in the large field that contained it. Though it wasn't large—no more than an acre or so—the pond sustained us and lifted our spirits in every season.

In summer we would lie in bed and listen to the sound of spring peepers, hundreds of them, calling and squeaking in a marvelous cacophony. Later in the season came the bullfrogs with deep, rumbling croaks that cut across the still night air.

In the fall, ducks alighted on the pond. Mallards and wood ducks were always flying overhead, quacking signals and flight directions and splashing down on our private preserve. We were only a mile from the river, so many water birds used the pond as a rest stop on their way to larger winter quarters. But no visitor ever meant more to us than the great blue heron.

I noticed it one day as I walked past the upstairs window. I had such a paternal feeling about the pond that I rarely went long without checking its perimeters. Perhaps I feared it might drain away. (Nathan called me his "game warden.")

Then I saw it. A bluish figure so large I took it at first to be a child standing on the broken dock on the pond side. I grabbed for the binoculars and stood riveted when I realized what it was—a magnificent bird, storklike, bluish-gray, almost four feet tall. It was standing on the edge of the dock, almost motionless, as though deep in contemplation.

This was the first of many visits throughout the fall. So regular was the heron's arrival that we became worried when a day passed without seeing it. Most dramatic of all was to see the heron land or take off. The large wings beat slowly, powerfully. When landing, the heron drops easily, extending its reedlike legs until they touch ground. Then, in slow motion, the rest of the body settles atop the legs, the wings fold, the long flexible neck retracts into a U-shape, and the creature gives a slight ruffle as though to settle all its ungainly parts together.

The take-off is pure fascination for me. Seeing the heron lift off is like watching a small man struggle into the air. Too big to leap skyward, the crane must beat those huge wings against the air, pumping steadily until it lifts off by inches, then floats and rises and wheels off with a grace that never fails to leave me wonderstruck, as though I've just seen a flying carpet sail past. In a way, the great blue heron is *my* flying carpet. When it flies, so do I.

Once I looked out the window and saw the heron standing on the dock in a torrential rain. Water was coming down in sheets, slamming against the roof and tree limbs. The heron stood, one leg tucked up against itself, its head bowed, waiting, unflinching, accepting.

All these views were through binoculars. I was never able to get close to the bird no matter how stealthy my approach. And let me tell you, when it comes to stealth I sneak with the best. Once I stalked a female mallard who'd alighted on the pond. It took me 20 minutes of crawling and tiptoeing with camera in hand to get close enough to snap the picture I wanted.

I tried the same techniques on the heron to no avail. I never got within 100 feet no matter how crafty I was. But this pleased me. I'm glad the heron is so sensitive to intrusion. Perhaps that will help insure its survival.

Along the river all stealth seems to belong to the heron, not to me; instead of my surprising it, the heron is always startling me. There are more herons at the river and I am constantly being scolded by one or two as I run along the towpath next to the canal. As I run, a flash of blue will lift off 50 yards ahead of me, the magnificent wings pumping in slow motion, the large body soaring as I run into its territory. And always I am scolded by the herons' raucous voice; "Rooaark! Rooaark!" they admonish me, as they push against the air and fly over the river.

Betsy and I often used to take Noah and Rachel to the pond. We'd sit and discuss what they saw and were thinking about. Once when I had both children with me sitting on the pond's edge, watching the late summer sun turn the pond's surface into the colors of molten lava, we saw a baby turtle waddling along the shoreline.

"Look! Look!" Noah cried, and I gently picked the creature up for us to inspect. That moment is frozen in memory for me. Noah was five then, Rachel was two; both were dressed in bib overalls, sneakers, and tee shirts. They huddled around my outstretched hand, the little turtle glistening in the roseate sunlight. Their eyes were wide. "Can I touch it?" Noah asked.

"Of course," I said.

"Me too," said Rachel, breathlessly.

Their tiny fingers prodded the turtle's shell, gently, questioningly. No bigger than a half dollar, the turtle pulled its head and legs into its shell, hissing almost inaudibly as it shut us out.

"What will we do with it?" Noah asked.

"We'll let it go," I said.

"Can't I keep it?"

"No," I said, "not this time. Maybe when you're a little older we can keep a turtle for a day or so and then let it go. But wild things belong in the wild, not in houses."

"Sure is cute," said Noah.

"Is coot," echoed Rachel.

"Yes," I said, kneeling near the water's edge. I set the turtle down in the wet mud and moved back. We watched for a few moments until the creature poked its head out and decided all was well. Then it skittered into the water and paddled off, heading for the tall grass and safety.

Our experiments in homesteading have brought us many moments like these, when the beauties of the natural world are almost overwhelming in their clarity. Yet equally overwhelming is the irony that our discoveries have been made against the backdrop of a monstrously sprawling metropolitan area, that our search for self-reliance and a simpler life-style should take place here in affluent Potomac, just outside Washington, the seat of power and megabucks. Writers used to describe Washington as a "sleepy little Southern town." Now its prices for goods and services are among the highest in the country. Its real estate costs, especially in Potomac, are astronomical. And while the streets aren't yet paved with gold, the presence and importance of money in Washington is flagrantly obvious. Living here, trying to fashion a simpler life, a homestead existence, is like going to the Land of Oz to study political science.

Shopping malls spread across the land like algae blooms on the pond, all of them furnished with climate-controlled teenage loiterers, chlorinated fountains, potted plants, and acres of tiles and plastic laminate. Some boast glass elevators, the wonder of the age. Shaped like an ovate capsule, its outer edges festooned with frosted makeup mirror light bulbs, the elevator rises and falls the 20 feet between store levels, looking like a giant neon suppository.

But in Potomac, it's houses that count even more than stores. Not just houses, places for people to live; not simply homes, but estates and mini-estates and baronial spreads with underground lawn sprinklers. Here are hyperthyroid Swiss chalets and ersatz English Tudor mansions with heat pumps—the Holiday Inns of residential architecture. (You too can play the country squire in your Gucci overalls.)

Take a drive with us through our changing countryside. See the instant communities: Quail Run, Fox Hunt Estates, Silver Lake. But suspend your disbelief. The real estate advertisements promise "clean air and relaxed living," never explaining how Washington's heavy air pollution magically disperses within 20 miles of the city.

The advertisements for "Country classics with two-car heated garages, swimming pools, and clay tennis courts" never explain how the living can be relaxed when your mortgage rivals the national debt and bored adolescents get their kicks blowing up mailboxes with pipe bombs.

The marketable idea is to have a "country life" without having to suffer the problems inherent in a real commitment to rural living. That's why real estate agents and builders give their developments such alluringly bucolic names: Colonial Falls Vista; Summer Ridge Landing; Olde Horseshoe Farm. Ever wonder where they get such names? After years of research, I've finally discovered the secret. The builders of these suburban dreams use The Master List of Country Names. Here's how it works:

Red	Ridge	Acres
Silver	Mountain	Estates
Blue	Falls	Landing
Harvest	Creek	Glen
Hunt	Hills	Farm
Summer	Spring	Retreat
Colonial	Horseshoe	Valley
Olde	Quail	Highlands
Heritage	Lake	Vista
Rustic	Fox	Village

All you have to do is choose one word from each column, starting from the left, arranging them as you please, and ending with a word from column three. Simple, right? And very profitable: Blue Mountain Estates; Silver Creek Village; Heritage Hills Highlands. The names just sing!

Of course, if builders and real estate people were honest about the reality of rural living, they'd choose from another Master List of Country Names. This one has the same words in column three as above, but columns one and two are nearer the truth:

Broken	Pipes	Acres
Dead	Tractor	Estates
Frozen	Chickens	Landing
Tangled	Gardens	Glen
Sick	Barn	Farm
Lost	Cows	Retreat
Leaky	Roof	Valley
Dry	Pasture	Highlands
Rusted	Silo	Vista
Busted	Assets	Village

Now we have Frozen Pipes Farm; Busted Assets Landing; Tangled Gardens Valley. This is closer to reality, but less romantic and certainly less marketable than the idea that you can somehow simplify your life merely by leaving the city.

So welcome to the sanitized, disinfected, well-groomed country life. And don't worry about quail droppings on your lawn at Quail Run or rabid foxes at Fox Hunt Estates. The quail habitats vanished when the bulldozers cleared away the brush. And the foxes are gone for good, some hit by cars, some frightened off by the constant flow of people.

And don't worry about Silver Lake becoming an ol' swimmin' hole or a breeding ground for mosquitoes. The "lake" is only a real estate agent's exaggeration, nothing more than an erosion control pond, a shallow basin with pop-top tabs littering its muddy bottom.

Thoreau was right: you go from the desperate city to the desperate country.

Our need to confront nature hasn't waned in the years since we left the city. Our passion for the natural world, in fact, is even greater now than when we were smuggling animals into our apartment. Back then we tried to create our own little world. But now that we live in the real world—one on the edge of an advancing tide of development that's putting awful pressures on wildlife and open spaces—we treasure every small encounter with nature even more.

One day, I was working upstairs, struggling with the English language, when I heard Betsy call, "Vic! Hurry! Come here!"

I jumped up thinking, what now? Disaster, from the way she's shouting. "Hurry!" she called again. Rachel fell and hurt herself. A goat is sick. The house is on fire. Our account is overdrawn.

"What's wrong?" I said breathlessly, running into our bedroom. "What happened?" She was looking out of the window.

"Shh," she said, a finger pressed across her lips. "Look. There's a woodpecker."

"What!" I shouted in outrage, my adrenalin pumping. "You called me all the way from downstairs for a . . . "

"Shush!" she hissed. "It's a *pileated* woodpecker. On the bird feeder."

"I thought something was wrong . . . "

"It's as big as a crow, isn't it?"

"Yes," I said, relieved her call was only another triumph at the bird feeder. The woodpecker *was* a thrilling sight. Almost a foot and a half long from the top of its bright red crest to its black tail, its white neck and wing stripes gave it an elegant air.

"You hardly ever see them even in the woods," Betsy said in a whisper. "They're very secretive birds."

"Cuk-cuk-cuk-cuk!" the woodpecker called, flying up into a large pear tree.

I went back upstairs mumbling to myself about the irony of it all. People move from the city and congested suburbs looking for the comfort they think a natural setting offers. But their moving—plus the greed of developers trying to turn every green space into lawns and asphalt and profits—destroys whatever they hoped to find in the first place.

You see the evidence of this in little ways. Bluebirds vanish from the countryside, their habitats, hollow trees and wooden fence posts, bulldozed away by builders constructing new developments with names like "Bluebird Haven."

On suburban roads, there are carcasses, shattered proof of the clash between man and nature. In a week, one September, when animals were getting ready for winter, I counted more than 18 raccoon corpses on area highways. Add to this the numerous 'possums, skunks, squirrels, foxes, snakes, turtles, and deer struck down, and you wonder how anything but the automobile can survive in the suburbs.

Not far from our house there's another symbol of what happens when the countryside is assaulted. The owner of a small horse farm (his avocation, not a business) has erected an eight-foot chain-link fence around his land, prison-yard style, topped with four strands of barbed wire angled inward. Every time I drive past I wonder when he'll add the watch towers and armed guards.

His horses graze behind this monstrosity, protected from whatever the owner sees as threatening—vandals? Horse thieves? Door-to-door salesmen? I don't know. And even if I knew the man well enough to ask him why he built such a hateful sight, I couldn't get to him. His house is locked behind the fence too.

But I suppose I should be more tolerant, if not charitable, toward this man. Haven't I dreamed of erecting a fortress wall to protect our goats? My fearful neighbor has simply turned my paranoid fantasy into his own chain-link reality.

One night I was driving home, rounding the corner where his fence looms over the road. The diamond pattern of the woven links caught my headlights and reflected them down the fence in a kaleidoscope pattern of shadows and flashing lights. Suddenly, I hit the brakes.

Something was running up and down the fence line. A horse? No. I leaned forward, peering into the dimness. A deer. A buck was frantically running up and down along the fence, trying to get through. The glare of my headlights added to his terror and he threw himself hard against the fence. Then he ran a few feet and hit it again and again, trying to get through.

I sat there, helpless, watching. The night was still and cool; the only sounds were the car's engine throbbing and the terrible metallic rattling of the fence as the buck rammed into it.

What could I do? I felt sick watching the creature's confusion and panic. Deer had probably crossed these fields for ages on their travels. As the land was populated they adapted and leaped fences on their way to the woods and fields. But what creature could leap *this* fence, this final barrier?

I thought of getting out of the car to shoo the animal away, to coax it off to a different, safer direction. But you don't "shoo" a frightened buck, his hooves and antlers flailing in panic. So I sat there, sharing its agony, both of us wondering what to do next.

Then the buck broke away and began running down the road, right down the yellow line. I drove after it, pacing it, trying to keep it illuminated so a driver coming the other way would see it racing down the road.

But the buck had had enough. It veered to the right and leaped the slat fence on the other side of the road. This was a four-foot rail fence. He cleared it with several feet to spare and bounded away across the fields to the woods in the distance.

I drove home, parked in my driveway, and sat in the car for a long time, feeling my heart pound. I looked at the stars through the dirty windshield. And I felt empty. Drained.

There are other times when I—a self-appointed protector of wildlife—am more successful, though.

I am a rescuer of turtles.

I see the lumbering creatures crossing the roads and I stop my car to help them. At least I hope I'm helping them. So often I see them squashed flat on the road. I used to stop and grab them and hustle them over to the side of the road they were heading for. But now the roads are so busy with traffic that I put the turtles in my trunk and drive them to a secluded place and freedom.

I hope I'm doing these reptiles a favor. I know I'm rescuing them from death on the highway, but am I forever disrupting their lives by transplanting them miles from where I found them? I know that turtles are not gregarious creatures and that they form no family attachments, so I'm not a home-breaker.

They lay their eggs in a warm place and they move on, never to see their young unless by accident. Would a mother turtle even recognize her young? Science says no.

Still, I always wonder if the turtle I see slowly moving its way across the asphalt is on its way to a rendezvous of some reptilian kind, a meeting of importance beyond our narrow human understanding.

After all, we have learned only recently that dolphins are highly intelligent and communicate complex data among themselves. Turtles have no brain at all compared to the dolphin or to any number of mammals, but is cranial capacity the sole determinant of purpose? It's we who have defined intelligence.

Perhaps turtles and other creatures have their own definitions. I rankle when I hear people describe one or another animal as "stupid." Every creature is as smart as it needs to be, isn't it? A turtle doesn't need to be able to whistle a Bach fugue as it crawls along.

But then, scientists have found that even so basic and "primitive" a creature as a flatworm is capable of memory. Researchers have developed an interesting method of demonstrating this. They expose the flatworm to a stimulus of some sort, repeating the experience several times. Then they cut the worm up, whizz it in a blender, and inject it into other worms. These worms, who were not subjected to the stimulus, then show evidence of "remembering" what the deceased worms experienced.

Fascinating, no? (Not only does it show how much we have to learn about flatworms, it demonstrates the lengths some people will go to get a government grant.) A turtle is certainly higher on the scale of intelligence we've created than a flatworm, but the common assumption is that turtles, like other reptiles, are merely creatures that play out their lives with no real purposes other than as parts of the food chain.

Now don't get me wrong. I am not arguing for a *Secret Life of Turtles*. I am not suggesting, as the new nonsense does of plants, that turtles think profound thoughts, read our minds, or predict the future. No turtle I've handled—and there have been dozens—has ever led me to suspect that I hold in my hands the chelonian equivalent of an Einstein or a Picasso.

There are differences between turtles, however. Some I pick up are timid fellows, retreating into their shells with a snap and a hiss. Others are bold. They crane their baggy necks and claw at the air, trying to escape. The boldest ones open their mouths and try to lop off one of my fingers.

Some, on being set down in a new location, will stay clamped into their shells a long time before venturing out. Others will take off at a run as their feet touch the ground.

Most of the turtles I rescue are common box turtles, though I have also handled wood turtles, eastern painted turtles, and, occasionally, spotted turtles. I've even learned to tell a male box turtle from a female (males have red eyes; females, brown), one of my more precious accomplishments. Most turtles I encounter are small, up to six inches in length. But once I faced the rescue of a more formidable one.

I was driving home from work late one summer afternoon when I stopped for a dump truck that had parked almost in the middle of the road. The driver and his helper were out of the truck, looking at an object on the road. It was a huge snapping turtle, about 18 inches long not counting its head, which was as big around as my fist.

"Ever see one that big?" laughed the driver.

"No," I said. "What are you going to do with it?" I was feeling very protective. Turtle Man strikes again.

"I don't wanna do nothing with it. I'm just trying to get it outta the road, but it don't wanna move."

"It's confused," I said.

"It's ugly," said the driver's assistant. "Like somethin' out of a horror movie."

"Another turtle wouldn't think so," I said.

"What?" snapped the assistant, suddenly threatened.

"Can't tell by me," I laughed, trying to relax him, "I like hyenas and snakes, too." The driver laughed with me, but his assistant snorted and sniffed, wiping his nose on his arm in the proximity of a mottled purple tattoo, a poor representation either of a snarling panther or the map of Vietnam, I couldn't tell which.

"Ugliest damn thing I *ever* saw," he repeated. The driver nudged the turtle with his foot, trying to ease it toward the roadside. Snap! Hiss! The turtle lurched at us, clamping its powerful jaws on the air. We leaped backward like dancers. "Gah-damn," growled the assistant, "that sucker bites me I'll stomp his ugly head in!"

A pickup truck with a broken muffler rumbled alongside us. Its driver, a fat, red-faced man wearing a baseball cap, called out: "Whatcha got there?"

"Turtle," said the dump truck driver.

" 'At's a giant snapper you got there, boys. Musta come up outta a culvert or somethin'. We're tearing up all these old farms round here for houses, you know. Makes the wildlife keep moving."

"Ugly bastard," said the assistant.

"Say what?" scowled the fat man, getting a better grip on his steering wheel with hands the size of baseball mitts.

"Said it's an ugly turtle," the assistant said.

"Oh," smiled the fat man. "Okay then. Yeah, right, but them snappers make fine eatin', you know."

"The hell," said the driver.

"Chop their head off, pull 'em outta the shell. Turtle soup."

"You want him?" asked the assistant.

"Hold it," I said, Turtle Man about to reveal his secret identity. "I got here first, after you," I nodded to the dump truck driver.

"Don't want 'em anyhow," said the fat man. "I'm late now. Enjoy your soup!" He waved and drove off, choking us in a cloud of blue smoke.

"You gonna eat this thing?" the assistant asked me, curling his lip.

"No. I'm going to let him go at the river."

"You gotta pick him up first," laughed the driver.

I was thinking about that. I was looking at those jaws, the sides as sharp as scissors, thinking what I'd look like with a four-fingered glove. " 'At sumbitch'll take your thumb off, you ain't careful," said the driver.

"You're a mind reader," I said. The turtle hadn't moved all this time. It sat at our feet on the asphalt, its snakelike head thrust out in what passed for defiance, looking at nothing, at everything, waiting with reptilian patience for whatever would come.

The theory was simple: a turtle can't bite behind itself. I knew that. Did the turtle know that? I took a breath, exhaled, and dropped into a squat, grabbing the turtle from behind.

"You're nuts!" the assistant said.

"Hoo-eee!" the driver said.

"Hisss!" snapped the turtle.

"Open my trunk," I said to the driver. I was holding the creature at arm's length, straining against its weight and twisting feet. It snapped viciously, trying to get at me. I knew exactly how a bomb disposal crew felt. The trunk open, I laid the turtle flat and whipped my hands away.

"Shoulda just kicked it off the side of the road," the assistant said. I slammed the trunk lid shut.

"You must know a lot about turtles," the driver grinned.

"I'm learning," I said.

I drove straight to the river. This was a weekday, now almost early evening, so the towpath along the C & O Canal was deserted. I parked, grabbed the turtle from behind again, and headed for a large pond, part of a state game preserve, a swampy area where turtles congregated.

I stopped on the pond's bank and gingerly set the beast down.

It sat still, blinking at the light. I stepped back. The creature paused for half a minute, swayed its head from side to side, then lumbered toward the water. I watched as it crashed through some brittle reeds, slipped into the brown water, and vanished, leaving a thin stream of bubbles and a swirl of bottom mud in its wake.

Do turtles think of me as God? Is my hand that lifts them and plunges them into the darkness of my car seen as a divine hand, my meddling as divine intercession, chelonian cosmic consciousness, my car a chariot to whisk them across the universe to the Promised Land?

And do turtles wonder whether I am essentially good or evil? "True," says a sage turtle with a chipped shell, "he rescues us from death but we die anyway in time. Does he not disrupt our lives and cancel our notions of free turtle will? I, for one, would rather take my chances than be plucked up and manipulated."

"God cannot be all-powerful," says a young turtle, "He acts too much like a turtle."

Another turtle muses, "God cannot be good, else why does He let baby turtles die?"

"I *believe*," says a terrapin sunning on a rock. "I have felt the touch of His hand."

So it goes. Still, I keep rescuing turtles. I cannot bear to think of them being killed when I can save them, no matter that I might be meddling in things I don't understand.

Perhaps God has the same problem dealing with us. He cannot stop helping us, though His help is often the cause of misunderstanding. When are we being helped, we ask, and when is it chaos, a disordered and risky universe? Like the turtles, I wonder.

Sometimes my interference with nature doesn't work out quite the way I plan.

Once I was digging into a pile of rotted chicken manure when I discovered a neat pile of snake eggs. I'm always thrilled by moments like this, but also a little embarrassed. Entering into a secret corner of the natural world is exciting, but at the same time I always feel as I did with the turtles, as though I'm barging into some creature's personal life.

What do you do when you find 16 snake eggs? The first thing I did was to call Betsy and Noah (he was three then) to see the discovery. Snake eggs are off-white and flexible with a leathery unegglike feel to them. We marveled over the pile of eggs, sharing what we knew with Noah. Then I covered the eggs with a sheet of black plastic and resolved to protect them until they hatched.

I was worried about them. It was late August and I thought that was a terrible time to lay eggs containing creatures who couldn't survive a hard freeze. The chicken-manure pile was a good spot, being warm and moist, but still the eggs would need protection, I thought, against animals that might feast on them. So I became a snake godfather.

I checked the pile every day, kept the eggs covered and secure. Weeks went by, and I began to despair that they would never hatch before the first frost. I was sure the female snake had erred somehow and laid her eggs too late in the season.

But one day I uncovered the pile and found 16 eggs that looked as though they'd been slashed by a razor. The empty eggs still kept their shape, though. The leathery texture saved them from shattering like chicken eggs as the baby serpents used their egg teeth to slice their way out.

I saw no snakes at first. Then I stood still and saw a flash of movement here and there in the grass, among the weeds, and on the edges of the compost pile. A half-dozen baby snakes were heading off in different directions. I knelt down to look at one and got the shock of my life.

In all my godfathering and care I had never stopped to think what *kind* of snakes the eggs might contain. I've never seen snakes of any sort as my mortal enemy, so it never occurred to me that the eggs might be anything but benign. But this infant snake slithering past my heel chilled me; its markings were similar to those of a copperhead, dumbbell-shaped patches of color against the lighter background of its body.

Poisonous snakes aren't a major problem in our area. Rattlesnakes are rare, though I've heard a few stories of people who've encountered them in nearby woods. Water moccasins are supposed to inhabit the river area, but I've never seen one.

Copperheads are another story. They live among us in abundance, though, again, in decades of hiking and running around the area, I've seen only a few.

Of course, I do remember running along the river one evening in late summer when I had an unexpected meeting. I had misjudged the time and was completing my run in semidarkness, the full moon illuminating the shoreline path with a silvery glow. I was in a reverie as I ran, totally absorbed, not paying attention to where my feet landed. I've run the same path for so many years that I just go on autopilot after awhile.

But then everything happened at once, all in a second or two. A shape on the ground in front of me. Running too fast to stop. What is it? Dim moonlight.

A coiled snake right under my feet! A huge copperhead lying in the path, soaking up the radiant heat from the ground. I'm right on top of it, my foot almost plunging into its coils. I see its head snap back, the white of its open mouth . . .

That was the night I broke the world's record for the high jump. Straight up, friends, and nobody there to hand me a gold medal. I landed a few yards away and looked back at the snake. Biggest copperhead I ever saw. Thick as my wrist. (And it gets bigger every time I tell the story.)

Still, I don't live in fear of copperheads. I try to watch out for them and avoid them. They have a reputation for being pugnacious and for not easily yielding ground—as I learned. But they're not overly aggressive, either. They don't drop down out of trees or sneak up on unsuspecting sleepers the way snakes do in all those Tarzan movies.

And copperheads aren't all that poisonous; their venom, like the rattler, is a muscular toxin, less deadly than the nerve toxin of cobras or coral snakes. Few adults die from copperhead bites if they get medical attention and are in good health to begin with. But children and animals are a different matter.

My heart sank into my socks and I had a pain in my stomach. "My God," I said out loud. Have I played midwife to more than a dozen copperheads? Have I loosed on our land a little Biblical plague of poisonous vipers? I had awful visions of Noah skipping through a lawn heavy with snakes that could easily kill or sicken him.

I told Betsy. "The snake eggs hatched."

"Wonderful," she said, brightly, "have you seen the babies?"

"Ah. Yes."

"What's wrong?" She reads my face like a map.

"They might be copperheads."

"Oh no." Her complexion went gray, like mine. We looked across at Noah playing, laughing to himself and tumbling in and out of the hammock. "How do you know?" Betsy asked.

"I don't. But the coloring looks like copperheads."

"How many hatched?"

"Sixteen. All of them."

"Are they dangerous now, as babies?"

"I don't know. Some snakes are venomous just as they come out of the egg. I think I'd better catch a few and have an expert look at them."

Catching them wasn't hard. Most of the hatchlings had stayed close to the chicken-manure pile. When I peeled back the sheet of black plastic I found a squirming pile of little snakes who looked remarkably like pictures I'd seen of copperheads, not the same coloration, but the same type of markings.

I put on a pair of heavy gloves and began gathering as many as I could into a bucket. And I felt awful, sick at the prospect of living with a danger I'd inflicted on us, guilty as hell. Yet what should I have done? I thought. I couldn't have destroyed the eggs, any more than I could have knocked down a wasps' nest. I wanted to take care of the eggs. I wanted them to hatch and increase our snake population. But I expected the offspring to be black snakes or green garter snakes. It never entered my naive head that a copperhead might have left her spawn.

The nearest place to get what I hoped was an expert's opinion was Great Falls, a national park on the Potomac River. If the answers from park rangers didn't satisfy me, I could always head into the city for the National Zoo. I put the bucket in the car and started to pull out of the driveway. "Wait," Betsy called, "Noah wants to go with you." Big kick for Noah, to go for a ride with Daddy.

I didn't talk much on the drive. Noah was full of questions about the snakes but my answers were monosyllables snapped out. I was angry at myself and even angry at Noah for being so vulnerable. This is what you get for fooling around with Mother Nature, I thought. Jerk. What are you going to do if your 16 little friends are venomous? We'll invite all our friends over for a giant snake hunt. Call in the neighborhood kids. A dollar a snake. Dead or alive.

I uncovered the bucket for one of the park rangers I found in the administration building at Great Falls. He looked into the pail. He answered in a split second, but not before my throat went dry.

"Black snakes," he said, flicking the word out as fast as a serpent's tongue.

"But they're not black," I said weakly.

He looked up from the pail and smiled. "They will be. This is the way they look when they're young. They turn darker as they get older." I looked into his smiling face. Blond hair. Fresh scrubbed. Dark green uniform. Maybe 22 years old. A Boy Scout. Does he know what he's talking about? I wondered.

"You're sure," I pressed, wondering whether I needed a second opinion.

"Yeah," he said easily. "Hey Harriet, c'mere," he called a woman ranger over. She looked even younger than he did.

"Baby black snakes," she said. "Cute. Where'd you find them?"

"I'm a friend of the family." Harriet raised an eyebrow a bit, then laughed uncertainly. Park rangers, like cops, see a lot of nuts. Harriet was sizing me up, this bearded guy with a bucket full of baby snakes.

"What are you going to do with them?" she asked.

"Well, if they're *really* black snakes . . . " I said, leaving an opening.

"They *are,* " both rangers said in chorus.

". . . then I'll just let them go around my place."

"Good," Harriet said, lifting her chin. "A lot of people are afraid of snakes and see them as dangerous creatures, but they're an integral part of the ecosystem, you know."

"I know," I said.

"Did you know that of all the world's snakes only 8 percent are dangerous to man? And most of them are in the tropics."

"I didn't know that," I said, enjoying her impassioned Zoology 101 lecture.

"Yes, and people don't realize what a valuable contribution snakes make to our economy. Oh, they may eat an occasional bird or chick, but the vast proportion of a snake's diet consists of mice, rats, insects, and other creatures we regard as pests. I wish people wouldn't regard snakes with such horror," she said, shaking her head slowly.

"I *like* snakes," I said. "I really do. I wouldn't hurt a scale on their wiggly bodies. I just wanted to be sure these weren't poisonous. I *like* snakes," I said again. She was making me feel guilty.

"Okay," she said, still sizing me up. "Just remember what they call the black snake."

"What?"

"The farmer's friend," she said, unsmiling.

"I'll remember," I said.

I let the babies go when I got home. Noah helped me, giggling at the squirming creatures as they slipped into the grass and underbrush. We let them go selectively, some at the goat shed, sóme near the old barn where we stored our hay.

We only saw a few again after that. One found its way into our living room, working its way up from the crawl space. But our place was never overruun with snakes. We still see black snakes about as often as ever, which isn't often enough, I think. And whenever I do see one, its powerful blue-black body slithering through the grass, I wonder if it's one of my godchildren.

Beyond rescuing snakes and other creatures, though, our biggest involvement with wildlife is running a free lunch program for the neighborhood birds. But we've come a long way from narrow windowsills and warnings about the horrors of bird-doo. We put up bird feeders as soon as we moved into the Potomac house, and Betsy began buying seed, suet, and peanut butter to make various winter feed concoctions.

We hung feeders from trees, mounted them on posts, and scattered seed on the ground. We put up birdbaths, hummingbird feeders, birdhouses, and—in winter—bird roosting boxes where a variety of birds could escape from the cold.

Birds moved in from everywhere. Meadowlarks, evening grosbeaks, tufted titmouse, cardinals, scolding blue jays, grackles, starlings, mockingbirds, catbirds, barn swallows, and lots more we struggled to identify. We had hundreds of English sparrows, too, and an occasional kestrel (sparrow hawk) flew in from time to time to keep things in balance.

Betsy even fed the crows, scattering handfuls of dry dog food nuggets on a picnic table. A dozen crows flew in at a time, wary, posting lookouts high in the catalpa trees, chattering and growling among themselves.

Screech owls took up residence in the small patch of woods at the south end of our land. They'd awaken us at night or early in the morning with their unearthly yowling. The first time I heard that string of banshee yips, hoots, whistles, and hollers I thought UFOs had landed. In time, though, the sounds became reassuring, a part of our lives.

Our regular feedings in winter, plus our studied neglect of the brush and weeds that ringed our land, created a sanctuary. Birds flocked in from all directions, roosted in trees, on the rain gutters, along the fence, in the shrubs in front of our house. They'd wait, scolding, on winter mornings, upset when Betsy didn't appear at her usual time with a bucket of seed and treats. The cacophony of calls increased in intensity as she dumped the seed in the various feeders. Then, even before Betsy stepped back, hundreds of feathered bodies swooped down, the bold little tufted titmouse actually brushing past Betsy's hat to be first at the feeder.

We had a visible increase in the bird population over the years. Bird calls and songs constantly filled the air, a wonderful sound in early spring. We even benefited beyond the simple pleasure of just seeing and hearing birds; our garden, constantly patrolled by a variety of insect- and grub-eating birds, seemed to have fewer insect problems as time passed.

And birds improved the garden in more subtle ways. Many summer evenings I would stop my cultivation and lean on the hoe, enthralled at the musical repertoire of a mockingbird roosting in a wild cherry tree. Dusk would settle and I'd watch the barn swallows (they'd made their nest in the goat shed) darting acrobatically and swooping as they caught insects I couldn't see.

But what started off as a few bags of seeds and some chopped-up apple has become an avian welfare system. Frankly, I have stopped counting. It hurts less that way. Betsy comes home throughout the winter with one 50-pound sack after another of sunflower seeds and thistle seed and millet and cracked corn. She mixes her own bird feeds now. The commercially bagged stuff, she says, is mostly rough seed not worth the cost.

What do all Betsy's sacks cost? I don't know. I've stopped counting, remember? But if I *was* keeping track I'd guess that the birds are costing us several hundred dollars a winter. I raised this issue once, but felt like a Scrooge questioning Betsy's compassion and good works. Besides, even if I did complain, she'd keep on buying seed anyway. "Once you start feeding them in winter," she says, "you can't stop. They become dependent."

"Is it right," I ask, "to have them dependent? Shouldn't they be able to make it on their own? What did the birds do before we moved here? Before you were born?"

"I'm helping to right the balance of nature," Betsy says archly. "I'm offsetting the destruction of all the bird habitats and food supplies by suburban development."

I am married to the Mother Theresa of bird life.

But I have this great idea. I'm going to write off all these birdseed expenses on my income tax. Betsy says the birds are dependent on us, right? Okay then: *Dependents*. If I give money to an ecology group, it's deductible. If I contribute to a charity, it's deductible. Then why shouldn't the government give me a little help when I *directly* support an ecological balance? Why shouldn't I be given credit for growing an organic garden—protecting the topsoil and insect life?

And if I can deduct money spent on medical supplies and hospitalization insurance, why can't I get a break for protecting the greater health of the total organism, our natural environment?

It's a great idea.

I'll start this April with a test case. I'll list all the birdseed and supplies we buy as a deduction, all the birds we feed as dependents.

Expenses incurred for families I support: the Sparrows, the Robins, the Grosbeaks (Muriel and David, a lovely couple), the Baltimore Orioles—that's it! I'll demand that the Internal Revenue Service grant me an oriole depletion allowance!

Come visit me in jail.

I guess you've gotten the idea by now that the so-called simple life isn't necessarily a passive life, not even a quiet life. Not in our house anyway. So often, I like to slip away to my special refuge. Not a neighborhood saloon, but the shores of the Potomac River, the one place in the midst of this suburban sprawl and endless traffic where I can always recharge my spiritual batteries.

We're lucky that we live only five minutes from the river and the adjoining Chesapeake and Ohio Canal—the C & O Canal, as everyone calls it. The river has been a lure for me since I was a teenager. I live on the Maryland side of the river now, but I can look across to places on the Virginia side where I canoed and camped 25 years ago. Yet the contrasts at the river always strike me as though it was the first time I'd become aware of them. Commercial airlines use the river as a flight path for landings at National Airport, only 25 miles downriver. Military helicopters go pocketa-pocketa-pocketa over the treetops, in formation, on their way to an airbase or federal installation.

Mileposts set up by the National Park Service tell you how far you are from the canal's origin in Georgetown. I stand at mile marker 20 watching a great blue heron take off from a mud flat. Downstream, at mile marker 1, cars thump over a bridge that spans the canal in Georgetown. The drivers are looking for a parking place, an impossible dream in trendy Georgetown, with its dozens of bars and restaurants.

On a map, the blue dot where I stand is only an inch or so from the Pentagon, the White House, Capitol Hill, the State Department. Sometimes I come to the river and I think: I am 40 years old and I am plunking pebbles in the river. Downstream there are people making laws and policy and wars. I'd rather they were plunking pebbles in the river.

But that this magical preserve exists at all is due to the workings of our government and the courage of one man who believed in its processes. It sounds corny to say so, but I think of Supreme Court Justice William O. Douglas often as I walk along the canal. Back in the 1950's a group of nearsighted politicians wanted to turn this 180-mile hiking and biking path into another highway. "When this highway is completed," a developer crowed back then, "you'll be able to jump in your car in Georgetown in the morning and have lunch that afternoon in Cumberland, Maryland."

I didn't want to have lunch in Cumberland, and neither, I'm glad, did Justice Douglas. He walked the entire 180 miles of the towpath to dramatize its importance as a refuge. And he walked it every year for years, picking up supporters, until the C & O was first made a national monument and finally a national park.

The spirit of that rugged man is as much a part of the river and canal as the bark on the trees that tower over me as I walk, and I say a silent thanks to Justice Douglas whenever I step onto the towpath.

In all of Washington and its suburbs, only this place, the river, makes sense to me anymore. Only here do I really find solitude and an unraveling of tension. Well, most of the time, anyway. I am not the only one who comes to the river, though I regard it as my personal property.

On warm weekends the towpath is a magnet. Downstream from my area is Great Falls of the Potomac, a "civilized" part of the canal and river, complete with fast food and rest rooms. On a pleasant Saturday or Sunday it can rival the boardwalk at any ocean resort for its glut of humanity.

But even upriver, the path is crowded: briskly striding hikers; campers carrying their dreams in overstuffed knapsacks; fishermen carrying their catch of carp in old dry-wall-compound pails; canoeists in day-glo life vests portaging around a canal lock; mooning lovers strolling slowly hand in hand, whispering and giggling; flocks of birdwatchers on tiptoes, peering through binoculars; bicyclists zipping past, perched high on ten-speeds; elderly women in corrective shoes, clutching their handbags, trying to keep up with the grandchildren; anthills of Boy Scouts, Girl Scouts, and Cub Scouts boil up along the path, all of them shouting at each other in the blare of portable tape decks. Miraculously, somehow, the towpath and the woods accept them, stretches their numbers out, and there is little sense of crowding.

But early in the morning, at sunset, and especially in winter, when the area is all but deserted, then the river belongs to me again.

If I were to fall into a Rip Van Winkle sleep and my comatose body was hauled to the river and stretched out under a tree, I could, on the opening of only one eye, tell you the time of year from my first glimpse.

Are the turtles sunning themselves on the half-sunken trees that reach up from the canal's murky water? Is the air thin and cool, the sunshine as penetrating as a wood stove? It must be spring. The eastern painted turtles and the diamondback terrapins have awakened from hibernation, pushed free from the ooze they've hidden in, and struggled to the surface, reborn. Arranging themselves on logs, their black shells caked with dried mud, they close their eyes, extend their necks, and hang limply, absorbing the sun.

Is the air dank, filled with clouds of gnats in hurried orbit around themselves? Is the sound of cicadas, tree frogs, and bullfrogs a wall of noise? This is summer on the canal. Skunk cabbage grows in rank profusion near the bank; poison ivy leaves as big as dinner plates hang from vines twisted around decaying sycamores, their bark falling away like giant flakes of peeling paint; green frogs and leopard frogs hide in the grass near the canal's edge. They leap into the water as I pass by; the plops are rhythmic and comical.

Are there mallards and wood ducks quacking loudly, nervous grebes fluttering and scolding each other in the canal, Canada geese honking in counterpoint? Fall has arrived. Dead leaves mat the towpath and obscure the canal's still water. Muskrats paddle through the leaves, pushing them aside as they squirm quietly across the surface, hurrying to prepare for the cold. The green of late summer is vanishing, the woods are opening up, looking bare and resigned.

Are those pokeweed stalks lying limp and tangled in death, their succulence turned to black ooze by a killing frost? Do the branches that dip into the river where the current is swift have ice balls clinging to their tips? Do they clink like glass when the wind blows? This is winter. The stillness is broken now only by sparrows fluttering in the brittle underbrush and by the creaking of dead trees. Bleak and beautiful, the river completes its year. And mine.

But I have no illusions about the river. My life has been wrapped up in it too long for that. To the casual observer it seems benign, only a river. But it's many things, all things. Power, peace, creation, and destruction, and all of them at once.

At least a half-dozen people drown in the Potomac every year, mostly in summer when the shoreline upriver is crowded. At Great Falls, people scramble over the slippery rocks, trying to get close to the cascades of leaping, roaring water. There are signs here and there that warn "Keep Off The Rocks." And park rangers do the best they can to stop people from killing themselves. But the only thing that would stop these rock scramblers would be to close the park to everyone.

So every year people slip and fall in, screaming as they go, some of them laughing, unaware of the river's power. The lucky ones are plucked by helicopter from the rocks they cling to, but many others are sucked under, found hours later downstream.

Why do they misjudge the river? An old fellow I know who was born on the river—his family were lock tenders—has this theory: "This here's the can't do generation. Get 'em outdoors, away from their TV sets and they're helpless. They figure this river runs through a modern city, so it must be modern too. Must be *like* the city it runs through. Orderly, working by push-buttons and rules. But this here river makes its own rules. Always has. You gotta follow its lead. That's something, ain't it? This wild river running through this tame town?"

One morning in fall, stifled by a writer's block, I hurried to the river. I sat on a bank overlooking what had become a raging Potomac. The waters were swollen by heavy rains from the tail end of a hurricane. The roar filled my head like white noise. Huuuuuussssssh, endlessly. This must be the sound we hear in the womb. I hear it at the ocean, when it rains, when the wind blows. This is the sound of continual creation, the harmonic of our existence.

Sitting there, I think of my father. Years before, in Florida, my mother and I had placed his ashes in the ocean. We walked out along a rock jetty and tossed the small cardboard box into the water, watching it sink, tumbling end over end. When it settled on the sand, small fish darted in, attacking the thin line of silver bubbles that escaped from one corner of the box.

A grave scraped out of the coral in South Florida would have left him buried, Mom, my sister, and I agreed, but the ocean, scattering his ashes, completed the circle. And now, when I sit near the river, a thousand miles from where I wept and said goodbye, seeing the foam and the rush of waters headed for the bay and the ocean beyond, I think of him with love.

The hurricane has filled the river with the flotsam of man and nature. Whole trees float by, slowly, like Egyptian barges proceeding gracefully to a rendezvous. Oil drums bob and twist like fat men caught in the swift water. Small boards and twigs rip past, pitching and submerging, dragged under by whirlpools, then popping up as though frantically gasping for air or rescue from the river's cold grip.

As an experiment, I sit and concentrate on a tiny area of the rushing waters. I notice that the river flows not just downstream but in all directions at once. I feel an invitation to join in, to leave my sandy perch and meld with the waves.

A voice calls from the sucking and swirling water, begging me to yield, to merge. Suddenly a tree floats into my field of vision and I am distracted from the siren's call. I turn away and look at the ground. The afterimage makes the shore heave and twist.

I become slightly riversick. Watching the river flow past isn't like sitting on the shore watching the ocean waves roll in. Waves come toward you, then recede. On the river bank you sit and watch the water go past you, always pulling your consciousness downstream. The effect disorients. My body seems to lean downstream. Perhaps I should balance my river viewing by shifting to the Virginia side from time to time.

I move on to another part of the shore, to a quieter section, far from the rapids. The sun is bright and warm, the temperature in the 60's. It is noon when I step down into a wooded pocket on the bank. The towpath and the river are deserted on this weekday. Only the jets overhead tell me a civilization is near.

A tree lies half submerged in the shallows. It is forked and looms over the clear water. Caught against the trunk is a smaller branch, four inches in diameter, pinned crosswise against the current. The river flows over and around the wood, washing it and wrestling with it. Like a dog with a rag, I think.

The sound is hypnotic, the siren's song again, in a gentler tone. All the descriptions of babbling brooks are made real by this sound. Tinkling, rushing, bubbling, sounds so beautiful that I'm forced to lie back on the bank, to close my eyes, to listen. I laugh out loud. The bubbling sounds like the noises Noah and Rachel made as babies in their first baths. They'd lift a washcloth and watch amazed as the water trickled back into the tub. The sun is warm and penetrating without being hot. I fall into a half sleep. The tension dissolves and floats downstream.

The Song of Uvanuk

The great sea
Has sent me adrift
It moves me
As the weed in a great river
Earth and the great weather
Move me
Have carried me away
And move my inward parts with joy.

—*Touch the Earth: A Self-Portrait of Indian Existence,* by T. C. McLuhan (Promontory Press, 1971).

Sometimes nature barges in on us.

One day, Betsy was working in the goat yard when she heard a strange sound. She investigated and found a baby crow tangled in the wild blackberry canes that grow along our property line. Noah, who was then two years old, and I came running when she called. And there stood Betsy, as I have so often seen her, cradling an animal in her hands.

"Is it hurt?" I asked.

"I can't tell," she said, "it seems okay." We held the bird gently and ran our fingers over its wings and legs looking for signs of a fracture. The crow took this calmly, looking directly into our faces, with no struggle at all. It was fully feathered, about ten inches long from its feet to the top of its head.

"Here's some blood," Betsy said, fingering one of the wings where the pinion bones met.

"It's dried blood," I said. "I wonder how long it's been in the bushes?"

We took the bird into the house and settled it in a cardboard box until we could figure out what to do. The first thing we did was to call Mrs. Winslow, a local woman known for her skill in caring for injured wildlife. Mrs. Winslow has filled the gap between death and the veterinarian. By experience and determination she's learned how best to care for creatures hurt by man or natural circumstances, creatures few veterinarians know much about or would minister to.

We had brought Mrs. Winslow other creatures in the past—baby birds tossed from the nest, a blue jay torn up by one of our cats. And always a visit to her home was like stepping into a magic place. Here were cages with bandaged squirrels, birds, even a box turtle injured by a dog. Mrs. Winslow turned no creature away, tended them all, and released them as they mended. We called her about the crow.

"Any injuries?" she asked gruffly. Mrs. Winslow reserved her manners for her wild charges. With humans she was always direct, short, and snappish. We explained about the blood and said we could find no other damage.

"Probably got separated from the flock," she said. "Get some food into it and let it go in the morning. They'll be looking for it. Any problem, call me back." End of conversation. Before she hung up she suggested feeding it hard-boiled egg.

We uncovered the box and looked in. Darkness always calms wild things, and calm is especially important if they're injured. The crow peered up at us, now looking a bit peaked. How long since it had eaten? How did it get separated from the flock? We had no answers.

We dug an old kennel crate out of the barn and fitted it out with a branch perch. We put the baby into the cage and eased it onto the perch. It sat passively. Betsy cooked some eggs and we offered the cooled mash to our visitor. It gave us, then the egg, a baleful eye.

"I don't think it can eat out of a bowl," Betsy said. I smeared some yolk on the tip of my finger and held it under the bird's beak. Nothing. I smeared a little on the tip of the beak. Nothing. "Birds don't have a sense of smell," Betsy said.

"Great. Let's go out and mash up some worms."

We had a problem. If the baby was to survive it was going to have to eat something.

We called Mrs. Winslow again.

"Gone out," said her husband. "I don't know when she'll be back. Fellow found an injured sparrow hawk. She's gone up-county to bring it back." Did he know how to feed a baby crow? "Naw," he said, "that's her department. Sorry. I'll have her call you when she gets back." Would the bird be alive by then, we wondered?

"Maybe it'll eat some worms," Noah said helpfully.

"I was afraid you'd suggest that," I said. A most unpleasant prospect, I thought, digging up worms to feed to a crow. I don't like killing and it didn't please me to think of killing one creature to aid another. "All right," I said, "let's go out and do some digging."

Out we went, shovel in hand, and dug up a cupful of squirming nightcrawlers. The crow wasn't interested. Betsy held a fat, wriggling worm right under its beak and got no reaction. She held it over the bird's head as the mother might have done. Nothing. "We could mash the worms up," Betsy gulped, her throat tightening at the suggestion, "and try to feed it a puree. Its mother regurgitates the worms and . . . "

"You do it," I said, ever the gallant one. "I draw the line at whizzing worms in the blender. And throw the blender away when you're done." We were stymied, caught between our compassion, the urgency of the bird's condition, and our aesthetic senses. Then I got an idea.

"I once had a parakeet," I said.

"How exciting for you," Betsy cracked, not taking her eyes off the bird who was beginning to look weaker, the sheen of its black feathers getting duller as we watched.

"No, wait," I said, "we trained the parakeet to sit on our fingers by touching its chest. Maybe . . . "

"Then what?" Betsy said.

"One thing at a time." I opened the cage door and slowly reached in. The crow showed no fear at my advance. I gently pressed the back of my left hand against the bird's soft chest. "C'mon, c'mon," I said softly, pushing the crow back, trying to encourage it to lift a foot. It did! Just as though it had been trained to do so, the crow lifted one foot and gripped the base of my index finger. Then, with no prodding, it pushed off from the perch and gripped my hand with its other foot.

"Look at *that!*" Betsy said in a whisper. The crow sat on my hand, placid as ever. Now what? I thought. This must have been my day for flashes of intuitive wisdom because I called to Betsy, "Get me the egg again." Once again I smeared a dollop of egg yolk onto my index finger. Then I carefully and slowly removed my left hand from the cage, hoping the crow would stay in place.

"Wow," said Betsy as I stepped away from the cage, the crow firmly perched on my hand. "Now for the food," I said a little too confidently. But again the crow refused to show any interest in the egg or even a live worm I held at various angles over its head. I was beginning to think the obvious, that maybe the bird just wasn't hungry. Then, for no good reason I can remember, I looked the bird right in the eye and said, in my best imitation of a crow, "Caw!"

The bird reacted as though I'd touched it with a live wire.

"Aw! Aw!" it repeated to me.

"Caw!" I said in return, wondering just what it was that I was saying.

"Arrgh!" the baby replied. We were having a helluva conversation here, the meaning of which escaped me completely.

Then, figuring this was a perfect moment to introduce some nourishment, I again offered my finger with the egg smeared on it. This time the baby almost swallowed my finger trying to get at the yolk.

"What did you do?" Betsy asked in delight.

"It must have been something I said." The crow attacked every bit of yolk I offered it. I tried a worm a few minutes later but even with another exchange of "caw" and "aww" and "arrgh" the baby showed no interest. The hell with mashed worms, I thought, "Let's try canned dog food. Crows are omnivorous and it might do."

It did. The baby eagerly took several helpings of dog food along with the egg. The sheen returned to its feathers almost magically. By this time the creature almost seemed relaxed and had abandoned my hand for my forearm, then walked up my arm to settle on my shoulder.

Betsy and I were amazed. Here was a wild creature who had accepted us fully. We discussed the chance that it could have been someone's pet, but dismissed this as impossible. There were no houses anywhere near us and we had found the bird far from the road. We decided Mrs. Winslow was right, that it somehow got separated from its flock and had been slightly injured.

"Awwk!" said the crow and jumped from my shoulder to the top of my head.

"You never looked better," Betsy said.

We fed our guest again that evening. Its appearance had changed in just a few hours. Its bedraggled feathers now shined—the result of a careful preening between meals—and its eyes and manner were fully alert. I spoke to it as I did earlier and the response was just as electric.

The funniest thing was the way the crow looked at me when I cawed. Each time it cocked its head and peered into my face before cawing in return. Its expression seemed to say, "What's a nice crow like you doing in a place like this?"

That evening we covered the cage with a blanket and after putting Noah to bed—he wanted to know why the crow couldn't sleep in his room—we discussed what was on both our minds.

"I don't want to let this bird go," I said.

"I know," said Betsy, "there's something special going on. I've never seen anything like this."

"I've known people who had crows as pets. Crows are remarkably intelligent." I lay back on my pillow, staring at the ceiling. I hate the word pet, I thought. It has the connotation of some fluffy little mutt with ribbons in its hair. This crow wouldn't be a pet, it would be a companion. Suddenly I was fantasizing myself walking down some busy street with a shiny black crow perched on my shoulder. Caw! Caw! Sussman, the life of the party.

The next morning I fed the crow again. It was much stronger now and more alert. I tried not to project my feelings, but it did seem even more at ease with me, sitting on my shoulder and pecking gently at my ear and eyeglasses. I was falling in love. Betsy held out her hand to the crow and it easily stepped off my shoulder, ran up her arm and nibbled on her braids.

We were laughing at this when reality burst in. "Caw!" came the sound of a crow flying over the house, then "*Caw!*" louder as it crossed directly overhead. Instantly the baby leaped from Betsy's shoulder and smashed into the closed porch window. "Aw!" it screamed in return, then fluttered into a heap on the floor.

It was unhurt, but its eyes were wild and I could feel it trembling as I picked it up and smoothed its feathers. We knew then who the crow really belonged to. All my fantasies of playing Long John Silver for the tourists vanished in the flap of a wing. "I guess it's time," Betsy said, softly, as much to the crow as to me.

"One more feeding," I said, "just to make sure it's strong enough."

"Sure," Betsy said, and touched my arm.

A few minutes later, after we had returned the baby to the cage, another loud "Caw!" came from over our rooftop. And again the baby screamed in return and thrashed against the cage bars. I ran out the door this time, determined to see what was happening over our house.

An adult crow, very large, was flying slow, in crisscross patterns, circling over the brushline, swooping over the tall oaks at the south end of our two acres, then flying low back over the house, calling intermittently. I heard other crows calling in the distance. A search and rescue mission.

There was no last feeding. The baby was too frantic to eat. The egg yolk smeared on my fingers was of no interest, nor were there any more pecks at my ears.

"Time to go," I said, running my hand gently down the iridescent wing feathers. Then I gathered the crow in both hands, encircling its body and holding it firmly. "Open the door, please," I said to Betsy, and we walked outside.

There was no need to open my hands. The baby struggled free, almost pushing me away, and leaped into the air. I could feel the rush of air on my face as its wings stroked hard, forcing it almost straight upward. About 20 feet up, the baby veered right and landed on our chimney. It sat still for a minute, looking in all directions, never looking back down at Betsy or me or Noah, all of us standing with our necks craned like yokels seeing a skyscraper for the first time.

"Will it come back?" Noah asked.

"No," said Betsy.

"But who does it belong to?" Noah asked.

The answer to his question came with a "Caw!" from the north, above the meadows that surround our house. The adult crow was making another pass, its call getting louder as it approached. I watched the baby on the chimney as it jerked its head around and stared up into the sky. Its body tensed into a slight crouch.

Then the adult passed overhead, cawed twice loudly, and swooped low over the baby. Instantly both of them seemed to explode upward, dipping slightly as the baby leaped from the bricks. Then they flew in tandem toward the south.

The tears backed up into my throat as I watched this. I heard a characteristic sniff from Betsy, though neither of us looked at each other. Noah clapped his hands and ran forward. "Goodbye, Crow!" he called, waving both hands over his head. In seconds the baby and adult were over the tall oaks, then gone.

We stood for awhile, staring into the southern sky, though there was nothing left to see. We could still hear a faint cawing, though which crows it came from we couldn't tell. Then we went into the house and began dismantling the cage. As I pulled out the branch we'd wedged between the bars as a perch, I noticed the yellowish cast on my fingers. A little dried egg yolk. I brushed it away. And I cursed myself for not having wings.

There is more to this story, an incredible incident that I still find difficult to believe.

Three weeks after we released the crow, I was working in the garden.

The day was bright and cool. It was about ten in the morning and I was cultivating with a hoe when a flash of movement or a quick shadow caught my eye. I looked up just in time to see a young crow dip about ten feet over my head. My jaw dropped and so did the hoe as the bird flew off, then veered back, buzzed me again, then perched on a low limb in a pear tree that borders the garden.

I've been around crows for a decade—or at least, they've flown around me during that time—and nothing like this ever happened. Crows simply don't like humans (with good reason) and never land near them. Nor do they often travel alone. One or two always act as lookouts, cawing the danger signal if you so much as cough.

Could this be our old friend and guest returning after three weeks? There was one acid test. The crow paid no attention to me as I approached the tree where he sat. I stood directly under the branch, the bird only about four or five feet above my reach. Crows don't do this, I thought, skeptic to the last. Then the test.

"Caw!" I said.

"Caw!" said the visitor, ruffling its feathers, cocking its head, and staring down at me. My God, I thought. My God!

"Awww!" I said again.

"Awwk!" came the answer. I began to laugh, giggling as though I was being tickled by a feather. "Don't go away," I laughed, shaking my finger at the bird, "don't move!" Then I ran toward the house yelling as loud as I could, "Betsy! Noah! Come here! Come here!" all the while looking back over my shoulder, afraid our friend would vanish at the sound of my shouts.

They came running from the house, Betsy with a what's-happening look on her face. I was dancing a jig and pointing up into the tree. "Look! Look!" I said, bursting at the seams. Betsy stopped short. "No," she said, "it can't. . ."

"It's back, it's back!" squealed Noah, rushing to the base of the tree and arching backward to look up at the bird, who was still preening as though we weren't even there.

The three of us stood for a long time under that pear tree, looking up at our visitor, with me occasionally saying "Caw!" and getting an answer and a ruffling of feathers. Whatever I was saying in crow talk must have been memorable.

The crow attended to its preening and seemed to take no notice of us. We sat under the tree for a while until Noah got restless and asked to go back to the house. I returned to the garden and my hoeing, all the time watching the bird. Then, its visit at an end, the crow leaped off the branch, and swooped within a few feet of me. "Awwk!" it said as it flapped over my head. "Caw!" I said in return. Then it gained altitude and flew southward over the tall oaks.

I leaned on the hoe, looking into the sky and treetops. I felt an ache deep within as though I wanted to reach out and touch something but couldn't. The gulf was too wide.

We were never again visited in quite the same special way, though for weeks and months afterward we jumped whenever we heard a "caw" overhead. From time to time, we'd see a single crow, a young one, sitting in a tree near the house, nearer, we thought, than most crows we'd seen. And months later a mature crow, shiny and velvet black, roosted on our chimney, and cawed loudly. I cawed in return but got no answer. Then, with strong wings, it flew away, cawing once as it gained altitude over the meadows.

Other wildlings have burst into our lives over the years. Once we found a half-frozen cricket in October. Betsy rescued it and set up a cricket house in a small aquarium. We kept it in the kitchen on a countertop where all of us could watch our houseguest. Winter came and the crickets outdoors died but she lived on, thriving on bread crumbs and fruit. Life is precious and it gave us pleasure to know that we had extended this tiny creature's existence. Our cricket never chirped (females don't) but she did, near the end of her life, thrust her spear-shaped ovipositor into the damp earth on the aquarium's floor, and lay her eggs, ensuring another generation of her kind. She died quietly on New Year's Eve.

Another time we used the same aquarium to rear caterpillars, feeding them milkweed leaves. Noah and Rachel watched in fascination as the creatures spun cocoons while hanging upside down from the aquarium's glass cover. When the cocoons had hardened, we transferred them to a curtain rod above our bedroom window, taping them in place. Then we read all about butterflies, sharing the information with Noah and Rachel.

What an amazing process goes on in those cocoons! The caterpillar actually turns into a liquid and from this ooze are formed the new parts of the butterfly. Then, after 9 to 15 days of incubation, the cocoon splits and the monarch butterfly emerges, as four did in our bedroom. Fortunately, we were home when it happened. We watched, spellbound, as the bedraggled creatures struggled to free themselves of their cocoons. Wet with birth liquid, they clung to the curtain rod, slowly pumping fluid into their wings, expanding them as we watched. Then the butterflies flexed and stretched their wings, fanning them open and closed, readying themselves for their first flight.

Butterflies are remarkably tame, we found, and we were able to coax them onto our hands, the better to lead them to the open window. "Do you know where these monarchs are going?" I said. We had read about their incredible journey but it was only then, as we prepared to see them off, that the wonder of their odyssey struck me. "They're going to fly from here to the Gulf of Mexico, to the swamps of Louisiana, to the Texas coast, to Apalachicola in Florida. Thousands of miles on those tissue-paper wings."

Other monarchs west of the Rockies would head for Monterey, California, for the pines in Pacific Grove. And the wonder of it all was that none of these insects knew where it was going from memory. None of them had ever made the journey before. Somehow they return to the same places every year, to the same areas their ancestors came to generations before. I looked up at the empty cocoons on the curtain rod. What secret flight instructions had they held? How was the information encoded? How was it released as caterpillar melted into transmogrifying ooze?

I turned away from the empty husks and looked at Noah and Rachel. Each stood before the window with a butterfly perched on a finger. I would have expected the children to giggle, but they stood still, transfixed by the exquisite beings slowly flexing on their outstretched hands. Then, as though responding to a signal, the butterflies lifted off together and glided out of the window.

"Goodbye! Goodbye!" the children called as the monarchs caught an autumn breeze and drifted past the red maple, then over the fence and out of sight.

Not all of our conclaves with the natural world have been as successful or as mystical. We've cared for infant rabbits and for abandoned baby birds and for turtles whose shells have been cracked by passing cars. Some of our foundlings survived and were returned to their own world. Others died no matter how diligent our efforts. The tragedies we relegate to painful memories. The successes become part of our family lore. And sometimes the successes even become part of the family.

One night, Betsy came in from the goat shed with her hands cupped in front of her and a light in her eyes. "What's going on now?" I asked suspiciously. I know when that light glows it means something out of the ordinary is happening, something that will cost time or money.

"I found something," she said, suppressing a smile. Then she opened her hands, revealing a tiny, almost fetal, baby mouse.

"Is it alive?"

"Yes. I saw it in a feed bucket in the barn this morning and figured the mother would come back for it. She didn't."

"Wonderful," I said, "so now you're a foster parent."

"Ohhh." Betsy moaned and laughed. I knew that moan. It meant "here we go again." Another round of deep involvement with a helpless creature, with unseen and unfathomable quirks of nature, with expectation and hope, and perhaps, sorrow at the end.

"How old do you think it is?" I asked, hearing the children running down the hall.

"I think it's only . . ."

"What is it? What is it?" yelled Noah, bouncing into the room.

"Whatcha got, Momma?" yelled Rachel, dancing around us, pushing at our knees.

". . . . about a day old?"

"A *day?*" I said, aghast. It's hard enough trying to nurture baby birds that have tumbled out of the nest fully feathered, but a day-old mouse? I looked down at the tiny, hairless, eyeless, earless speck of pink flesh quivering in Betsy's palm.

"Let me see! Let me see!" the children chorused. Betsy knelt down and held her hand out. Noah and Rachel pressed in, their eyes wide, holding their breaths in wonder. "What is it?" Noah asked.

"A baby mouse."

"What will we do with it?" he asked, not taking his eyes from the mouse.

"We'll try to save it," Betsy said gently. "We'll do our best."

Betsy caught my eye and I knew exactly what she was thinking about, the struggle ahead. "I found it this morning," she said, guilt in her voice.

"Why didn't you bring it in then?"

"I kept hoping the mother would come back for it," she said. "And I guess I hoped if she didn't that it would die."

"Why do you want it to die, Momma?" Noah asked.

"Oh, I don't want it to die, Noah. But sometimes baby animals don't survive no matter what you do. And I thought it would be easier if it just died right then and there."

"It's hard to understand, I know," I said, "but both of you have to understand that your mom might not be able to save it. That it might die no matter what we do. Okay?"

"Yeah," said Noah, solemnly.

"Yes," whispered Rachel, her eyes still very wide.

Betsy started right away. She poured some fresh goat's milk into a pan to warm it to about 100 degrees F. I went for a heating pad and a box. We were somber about this business, though the children were excited and full of questions. "What's that for?" "Can a mouse drink goat's milk?" "Is it still alive?" How many baby rabbits have died in our hands? How many times have we opened the shoe box in the morning to find the baby bird dead and stiff? But what can you do? You give it a try, always.

"This is ridiculous," I said. "Look at it. You can see its organs right through the skin. This one doesn't have a chance."

"I know," Betsy said, "but maybe it's tougher than we think. After all," she said, filling an eyedropper with warm milk, "it sat all day in a cold bucket and it's not dead yet."

The tiny creature was alive and kicking, all right. Betsy gently picked it up and cradled it in her left hand while she tried to angle the milk dropper with her right. "My God," she said, "it's so tiny the eyedropper could drown it."

And then, a miracle. With all of us gathered around the kitchen counter, the children snuggled next to us, standing on their chairs, the mouse eagerly and blindly sucked at the drop of milk Betsy squeezed from the dropper. "Look at that!" Betsy laughed.

"Let's not get our hopes up," I said, ever the bearer of dark clouds. And though I didn't say it because the children were there watching the mouse feed, I thought to myself: it will probably be dead by morning.

It wasn't.

Betsy got up every three hours during the night—and every night for two weeks—to feed the mouse. I took over some feedings by day, but this was Betsy's show, her "foster mouse" as I called it. And, amazingly, she was right: this was one tough mouse, a survivor. "It," as we called it the first few days—you can't easily sex an almost-fetus—continued to grow stronger, frequently pipping in annoyance when the milk was slow in coming.

And, of course, I fell in love with Betsy all over again. Every time I stood there watching her cradle that speck of life in her strong hands, cooing to it and fussing over it and encouraging it to live, I crumpled. "You're quite a person," I told her as I watched her tenderly wipe droplets of milk from the struggling baby.

"What?" she said, sheepishly, embarrassed at being caught with her humanity on her sleeve.

I put my arm around her shoulder and hugged her close, kissing her cheek. "Earth mother," I said, "mouse mother."

"Is it still alive?" Noah shattered our moment.

"Is it still a-wive, Ma?" Rachel came in right behind. Both of them had been affected by my pessimism (I call it reality) about the mouse's chances for survival. They dampened their enthusiasm for our foster rodent by always assuming the mouse had died or was on its way out.

"It's very much alive," Betsy said, cupping the creature in her hands and holding it out for the children to ogle. The first critical nights and days had passed. We could see the rapid development of our foundling—fuzzy hair had started covering the naked pink, the torso showed some signs of growth, and now the pips and high-frequency squeaks became more numerous.

Obvious, too, was that "Mousie," as the children dubbed it, already preferred Betsy's hands to mine. Feeding it was a struggle for me, though it always took food. But when Betsy put her hand into the box, Mousie—still blind and with only the hint of ears—pipped and struggled in expectation. After a week it fed eagerly, now large enough to grab the tip of the eyedropper in its mouth.

Betsy wiped it down with an old diaper dampened with warm water, rubbing the tiny body briskly. "Its mother would have licked it, I guess, and roughed it up a little. All babies need plenty of physical contact, right?"

"Right," I said, "otherwise we could have an emotionally disabled mouse."

"Look," she said. There, nestled into the soft flesh at the base of Betsy's fingers, Mousie had burrowed down and fallen sound asleep, its fur rough and glistening from Betsy's rubbing.

The irony of all this is that Betsy hates mice. Or did. Old houses like ours are mice condominiums, especially in winter when the little beasts take up residence in the floors and walls. "I hate them! I hate them! Ugh!" were the shouts I often woke up to in winter when Betsy discovered some new mice intrusion in the kitchen. "One thing I can't take," she fumed one morning when I walked in to find her scrubbing out the silverware drawer with hot, sudsy water, "is *mouse turds in the spoons and forks, Godammit!*"

"Want to set some traps?" I asked. This was a regular routine with us. Both of us were annoyed by the mouse attacks on our food supply, books, and clothing—it wasn't unusual to find clothing or papers stored in closets shredded for a dimimutive nest—but neither of us enjoyed the idea of killing mice. Our anger at the rodents was always balanced by our discomfort at killing other creatures. Three barn cats kept the goat shed free from mice for us, delivering victims to our doorstep in the morning.

The house was more vulnerable. We couldn't set out traps. Neither of us could deal with the sight of tiny bodies mangled by assorted springs and wires. Live traps were another possibility, but I don't think either of us wanted to spend time transporting mice out of the house to new surroundings.

But finally the rodent attacks became so numerous as to be a threat to our health, if not Betsy's mental stability. So we took the coward's way out, one I am not happy to admit publicly. We rationalized that since we were under attack by mice, and since our two house cats were foiled by the rodents' ability to hide, we had to fight back. We used poison.

"We have to do it," we lied to each other.

"It's painless," we lied some more, knowing well that mouse and rat poison is made with an anticoagulant that causes death by internal hemorrhage. We were putting on blinders, setting out poison in places we didn't have to see to do a nasty job we didn't want to hear about or deal with. And we closed the doors and went away.

Within two weeks our domesticated Mr. Mouse—as the children now called him—opened his eyes, first slits, then dark and round. The first image to fill those eyes was, appropriately, Betsy, fully imprinted in the psyche of her miniscule ward. By this time we realized that Mr. Mouse was really Ms. Mouse, development having proceeded enough for positive identification.

As the mouse became part of our daily routine, we tried to make the children understand that there was still risk involved, that the mouse might not survive. The fact that things die is terribly threatening to a child. If things die, they reason, then they can die, their parents can die. It's an uncomfortable awakening.

The mouse didn't die, though for a long time I think Noah expected it to and prepared himself for that possibility. This seems maudlin, but it struck me as healthy that he realized life wasn't as TV portrays it—all happy with fully resolved endings and no risks.

Rachel's reaction was more difficult to see because she was only three. But several days after Betsy found the mouse Rachel sat with me in the living room and asked a serious question.

"When will we die, Dad?"

"Not for a long time, Rachel."

"But what if we don't?" I realized Rachel wasn't asking "what if we don't die?" but "what if it's *not* a long time?" What if it's now? This was her "what if" stage, distinguished by perverse questioning.

I looked at her sitting next to me. Hard to imagine serious concern etching the soft, round face of a three-year-old, but there it was. "Rachel, are you really asking me what will happen to us when we die?"

"Yeah."

"Well," I said, taking a deep breath, "when we die we become part of the earth again, part of the plants, and water and sky and trees. It's hard to understand, but we become part of everything there is." She sat quietly, thinking. I knew I hadn't given the standard answer—that we die and go to heaven or that God welcomes us with open arms. That kind of answer might be easier for a child to deal with because it involves a mental image of a place and a person, but I don't believe it and I wouldn't cop out with it.

"Does that help?" I asked.

"Yes," she said in a tiny voice. I knew I hadn't given her a concrete answer, but what *is* the answer? I like to think I gave Rachel a better question.

The children finally named the mouse Hunca Munca after the heroine of Beatrix Potter's *A Tale of Two Bad Mice.* We were able to stop the eyedropper feedings as soon as Hunca's eyes opened, so we could again sleep through the night. Hunca was now self-reliant, eating fruit, grains, nuts and—like her relatives in the walls—just about anything at all.

We bought a ten-gallon aquarium and fitted it out as a mouse heaven with several inches of wood shavings, cardboard tubes, and old wool socks for her to shred and nest in.

I know, I know. We should have set her free. "I can't," Betsy said. "I know I should, but winter is coming on and I've just given too much of myself to see her gobbled up by a cat. I didn't save her for that."

"What *did* you save her for?" I asked, a rhetorical question if ever there was one.

"What else could I do?"

Hunca Munca is part of the family now. She is fully tame, comes when you call her name, and jumps into Betsy's hand with great enthusiasm. Noah and Rachel delight in watching her feed, sharpen her teeth on the wood block we gave her, and explore her tiny world. She is a sleek, clean, rotund, white-footed mouse now, bright eyed and intelligent, but impossible to explain to people who think of mice as just mice.

No more poison for us now. Every mouse that might writhe in agony would be Hunca Munca. Is this sloppy sentiment? I don't think so. We've learned that what we believed only intellectually is true: you preserve and celebrate life whenever you can.

There's more to this story. About a month after Betsy found Hunca Munca I walked out into the driveway and found another day-old mouse on the ground, between the paws of Punchy Sally, one of our cats. That afternoon when Betsy and the children came home I stood in the kitchen doorway, a stupid grin on my face.

"What's going on?" Betsy asked suspiciously.

"Look on the counter," I said.

"Oh no," said Betsy.

"Another mouse!" yelled Noah.

"Yaaaay!" squealed Rachel. Betsy turned and grabbed my arm, laughing.

"What can I say?" I said. "We're the ultimate suburban couple. We've got *his* and *hers mice.*"

Some months after both mice were ensconced in their new homes, we chanced to read *The Complete Care of Orphaned or Abandoned Baby Animals,* an excellent book by C. E. Spaulding, D.V.M., and Jackie Spaulding. The Spauldings write that saving baby mice is virtually impossible because their mouths are too small to accept the tip of an eyedropper, something we discovered on our own. The Spauldings recommend feeding the mice by letting milk seep into their mouths from a piece of string. We succeeded, I think, because of Betsy's infinite patience and compassion. And it helped that we used fresh, unpasteurized milk. But we still keep a ball of string handy, just in case.

Hunca Munca and *my* mouse, Tom Thumb, now live in their respective aquariums atop a bureau in our bedroom. We've added plastic gerbil runs and exercise wheels to their homes so they have plenty of room to run and explore. We feed them a great variety of foods, their favorites being Betsy's bread, mixed seeds and nuts, fresh broccoli, and bits of apple (especially the seeds).

We no longer have any doubts about whether we should have set them free after weaning. That would have been their death sentence. Having been hand-reared, they have no fear of humans and regard us, I think, as giant mice. Both animals enjoy being handled and go into reveries when being petted. They particularly enjoy having their ears and bellies scratched. We've even been bold enough lately to take them out of their homes, letting them sit in our hands or run up onto our shoulders. They seem to genuinely enjoy our company. We certainly enjoy theirs.

For all my inherent love of the outdoors and natural phenomena, you'd think I would have been an avid gardener right from the start. A garden, after all, is one's own special nature preserve, a wondrous place where we're privileged to have a direct hand in the mystic circle of growth and decay. But it took me years to realize this. To say I started out in life with no particular interest in tilling the soil would be an understatement.

I remember my mother's vegetable garden when I was a teenager. Like most self-centered adolescents I had no qualms about eating the food she grew as long as I didn't have to do any of the work.

"Victor," my mother would say—she always called me by my full name when there was serious business at hand—"I'd like you to help weed the garden."

"Oh, gee, Mom. I wish I could. I really do, but I have this terribly important biology test coming up and I have to study for it."

"I thought you took biology last year."

"Uh, I did, but I'm taking it again. I've decided to become a surgeon."

"You?"

"Yes. So I'm sure you can appreciate that we don't want anything to happen to my hands. No calluses or anything that might ruin them for saving lives on the operating table."

"Weeding won't ruin your hands."

"What if I got my hands caught in a threshing machine?"

"Use a hoe. Get out there, please."

"Look, I'll be honest with you . . ."

"How nice for a change."

"I *hate* the garden. I really hate it. It's full of bugs and dirt."

"Victor, it's hard to have a garden without dirt. And the bugs won't bother you if you don't bother them."

"All right," I gave up, "if you think nothing of ruining a career in surgery that might have plucked innocent souls from the jaws of death . . ."

"Go pluck some innocent weeds. It'll be good for *your* soul."

So I went into the garden as reluctantly as one entering a penal colony. I pulled weeds and swatted the bugs that bothered me endlessly though I didn't bother them. Red ants bit my ankles, Japanese beetles got caught in my hair. How could anyone actually *enjoy* gardening? I wondered.

But lo, the reluctant gardener has changed, as years passed, into a natural foods enthusiast, an ecology nut, a concerned consumer. And the more I got interested in the notion of self-reliance, the more I realized that having a garden was the only sensible way to control the quality of the food I ate.

Besides, all my angry adolescent memories of weeding and bugs faded as I greedily looked through seed catalogs and gardening books. It all seemed so simple. Plant a few seeds, water now and then, and *voilà!* Instant groceries.

I was living in the city then, slowly going crazy in a cramped apartment, reading gardening books and *Organic Gardening and Farming* magazine. Having a garden became a cause. I sprouted seeds in the kitchen, but nothing would still my drive for a patch of ground to call my own.

My parents had already moved to Florida by that time, so I had no hope of having a garden on their land in nearby Virginia. (My mother enjoyed a long, ironic laugh when I told her over the phone of my new passion.)

Help finally came from a friend with a small patch of land behind his city house. We could garden there, he said, in exchange for some of the produce. What a deal, I thought. I had no doubt we'd be rolling in vegetables by midsummer.

I enlisted Betsy and we bought more books on gardening, found places to buy mulch and manure, and pored over seed catalogs together. Then we bought a hoe, a rake, a spade, and a ball of twine at the hardware store and rented a Rototiller. Gardening was going to be a snap!

"It doesn't seem like enough land for a serious gardener," I said as Betsy and I surveyed the garden site.

"Vic," Betsy said gently, as though speaking to a child, "this plot is 60-by-30 feet. That's 1,800 square feet."

"Well . . ."

"Probably enough to feed the neighborhood."

She was right, but I was gripped entirely by passion. Back to the hardware store where I was welcomed with a smile and an open cash register. I bought seeds, seedlings, stakes, another ball of twine, a watering can, 50 feet of plastic hose, various sprinkling devices, bone meal, blood meal, dried cow manure, powdered seaweed, rock phosphate, and limestone.

"Don't you think we've gone a little overboard?" Betsy asked one particularly hot spring day. We were stringing lines to mark another row. "I think we might have planted fewer vegetables to start."

"Don't be timid," I snapped. "I've read all the books. There's nothing to it. I don't know why everyone makes such a fuss about gardening. You just cover the seeds with dirt and nature does the rest."

"You really think we needed to put in 30 tomato plants?"

"I like tomatoes."

"How about parsnips? You planted a 60-foot row of them and I know you've never even tasted a parsnip."

"I'm willing to be adventurous. Pull that string tighter, please."

"When all this stuff comes up you're going to have to care for it, weeding and watering and controlling the bugs."

"I know that, I . . . hey," I stood up, the sweat pouring off my forehead into my eyes, "what do you mean *you're* going to have to care for it. What happened to 'we'? This is our garden, right?"

"Sort of. But it's your craziness and I'm willing to go only so far with that."

"You don't believe in this garden, do you?" I stood straddling the row like Moses confronting the Israelites.

"I believe in the garden," Betsy said quietly, "but I also believe you're going overboard as usual. I think we would have done just as well with a smaller garden. I don't think you should have planted 27 different things until you learned a little more."

"Yeah?? Well, I'm going to let you in on a secret."

"What?"

"Mulch."

"Mulch?"

"Mulch. That's the secret. After we get all done we're going to pile the mulch on—the bales of hay we bought last week—and then we just sit back and wait to harvest."

"It's that simple?" Betsy asked dubiously.

"The mulch will smother the weeds, enrich the soil, and discourage insects. We don't have to do anything but wait."

"I know, I know. But I'm sure there's more to it than that."

There was, of course. I had read Ruth Stout's *How to Have a Green Thumb Without an Aching Back* and got so excited I missed an important point. Ruth Stout used a foot or more of hay as a mulch. In my enthusiasm I came away convinced several inches would do. So we spread out the bales of hay we'd bought into a skimpy layer that I, in my stubbornness, really believed would end all our gardening problems. It did, actually, though not quite in the way I'd planned.

"That's it," I announced when the last wisp of hay was scattered. "Let's head for the beach."

"You're not kidding, are you?" Betsy said. "Don't you think there's more to it than that?"

"You'll see."

Off we went for a two-week vacation at the ocean. When we came back the garden was gone.

Vanished.

"Who would steal a garden?" I said helplessly, standing on the edge of what seemed to be a weed-infested vacant lot. Betsy walked into the waist-high tangle.

"The garden is still here," she said, "under here," and she knelt and disappeared beneath the weeds. Then she stood up again. "I think it needed a little more mulch. And a little less arrogance."

We visited the garden plot once or twice later that season, just for old times' sake. Our labors and prodigious layering of mulch and soil conditioners produced one of the lushest stands of mixed weeds in the hemisphere. There were even tomatoes beneath the heavy undergrowth. We never got any to eat, though. Turtles loved the cool plant cover and kept the plants well picked.

I was right about one thing, anyway. Gardening *had* been a snap. I was finished in no time.

My next attempt at gardening came after we moved to Potomac. We arrived in mid-August, too late to put in a full-fledged garden. But a friend had given me some leftover packets of seed—some bush beans and black Spanish radishes.

I spaded up a 2-by-4-foot section of ground on the south side of a toolshed. I didn't know it was the south side then, all I knew was that the sun seemed to shine there most of the time. It would take years before I knew one compass point from another, or cared.

"Nothing's coming up," I told Betsy. "I must have done something wrong again."

"When did you plant the seeds?"

"Yesterday."

"Vic . . ."

"Okay, okay. But I thought I might see a sprout or two."

I tried to be less impatient and only checked the plot twice a day. Nothing. I was sure my days as a gardener had ended in failure again. The curse of the brown thumb.

But one morning after I had almost given up, I checked the eight square feet again. I saw something. A tiny, fleshy sprout had pushed up near the marker that said "beans." I knelt down and stared at it. Another sprout was pushing up next to the first. And another.

"Hey!" I shouted. "Hey Betsy! Hey!" I ran for the house. Suddenly I knew how Pasteur and Madame Curie must have felt.

"Eureka!" I yelled at Betsy as she came out.

"What?"

"Beans!" I shouted, dancing in place. "They're up! Look!"

"The radishes are up too," she said, looking over the plot.

"What? Oh boy! Isn't that amazing!"

"Congratulations," she said. "Are you going to hand out cigars at work?"

That was a day of miracles—that a handful of dry seeds, nondescript pellets, could burst with hidden life. Botanical satori. And I was hooked on gardening.

When spring came I was ready for my first serious effort. On the first warm day in March, when the soil was no longer muddy, I hurried out to rent a tiller. I spent an afternoon running it over the 50-by-50-foot plot I'd marked off. Beautiful. Twenty-five hundred square feet of dark, rich soil.

That's what it looked like at first, anyway. But after a few hours of drying in the sun, the soil reverted to its true color of yellowish clay. The crumbly richness changed back to ceramiclike hardness. And even before I was ready to plant seeds, the grass sod I'd tilled under was struggling back up again. All I had really done was to turn a lawn upside down.

But when the going gets tough, the tough get great ideas. Oceanic concepts. Betsy can see them coming like bad weather blowing in. She gets a tight rein on her disbelief and on our checkbook.

"I have a great idea," I said.

"I was afraid of that," she said.

"What we need to do is compost all that grass."

"I thought you said it was too late for that."

"No, not if we build a *giant* compost pile. Not if we turn the entire garden into a compost pile!" My eyes must have blazed with an inner light.

The next day I drove to a wholesale dealer in plastic sheeting. "I want to buy enough black plastic to cover my garden," I told the owner. "Enough to cover an area 50-by-50 feet."

"Don't tell me," he said, "you just won the Irish Sweepstakes, right?"

"Why?"

"Because you're talking big bucks, that much plastic. Why do you want to do that anyway—cover your garden up? You hate plants or something?"

I explained how I wanted to create a giant compost pile. The black plastic would shut out all the light, trap the heat, absorb sunshine, and bake the grass and roots into humus.

"Crazy idea," he said. "Nutty. But maybe we can work something out."

A half-hour later I drove off with 2,500 square feet of black plastic sheeting. My mentor had sold me "end rolls," the tail ends of an assortment of rolls containing pieces too short to be sold easily. I paid $25 for the load, a terrific bargain. Getting the plastic down on the garden plot wasn't as easy, though.

Did you ever try to spread a blanket out on the beach when the wind was blowing? We had dozens of thin black plastic blankets, and trying to spread them out in the teeth of a March wind was like throwing confetti into a fan. Of course, there was no wind when we started the project. Dead calm. The wind didn't start until we had several sheets unrolled.

Every time we managed to lay a sheet flat, a gust of wind sneaked under a corner and snapped the whole business loose, showering us with the bricks, stones, and scrap lumber we'd used to weigh the sheet down.

We dragged out more ballast—cinder blocks, old locust fence posts, tires, hay bales, a broken easy chair—anything to peg the crazily flapping mess down.

The wind burrowed under the sheets, making them billow like angry black waves. A giant air bubble undulated beneath the sheets, rolling slowly from one end of the garden to the other, tossing up little piles of rummage as it passed by.

We were desperate, losing the battle, using anything we could drag to the garden to flatten the monster we'd loosed.

"I never knew gardening could be so much fun," Betsy shouted into the wind as she wrestled with a twisted swirl of sheeting.

"My God," I said, standing back to look at the wide expanse of flotsam and jetsam we'd accumulated. "We can have a wonderful garage sale when the wind dies down."

An hour later and we finally had all the sheets in place. They looked awful. Viewed from an upstairs bedroom, the garden looked like a junkyard floating on an oil slick.

"This is never going to win a prize from the garden club," said Betsy.

"Skeptical as always, aren't you? Ye of little faith. Just wait until the sun beats down on that plastic. Why, we'll have compost coming out of our. . . "

A huge piece of plastic suddenly ripped free of its moorings, rising like King Kong escaping from his jailors. We watched horrified as the plastic crouched, filled with wind, and turned into a boiling mass.

"Well, Dr. Frankenstein," said Betsy, "what's new in the laboratory?"

"Look at that thing," I said. The sheet had grown into a ball the size of a pickup truck and was rolling over the garden fence, gaining momentum, cartwheeling across the meadow.

I raced down the stairs and ran after it as it lumbered toward the houses on the far side of the field. I could see a woman hanging clothes on a line. The breeze was snapping the sheets as she clipped them in place. King Kong was bearing down on her.

I ran as fast as I could, but I was too late. She must have heard the crackling sound the ball made as it tumbled across her yard, because she turned just in time to see a tidal wave of black plastic engulfing her.

"EeeeeeEEEEEE!" she screamed and threw her hands in front of her face. "EEEEEEEeeeee! Fraaaaank!"

Oh Lord, I thought. I'm trapped in a "B"-movie.

I caught up with the tail end of the billowing mess, but not in time to save its screaming victim. The ball rolled over her and over the clothesline, crunching and snapping as it advanced. My neighbor's screams were muffled and frantic as she valiantly punched and kicked her attacker from the inside. I jumped into the fray, ripping and pulling at the sheet, but the wind and the fates were too strong.

"What the hell's going on here!" Frank came bursting out of the back door, murder in his eyes. "Louise! Louise," he tore at the other side of the plastic, "you in there?" Then, as he struggled, he spotted me on the other side of the ball. "Who the hell are you?"

"Hi," I said, as though I'd just dropped by. The plastic snapped under my nose. "I live across the meadow."

"Yaaaaaaa!" Louise screamed as she suddenly broke free and popped out of the center of the ball.

"Louise!" Frank grabbed her by the shoulders. "What the hell's going on here?"

"I'd like to apologize," I said faintly, gathering as much of the plastic against my chest as I could.

"I've been attacked!" Louise screamed, pointing a clothespin at me.

"Oh, Jesus," I said.

"Louise, calm down or you're gonna hyperventilate."

"And look at my sheets," she wailed, seeing the mud the billowing plastic had smeared across her laundry.

"See, let me explain," I said, clumsily, gathering up the plastic, stuffing it under my arms, trying to squeeze the air and the life out of it. "I'm an organic gardener. . ."

"You're an organic *nut!*" Frank shouted.

". . . and this is part of. . . "

"You best get your plastic and yourself outta here," Frank grumbled.

"I'm trying, I'm trying," I said, finally wrestling the last bit of life out of the sheet, compressing it into a ball the size of a bushel basket.

"You keep that thing tied up, y'hear?" Frank waved a fist at me and at the black ball. "I see that thing coming over the field again and I'll throw some buckshot into it!"

"Right, right," I said, backing away.

"Don't step in my flower bed!" Louise screamed.

"Right, right," I said, stepping out of the pansies. "Sorry about the trouble," I smiled weakly.

I hurried across the field, not looking back, holding the ball of plastic like the golden fleece. Even as I approached our property line I could see the other black sheets flapping and snapping in the breeze. Maybe a little buckshot *would* slow them down.

I found out later that Louise was the Welcome Wagon lady.

In matters other than community relations, the black plastic was a rousing success. Betsy had to admit that, for once anyway, one of my great ideas had worked according to plan. We peeled the sheets back layer by layer in mid-June and found crumbly soil alive with earthworms. All the grass, including the roots, had rotted away. We had a 50-by-50-foot plot of compost, a thin layer, but enough to get us started as serious gardeners.

Betsy and I folded up the plastic sheets and stacked them away. We used them again from time to time over the years to cover manure piles, lawn mowers, and other equipment, but we never laid any out in the garden again, not even as a temporary mulch. I was always afraid an errant piece or two might escape toward Louise's house.

I planted snow peas that first season, learning an unexpected lesson about gardening and nature. I was doing everything by the book then, with no experience or intuition to fall back on. And because I had learned as an urbanite to rely on invisible, predictable systems, I naturally assumed the garden would go as smoothly as mail delivery or garbage collection. I forgot about nature playing a role.

One morning I came down to the garden and surveyed the beauty. Delicate purple blossoms hung from the hollow, reedlike pea stalks. I stood there for a long time. Staring at the garden, now as in the beginning, has the same effect on me as watching waves break on the shore. I can sit or stand, in a reverie, totally at peace.

But the clouds darkened later that day and the wind blew in great huffs from the south. Going to be a hell of a storm, I thought. It was indeed, but not rain. Hailstones the size of lima beans pelted down. They ricocheted off the windowpanes and hammered on the roof. Betsy and I looked out the window and watched the white balls bouncing off the grass and tree limbs. We shuddered as a gust of wind threw hailstones against the window with a frenzy.

The peas were murdered, beaten into desolate tangles of broken stalks. Nothing else in the garden was far enough along to be knocked flat, but the peas were a total loss.

"I'm sorry," Betsy said, taking my hand. We stood there helplessly, looking at damage no gardener's skill can repair. "You worked so hard," she said.

"Yeah," I said, mournfully. I had spent hours digging shallow trenches where the pea rows were to go, filling them with compost to produce the healthiest plants. I had pounded in fence posts and hung chicken wire for the peas to climb on. I worried and fussed over the first sprouts like a mother hen. All for nothing.

But then I realized something strange. I felt saddened, but resigned. If a stray dog or vandals had destroyed the peas, I would have been enraged. But with nature, I thought, there's no meanness, nothing deliberate.

Betsy and I walked up to the house, talking quietly of planting peas again in the fall and making other garden plans. As we crossed near the brushline that borders the east side of the garden, something caught my eye. I stopped.

"Look at this."

"What is it?" asked Betsy.

"I'm not sure," I said, dropping to my knees to inspect a clump of green shoots. I pushed some tangled wild raspberry canes aside.

"Asparagus!" Betsy said with a laugh.

"Wild asparagus!"

We harvested about a dozen tender shoots from several clumps and hurried to the kitchen. To tell the truth, I never liked asparagus much, but I knew how Betsy loved it. Then I tasted a spear tip, fresh from the light steaming Betsy had given them. Guess who changed his mind about asparagus? That was the first of many times I realized the difference between vegetables that sit around in a supermarket produce section and those you grow or pick fresh yourself.

But a larger truth dawned on me as we ate, reveling in our discovery. "I can't put it into words, exactly," I told Betsy, "but I've learned something important today about nature—about its neutrality."

"Yes," she said, "loss and gain balance out—peas and wild asparagus."

"But it's also a little scary, realizing that we're no big deal in the scheme of things, no more than pea stalks waiting to be flattened," I growled.

"Oh come on," she laughed, "I'd rather think of us as wild asparagus waiting to be discovered!"

My skill at gardening increased with each new season. I continued to read everything on gardening I could find (as I still do) and I kept a garden diary to track my successes and failures. There were plenty of both. But each season held out another chance to learn, to experiment, to grow. And the turning point in my gardening career came because I'm so bad at arithmetic.

My first several gardens were what I call traditional. That is, they were laid out in rows, nice and neat and straight, just like in the seed catalogs. And they were productive gardens and very satisfying. I had no reason to change anything and no intention to do so.

But one evening in winter, when I was planning out next spring's garden on paper, I noticed something odd. I always planned gardens out on graph paper. With an area 50-by-50 feet, I tried to make the most use of every inch of space. As it was, I couldn't use all the space because I had to leave paths around the garden and a large path up the center so I could get in and out with a wheelbarrow or garden cart. And for ease of planning, I kept my rows uniform in length.

The rows ran north to south. All were about 22 feet long. But this evening I decided to lay out some short rows, 10 feet long, in an attempt to cluster some plants in blocks. I have trouble balancing a checkbook (I have been known to switch banks just so an old account goes dormant, balancing itself, in effect), so figuring all that square footage was heavy math for me.

What I discovered was that if you lay out short rows you get more growing space. In other words, let's say I grow carrots in one 20-foot row with a 12-inch-wide path on either side. That's 40 square feet given to carrots. But what happens if I lay out four 5-foot rows with 12-inch paths? I grow the same amount of carrots but only take up 25 square feet of garden.

Amazing.

Realizing my limited proclivity for math might be leading me astray, I had a friend, an engineer, go over my calculations. It took him a glance. "Yeah," he said, "so what?"

"You mean I'm right? Short rows take up less square footage and deliver the same amount of produce? How can that be if the total row length is the same?"

"Because, you dummy," (he is a close, personal friend) "when you put in short rows you're reducing the amount of space you're giving up to paths. Paths don't grow anything, right?"

Paths don't grow anything.

That phrase rang in my ears all the way home—a revelation as staggering as any theory Einstein might have dreamed up. Paths don't grow *anything!*

I got home and immediately began redesigning the garden. I shortened all the rows, reduced the size of the paths to just enough room to tiptoe between rows, and laughed out loud when I was done. What a discovery, I thought. I had dramatically increased the potential yield of my 50-by-50-foot plot by doing nothing more than breaking with tradition.

And I thought about something else that had always intrigued me. Why does it say on seed packets: "plant seeds 2 inches apart, leaving 18 inches between the rows"? Why, I wondered, can carrot or other seeds grow

2 inches apart in one direction but not in the other? Why can't a garden more closely resemble a natural setting instead of having plants arranged in long straight rows?

I began looking at gardens and garden books intensively after these revelations. And I began to realize that gardens are traditional in more ways than one. People lay out gardens in rows because that's the way it's always been done—no other good reason. Gardens are, after all, mini-farms. And farmers use long straight rows to make it possible for their tractors to roll along cultivating and tilling. But who has a tractor rolling through their backyard garden?

Right about this time I began hearing about the raised-bed method of intensive gardening, and all the pieces fell into place. The name Alan Chadwick kept showing up in various articles in alternative-life-style publications. Chadwick was an actor, mystic, and gardener who had come to the University of California at Santa Cruz. There, he and some students took over a plot of "useless" land and transformed it into an incredibly fertile biodynamic garden. Chadwick's method called, laboriously, the French intensive biodynamic method of raised-bed gardening, was based on principles used in Asian gardening, on the philosophy of Rudolph Steiner, who developed the concept of biodynamic gardening, a type of organic gardening, on methods used by French farmers a century ago, and on accepted principles of organic gardening.

No books or detailed accounts were then available about Chadwick's methods, but I picked up enough by guess to figure out what he was doing. It seemed revolutionary, wonderfully sensible, and startlingly close to what I'd discovered on my own.

So I completely transformed my garden according to what I'd gleaned about Chadwick. First, I did away entirely with the concept of rows, even short ones. Second, I tried to create a garden that was as close as possible to a natural setting with mixed varieties and equidistant plantings.

I laid out beds that were 4 feet wide and 22 feet long. It doesn't matter how long the beds are, but the width must be no wider than twice your reach. You must be able to touch the center of the bed from either side—with your hand, not a garden tool.

Then I double-dug the beds, a brutal job but enormously satisfying. Double-digging involves removing the topsoil from a trench dug across the bed. This soil is set aside. The subsoil is then loosened and broken into large chunks. Another trench is dug alongside the first one and the topsoil from the second trench is shoveled into the first trench. The subsoil is then loosened in the second trench and so on down the length of the bed. When the entire bed has been dug down to the last trench, you fill that with the topsoil saved from the first trench you dug. I found the work so hard I couldn't dig a 22-foot bed in one day. I'd work—and so did Betsy—a little every day. Six feet down the row was about my daily goal. At that rate a finished bed took about three days.

After all the trenching is done you have a huge mound of dirt. It looks like a mass grave or the attack of a giant mole. This is allowed to sit for several days. The action of wind, sun, and rain helps to break up the clods of dirt. Then you go back and break the clods by hand, chopping at them with a hoe or rake. Great exercise for the arms and chest.

The bed is then shaped, a pleasant task almost like sculpture. You add plenty of compost to the bed and reshape it. You end up with a bed of loose, compost-enriched soil—ground that's crumbly for about three feet down. (From the ground level down it's a friable two feet; on top of this you have a mound of loose soil that's about 8-to-12 inches above ground level.)

The soil isn't only loose, it's graded. Soil on top of the mound is fine. The subsoil is coarse and chunky. In between is a range of particle sizes. This means air and water can move easily from the top of the bed to the root zones and back again.

The key to the raised bed is this: you never step on the bed or compress it in any way. Beds are renewed by digging and adding compost each year—though gardeners disagree on whether you should double-dig each season. Some experienced raised-bed advocates believe one double-dig is enough, that the subsoil never really compacts again if you don't step on it or run equipment over it. Others think you should repeat the entire process yearly.

I've done both. I tend to agree that one or two double-digs are enough. And one nice thing about digging the beds the second year: even if you double-dig all over again, it takes far less time and energy. Now I can dig an entire bed in a few hours, instead of several days.

Once I tried making an ersatz bed by raking up topsoil and compost to form a mound. But I did no digging below the surface. I didn't keep scientifically accurate records on the results of piled mounds versus dug mounds, but I suspect garden production with a mound of any kind will surpass that of traditional "flat earth" gardening. And garden health and productivity is always going to be improved when you don't step on the plot.

I used to think about that when I gardened in rows. All season long I walked on the paths, compressing the soil and packing the clay down into the consistency of concrete. Then, next season, I'd be out trying to loosen the earth I'd spent the previous year compressing. Makes no sense. Why recycle your footprints?

I like double-digging, for all the work involved. I enjoy the exercise and I enjoy knowing that I've transformed the earth in a beneficial manner. Were you to step into the garden and see the beds (there are now 18 of them, all 22-by-4 feet) you would be unable to tell which were dug and which were simply mounded. But I know. That is important to me. When I look at the neatly sculpted beds I know that loose soil goes down for more than 2½ feet.

Sometimes I stand in the garden and just think and look. I look at the beds and visualize the rich, loose soil, the water moving up and down, the earthworms burrowing and laying eggs in the crumbly dirt, the insects, the bacteria. Never do I feel more like a child of the universe than when I stand in the garden.

The pleasure is cumulative. With each year's gardening the soil improves. And it changes much faster than in a traditional garden. "Coffee grounds." That's what someone called the texture of my soil. It does have that pelletized, crumbly appearance, the result of worms at work more than anything else.

Now, with an evangelist like me extolling the wonders of the raised bed, you'd guess most of my friends and gardening acquaintances employ the same methods. Wrong. After more than six years of raised-bed gardening I still know of only one person—my friend, Alan Pollock—who adopted the method. His results were phenomenal. He stuck a garden in the only place he could in his small, city backyard. Nestled close to the house, his garden consisted of boxed beds made of scrap lumber. He dug as far as he could into the subsoil and then filled the beds with a mixture of leaf mold, sand, compost, and various organic soil amendments like seaweed, rock phosphate, and dried manure. The harvests he got the first year were far better than either of us expected. He didn't feed his family out of the garden—there wasn't enough space for that—but he made a noticeable dent in his food bill and had a wonderful time doing it.

His garden became, as a garden will for most gardeners, a refuge rather than simply a source of food. Every night when he got home from his tedious government job, Alan entered the garden, moving into another, saner, more orderly world.

I'm not the first to think that gardens nourish us in many ways. They feed our corporeal selves, of course, but if food alone mattered, the garden would be no more than a machine, as the earth itself has become for so many agribusinessmen.

But the garden feeds our spirits, nourishes our souls. There, amongst the buzzing and droning of insects, in the light and shadow, we are closest to our true natures. We can yell and rail and give orders, but nothing happens. The garden moves at its own private pace. It moves according to principles we have only barely seen and understood less. We can, some think, hurry these processes and—God help us—"improve" them with an arsenal of chemicals and magic potions. Gardens, like the earth itself, are forgiving and they can absorb much of our heavy-handedness, but only up to a point.

In the same way, I suppose, we can improve poetry by programming poetic images into a computer. And we can improve religious services and spiritual experiences by using drugs or microprocessors. But I think a garden should be left alone except to augment the natural processes taking place.

The most important of those augmentations is compost, the heart of organic gardening and the soul of healthy soil. I'm a compost lover. I love to make it, smell it, run it through my fingers, and dig it into the soil. Nature takes a million years to make an inch of topsoil, but the harsh practices of modern farming can wipe that out overnight, as can indiscriminate logging or poor environmental planning.

Making compost, then, is a way to rebuild the earth, to nourish and respect it. Each application of rich, black humus improves the garden and enhances the earth—even if it's only a flyspeck of ground on the planet's surface.

Compost, compost, and more compost is the key to healthy and productive garden soil. Nonorganic gardening books and most professors of agronomy will tell you that compost has less nitrogen, phosphorus, and potassium than what you get in a sack of artificial fertilizer. Compost is important for its humus content, they say, but it generally lacks essential amounts of nutrients. But their explanation misses several important points:

Compost isn't just a substance. It's a process, a community of organisms, an organism itself, the living earth in a heap. Compost contains billions of varied bacteria, naturally occurring antibiotics, chelated nutrients, trace minerals, and complex substances not yet isolated in a laboratory.

Good compost not only nourishes plants, it conditions the soil and helps create optimum conditions for growth and soil health.

I make compost twice a year: in early spring for use at summer's end, and in fall for application the following season. I make a lot at both times, several tons, so I keep the process simple.

My compost frames are old 2-by-4-foot plastic fluorescent-light diffusers, tossed out when a government building was being remodeled. Alan, who has a sharp eye for useful trash, rescued hundreds of the frames. "They must be good for something," he said as we loaded them on my pickup truck. This was one of the few times we got something tangible back from the government.

The frames are easy to use. I tie them to steel fence posts pounded into the ground in a 4-by-4-foot square. Then I tie a second line of frames above the first ones. This gives me a 4-by-4-foot frame, 4 feet high. When filled, each enclosure holds about a ton of humus.

I follow the classic method for compost making. First, I loosen the ground where the pile will sit. This helps free soil bacteria at the pile's base. Then I begin alternating layers of various organic matter, occasionally spreading handfuls of rock phosphate, wood ashes, and other soil amendments. I sprinkle each layer enough to dampen it. A wet pile won't heat up properly, nor will a too-dry one. The materials should be as damp as a wrung-out sponge.

I also try to alternate very wet stuff like kitchen wastes with absorbent matter like hay or a thin layer of dry leaves. This stops the wet material from packing down and putrifying.

A putrid, foul-smelling compost pile is really a garbage pile undergoing anaerobic decomposition. I strive for an aerobic process, an aerated pile that heats up fast (160 degrees F. at its peak) and smells woodsy instead of rank.

Compost piles are supposed to be turned regularly every few weeks to subject all the ingredients to an equal rate of decomposition. I rarely get around to turning my piles with any regularity. This means my piles take longer to become finished humus, but then, what's time to a compost pile? After six months or so, even without conscientious turning on my part, the pile rots thoroughly enough for use in the garden. If I was in a hurry I'd turn the piles more often, but a ton of finished compost goes a long way.

I get intensely philosophical when I make compost. Even tossing on a bucket of slops from the kitchen and mixing it with manure can send me into a reverie. When I make compost I'm participating in the fundamental birth-decay-birth cycle of the universe. I'm recycling the atoms that were the stuff of countless lives and will be again. I look into the compost and see my protoplasmic past, my heritage as a life form, my future, better than I'd see it in a crystal ball.

Eternity is there. Immortality. Dust to dust, says the compost. "*Tat tvam asi,*" says the humus, the Upanishad's ancient Sanskrit phrase, "that art thou."

Oh bury me not on the lone prairie.

Compost me instead.

Let the cycle continue.

This is magic, this layering of slimy banana peels, pumpkin rinds, moldy bread with rotted hay, October's faded leaves, and the goats' manure. The changes occur almost at once. Bacteria multiply and their teeming masses soon generate the heat the pile needs to "cook" and steam. Yeasts and fungi bud and bloom. A thousand chemical processes lock into gear, the ancient programming code clicks the molecules into place almost audibly. All of this is invisible, yet the processes vibrate through me as I wield the pitchfork.

Did the alchemists know about compost? They sloshed about in search of a universal solvent, decapitated toads seeking magic jewels, and did their best to transmute base metals into gold. But the secrets were here all the time. In the compost. Black gold.

When I finish a pile I stand back and lean on the fork, staring at the heap. "Alpha and omega," it whispers. "Eureka!" it shouts.

These moments are what gardening is all about for me. There's a scene in Goethe's *Faust,* Part One, when Dr. Faust is about to drink a stinking witches' brew that will restore his youth and seal his terrible pact with the Devil. Faust wonders if there isn't an alternative, another recipe for youth? Mephistopheles replies:

> Without a doctor, gold, or sorcery:
> Begin at once a life of open air,
> To dig and trench and cultivate the ground,
> Content yourself within the common round,
> And for your dinner have the homeliest fare.
> Live with the beasts, on equal terms; be sure
> That, where you reap, your hands must spread the dung.
> And there, my friend, you have the certain cure,
> By which at eighty years you still are young.

Goethe. *Faust.* Phillip Wayne, trans. (Penguin Books, 1949).

Do I ever talk to my plants? There's been a lot of publicity over the past years about the alleged value of talking to plants, inquiring after their health, murmuring sweet nothings into their leaves, and even personalizing this repartee by giving them names: "Fred Philodendron, meet Peggy Petunia." I suppose this sort of thing is okay if it makes you happy and doesn't inspire your relatives to institute commitment proceedings.

Other people think playing music helps stimulate plants. One study says to play nothing but Vivaldi. Another says old Snooky Lanson records make pumpkins grow like crazy. Still another experimenter claims Little Richard's rendition of "Long Tall Sally" is a positive tonic to root growth.

Personally, I think all of this is wasted on vegetables. A bed of petunias might go into a swoon at the first notes of Beethoven's Fifth, but vegetables are made of sterner stuff. They have one season to fulfill their destiny—production. They're not supposed to stand around in light conversation.

Vegetables, after all, are the blue collars of the plant world, the hoi polloi, the Great Unwashed. Kids hate them. Your mother overcooks them. Supermarkets overprice them. And gardeners like me who specialize in growing vegetables suffer, in some people's eyes, from a lack of class. "Vegetables? Ah. Well. Actually, I raise dahlias." Wait a minute. Are some plants more *dignified* than others?

Dahlia. Even the name reeks with upper class. To say dahlia correctly one should have a southern accent like Vivien Leigh's in *Gone with the Wind* or diction so haughty it sounds like you cut the inside of your mouth. Go on. Say the names of flowers. Let the sounds roll around like fine cognac:

Alyssum. Calliopsis. Hibiscus.

("Tea is being served in the gazebo, Madam.")

Anthemis. Cerastium. Euphorbia.

("The Countess thinks the Côte d'Azur is divine, but I prefer Monte Carlo in season.")

Ageratum. Delphinium. Canterbury bell.

("No, *you* take the Bentley and I'll drive the Rolls.")

Some vegetables come close to this. Parsnip sounds patrician. Asparagus, continental. Endive, swank—but only if you pronounce it "ahn-DEEV." And even rutabaga has a slightly exotic air to it, sounding like the name of an exiled Serbian prince. But most vegetable names have solid, no-nonsense sounds. Even the word "vegetable" is a gumbo of syllables that catch in your teeth.

Cabbage. Broccoli. Turnip.

("The pigs has turned over the outhouse agin, Paw.")

Garlic. Squash. Horseradish.

("It's almost time for the county fair, Jim-Bob!")

Cauliflower. Beans. Leek.

("No, *you* take the Hudson and I'll drive the John Deere.")

But who says only flowers and ornamentals can nourish our deeper selves? Have you ever seen the lilylike beauty of okra blossoms? Or the delicate purple flowers of snow peas, the first of the vegetable blossoms in the chill of early spring?

And who's to say that the bright orange of young carrots or potato flowers winking out from under thick greenery or sturdy broccoli bursting with new florets or the vortex of emerging lettuce leaves is any less soul lifting than tea roses or carnations?

You might argue that a well-balanced gardener should grow both, flowers and edibles. You're right. And I do, whenever possible, interplanting marigolds and zinnias and calendulas throughout the garden. But vegetables take the forefront in my life because I can't stock my freezer with dried flowers or the memory of their beauty.

So when I talk to my plants I don't say dumb stuff like, "Have a nice day." I don't simper. Vegetables are tough. I've seen lettuce seeds germinate in the barren cracks of a concrete walk, bursting into leafy arrogance. And what about lichens? Not a vegetable, true, but a simple fungal plant that eats rocks. Eats *rocks?* Better watch what you say to some plants.

When I go down to the garden I swagger a little, fix a sneer on my mug, and do my best imitation of Edward G. Robinson as Little Caesar:

"All right, you plants! Frost is three weeks away and you guys are looking laid back. Time to shape up! You—cucumbers—repeat that! Sweet corn—get that silk out of your ears! Cabbages—let's pull ahead! This is a two-way street, see? I do my part, watering you, keeping the slugs away. And what am I getting for my troubles? Small potatoes. Get this, Gang, you're one stalk away from the compost pile, see? Here today, mulch tomorrow!"

Straight talk, right? But vegetables understand. Stow the sonatas, the sonnets, the idle chitchat. Give them air and water and protection. They'll do their part. That may be oversimplifying matters a bit because there are some factors affecting plants that you can't control, of course, like the weather.

And here I'm going to let you in on a secret: in Washington, Congress actually legislates the climate! It's true. Only a bureaucracy could deliver such a hodgepodge of obfuscating, unpredictable, and maddeningly inconsistent weather. Washington's climate, like the camel, was designed by a committee.

Summers are brutally hot and humid. July and August have weeks on end when the temperature and humidity are a matched set—both stuck at 97. (Local legend says British diplomats forced to endure Washington summers received tropical duty pay.)

Cool summer evenings are rare. Usually the temperature plunges to 80 degrees F. by midnight. Spring is beautiful, but brief, passing into summer's oven in mid-May when highs of 90 degrees F. are common.

Even winter in Washington acts like it can't make up its mind. Temperatures may shoot into the 60's or 70's in January, March may roar in with great bushels of snow.

Snow. Washington's nemesis. Though "the white stuff," as creative disc jockeys call it, arrives only in restricted amounts in January and February—if then—any amount of snow past a flurry is greeted as a blizzard.

A two- or three-inch snowfall is, in fact, enough to virtually shut down the city. Schools close early when accumulations reach one to two inches and stay shuttered for days if more than four inches fall.

Worst of all winter's threats are Washington drivers, known everywhere for their inability to negotiate anything but bone-dry streets. The lightest dusting of snow turns Washington and its suburbs into Clown Alley. Everywhere you look, on side streets, in alleyways, on major highways, cars are sliding crazily, out of control as drivers hit their brakes and horns and each other. Cars crunch into each other at every intersection, locking bumpers and shearing great chunks of metal and glass away.

Cars fishtail and slip backward downhill, the terrified faces of their trapped drivers floating by as they glide past, thudding into other prisoners all the way down. Detroit bumper pool.

All the scene needs is music—"The Skater's Waltz" would do. But the howl of furiously spinning tires, a chorus of outraged whines as rubber is spun into nauseating black smoke, is accompaniment enough. And the wonder is that the scene is repeated every winter as though choreographed and staged.

Why is this so? One theory says it's because Washington's population is made up largely of people from somewhere else on their way to somewhere else. The population is too varied and transient to have developed and internalized snow-driving skills.

Another theory has it that Washington drivers are just plain awful and that snow just brings out the worst in them. I have only one opinion. I am sure I will one day see this headline:

DC MAN STRUCK BY FALLING SNOWFLAKE
MAYOR LAUNCHES PROBE

Yet for all its horrors, Washington's weather favors the serious gardener. Before I knew much about gardening I began the season in April and ended it in August. But now that I've had some experience, my gardening season is almost without an end. I have mixed feelings about this. I enjoy gardening. I also enjoy *having gardened.* Sometimes I wonder how my simple life got so complicated.

The gardening season begins in January, the dead of winter, when the seed catalogs arrive. This is either the best of times or the worst of times, depending on how much experience you have as a gardener. For the inexperienced, January is the worst time to get enthusiastic about gardening because your guard is down.

The ground is frozen or snow covered. The garden tools are out of sight. The memories of last season have faded. Like a first love, all you remember is the beauty and warmth and happiness.

Seed catalogs are written and photographed by master propagandists.

The colors leap off the slick pages. Tomatoes were never so red, carrots never so orange, lettuce never so green and crisp. And nowhere in the catalogs are pictures of bugs and rabbits or gardeners wilted by heat prostration or the ravages of drought or air-borne plant diseases.

Seed catalogs sell dreams. And because it's January and you're stuck in the house and your bones are crying for spring, you write out a check and order your fantasies postpaid. What do I mean "you"? I'm just as guilty. Even after ten years of gardening I still occasionally order more than I can grow or sensibly tend. A new vegetable variety or the discovery of an old one can still seduce me, I'm glad to say. I'd hate to think my gardening had so settled down that I always grew the same plants year after year, blind to a challenge or impossible dream. But I have imposed some restraint on my appetite and imagination.

Good organization is the key to successful gardening, and the best way to impose order on the garden and the gardener alike. Concentrate on fitting yourself into the flow of each year's growing cycles. Especially if you're trying to achieve food self-reliance, it's important to be attuned to individual plant characteristics, and subtle seasonal demands.

That's why the most knowledgeable and successful gardeners are often people who've been at it for 30 years and more. They've sailed through enough snap frosts and dry years and leafed through enough tantalizing catalog pages to know the way by heart.

"To every thing there is a season, and a time to every purpose under the heaven," says the Book of Ecclesiastes, concise advice for gardeners. No matter how long the garden season, each plant or family of plants operates on a certain schedule. Determining individual plant needs can simplify your life and your garden, while producing the most from your labors.

Here's what I've learned to do: I break the growing season down month by month, using estimated dates of the first and last frost to establish the extent of the season, and then I count forward and backward from these dates to determine my planting time. I've kept a record of first and last frosts for ten years. They can vary by several weeks, but the last frost hits around April 20 and the first arrives in late October. My total growing season is in excess of 175 days—far more than I really need to produce what we consume in a year.

I begin indoors in late January by getting my fluorescent-light seed starter ready. This is an arrangement of metal trays lit by a bank of fluorescents. An automatic timer allows me to give the young plants a steady 14 hours of "sunlight" daily. Many gardeners do just as well with their plants arranged on a sunny windowsill, turning the seedlings every day or so to equalize the growth. I don't have a sunny window that's large enough to accommodate all the seedlings we raise, so we must rely on electric sunshine.

The energy usage is low, however, especially when you consider that the three-tray unit I use has 24 square feet of growing space per tray—enough room for hundreds of vegetable seedlings. The little we spend on electricity is repaid all season long in fresh food.

Next I assemble whatever containers I'll need for seedlings. Over the years I've used every imaginable vessel: clay pots, peat pots, peat pellets, old yogurt cups, tin cans, and Styrofoam cups. There are others I know about but haven't used, like seedling flats made entirely of compressed peat. I've avoided these because I think one goal for the home gardener is to keep procedures as simple and as inexpensive as possible.

I make my own flats from scrap wood. You don't have to be a carpenter to do this. Any junk wood from fruit cartons or crates will do. (The rear entrances of glass shops and grocery stores are a wood scavenger's dream. Ask the managers for the schedules of trash pickups so you can gather up the crates before the dump trucks arrive.)

Knock the flats together with nails and a spot of glue. Appearances don't matter and neither do dimensions as long as you don't make the flats too big. A too-large flat is clumsy to carry and may buckle just as you're walking across the living room. Flats 18-by-12 inches are a good standard size.

The Styrofoam cups I use are inexpensive and reusable for years. Unlike smooth plastic, Styrofoam breathes, admitting air to the soil and allowing development of seedling roots. I write the name of the plant variety right on the cup with a felt-tipped marker. Some of my cups have been through so many seasons there is hardly a place to write on them. The miserly gardener. And the cups are free if you work where cups are discarded after each coffee break.

Another type of container I use is one I discovered only a few years ago. This too is Styrofoam and goes by the brand name Todd Speedling Planter Flats. Each flat contains anywhere from 6 to 200 holes or "cells." But the Speedling trays have a new wrinkle; the cells are in the shape of inverted pyramids with a small hole at the bottom. You drop seeds in just as you would do with any flat, but something special happens as the roots develop. The sloping sides of the cells and the air holes promote strong growth and the development of many hairlike feeder roots. Because the cells are tapered, it's easy to remove seedlings as individual "plugs." It's even easier to transplant. I just poke a hole in the bed and drop the plug in place, adding water or a starter solution of compost "tea."

Next, I fill these assorted trays and cups with soil. But look in any garden book and you'll realize that the compounding of seed-starting mixes is only slightly less arcane than alchemy. Here again, I've tried most of the homemade and commercial mixes, sometimes mixing my own and feeling like Merlin at work. Great fun if you have the time. And commercial mixes are convenient if you have the money.

Unfortunately, you cannot simply fill your flats with garden soil, even if you take care to sift and screen it. The best garden soil settles and compacts in pots and flats, cutting off the air and water roots need. Unpasteurized garden soil also contains the spores of damping-off disease, a fungal killer that can wipe out a flat of seemingly healthy seedlings overnight.

Being essentially lazy, I don't pasteurize my soil, by the way. The process involves baking the soil for an hour at 275 degrees F. The soil must be wet so the steam can penetrate thoroughly. The problem with this is twofold: for the gardener like me who uses a lot of potting soil, the extra time pasteurization takes is considerable, and the process stinks.

Nancy Bubel, one of the country's more experienced and articulate gardeners, suggests you "plan a picnic supper or weekend trip [when you pasteurize soil] because the kitchen will smell *awful*." (Ms. Bubel doesn't pasteurize her soil either.)

Other gardeners suggest you use a potato to tell when the pasteurization is complete. You put the dirt in a baking tray and nestle a raw potato in the pan's center. When the potato is baked, so is the soil. Frankly, I think you have to be a little half-baked yourself to go to all this trouble. ("Hey, Mom—this potato tastes *funny.*")

Here's what I do to avoid damping-off disease and a lot of fussing around with soil mixtures. First, my mixture is elementary. I mix sifted and screened garden soil with equal parts of vermiculite and screened compost. Sometimes I toss a little sand in and a dash of powdered limestone to cut the acidity. You'll notice I don't do a lot of precise measuring. A little of this, a bit of that. Plants aren't that fussy. I try to mix up a sack of starter soil in the fall. That way I have it ready when I need it in the spring. (Otherwise you face the chilling prospect of poking around in a frozen garden and chipping away at a glacial compost pile.)

Second, I beat damping-off disease right at its source. I start all seeds directly in vermiculite, which is a sterile medium. True, you have to buy the stuff, which is increasing in price like everything else. But you don't need much, especially if you use the "sandwich" method of seeding.

I fill my pot or flat with the dirt-compost-vermiculite mixture, but I don't bring it to the top. I fill the top one-third of the container with straight vermiculite. What happens is this: the seed germinates in the sterile vermiculite, immune to damping-off disease. Because seedlings, until they produce their first true leaves, don't need any additional nutrients beyond what the seed supplies, the seedlings thrive in the vermiculite, assuming temperature and moisture conditions are adequate.

And by the time the seedling is large enough to be resistant to damping-off disease, it has sent its roots into the dirt-compost mixture and can begin taking up nutrients. This works beautifully for me every year. No muss, no dirty potatoes, and no dead seedlings, or stinky kitchens.

In addition to a disease-free growing medium, seedlings need optimum temperature and moisture conditions. Most beginning gardeners kill their plants by drowning. I water once a week, keeping the soil damp but not wet. As for temperature, our wood-heated house is perfect for hardy plants. I keep the seed trays upstairs in the coolest part of the house. Day temperatures under the lights (fluorescents produce a small amount of heat) rarely get above 70 degrees F. At night, when the lights switch off, the temperature drops into the mid or lower 60's, just right for hardy plants.

Once the seedlings are fully leafed out, I feed them a weak solution of manure or compost "tea" every ten days. You make this by soaking fresh or dried manure or compost in a bucket of water, and diluting the brew to the color of weak tea. The liquid can also be used as a foliar or leaf feeder. But don't get it into any open cuts on your hands.

Of course, none of this is necessary if you choose to buy your seedlings from a local nursery. I did this when I first started, but the cost of seedlings rose as my garden expanded. But now, even if prices were lower, I'd stay with growing my own. Few activities are more satisfying than participating in the entire process—from seed through harvest to eating. And if you choose to save some select nonhybrid seeds each year, as I do, then you control the entire process. Enormously satisfying.

By mid-April my flats and the upstairs room are filled with luxuriant masses of greenery. The room takes on a dank, rich smell. A miniature rain forest. But spring means the plants must be hardened-off, readied for transplanting. I move all my plants, except easily zapped ones like eggplants, squashes, melons, and peppers, to a cold frame. I keep them warm and protected from full sunshine for several days. Then, by opening the frame a bit each day, I acclimate them to a range of day and night temperatures and strong sun. If a chilly night threatens, I hustle all the plants back in for the evening. I have been known to leave this until the last minute, doing the job late at night in my pajamas.

I'm careful about the hardening-off process. I've learned the hard way that unseen chemical damage can be sustained by chilled plants. They look fine but they never develop or produce the way they might have if they hadn't been shocked.

Here's what I plant indoors: I start lettuce, parsley, cabbage, broccoli, collards, and brussels sprouts in mid-January for setting out in March; that's a little early some years, but I like to get a jump on the season. I use plastic milk jugs with the bottoms cut out as cloches or miniature cold frames.

A few weeks later I start more lettuce (I find it easier to transplant individual heads than to fuss with thinning minute seedlings), then kohlrabies, tomatoes, peppers, eggplants, muskmelons, cucumbers, and even a small flat of carrots. You can transplant carrots and get an extra-early crop if you transplant the entire flat at once, no thinning or pricking off. I usually use small flats, about 6-by-8 inches at the largest, carefully transplanting the entire mat of young carrots as a single unit.

The climate here is mild enough and the growing season long enough that I really don't have to start cukes and melons indoors. I could just as easily seed them directly. But starting them indoors gives me a jump on the season and gives the plants an edge against their insect and disease enemies. I set out mature plants resistant to much of what might kill them as sprouts. (More about pest control later.)

I also start herbs and flowers indoors if I have the space and time. Otherwise I direct-seed or buy seedlings. I've outgrown the fluorescent light trays, of course, and we should have a greenhouse. We didn't put one up at first because we didn't know enough to make proper use of it. Now we have a lot of knowledge but not enough money. There's a message there somewhere.

When March arrives the garden season begins in earnest. The ground is usually too wet and cold to work in the traditional gardens around here, but raised beds dry out and warm up faster than flat ground.

I begin by redigging and reshaping the beds, adding compost and soil conditioners like wood ashes, limestone (if needed), rock phosphate, and powdered seaweed. If the weather is uncooperative, a lot of rain and damp days, I will "mud in" some cabbage and lettuce transplants. I can't stand staring at the garden through the window just waiting for a sunny day.

I put in potatoes in March, planting them whole or cut up depending on my schedule. I've had good results both ways, though cutting them up into pieces with no more than two eyes is more economical. (I buy disease-free seed potatoes.)

I plant onion sets, poking them into the soil only enough to hold them upright. I also plant garlic (unless I was organized enough to plant it the preceding fall, the best time for the crop).

I also seed spinach, radishes, chives, and peas now. I've tried all kinds of peas over the years and have settled on using only full-size varieties. The dwarf types are supposed to save you the trouble of erecting pea fencing, but I think the extra yields from the full-size plants are worth the effort.

Besides, I've developed a system of pea support that involves a minimum of effort. I've made permanent frames of 1-by-2-inch lumber (furring strips) and chicken wire. These "modular units"—each frame is 6-by-8 feet—avoid all the wasted time and frustration I used to suffer when I was struggling to put up a new pea fence every season.

Now I simply take the pea frames (stacked against a barn wall all winter) and lash them to steel fence posts I've pounded in a row where the peas will go.

For lashing, I use scrap baling twine from the hay. It only lasts a season in the sun and rain. When I cut the frames free in the fall I let the twine rot where it falls. I don't know of many things more exasperating than struggling with chicken wire on a chilly March day and the frames save me from that hateful job.

As to pea varieties, we grow several. I seed double rows about six inches apart on both sides of the pea frames, planting an early, midseason, and late variety all on the same day. Their maturity dates range from 55 to 65 days, so the harvests are staggered but continuous. I also plant an edible-podded pea—Sugar Snap is our favorite.

Every year I plant more peas. We eat peas fresh and shell as many as we can for the winter. The Sugar Snaps rarely make it to the freezer. Noah and Rachel eat them by the handfuls right in the garden. We don't dry peas for winter. It's simpler to buy dried peas in bulk.

But we do shell green peas, blanching and freezing them for the winter. Now shelling fresh peas is a tedious job. Each pod only holds from five to seven peas, so you've got to shuck your way through bushels of husks before you can accumulate even a few quarts of peas. Besides, neither Betsy nor I can resist eating the fresh peas as we shell (and the children snatch what they can) so the work seems endless. That's why country women always got together under a shade tree and did all their husking cooperatively. The conversation and extra hands made the work go faster.

Not having access to country women or willing hands, however, Betsy and I have regretfully turned to a mechanical pea-sheller. This Rube Goldberg contraption, whose catalog description exceeds its actual performance, is faster at pea shelling than we are, but, as always, technology extracts a price for increased production.

The device consists of two rubber-covered rollers attached to a hand-crank. You're supposed to turn the crank and feed the pods into the rollers, which, theoretically, are supposed to squeeze the peas out of the shell. We found it a wonderful invention for lovers of mashed peas. After some experimentation we found the device would expel whole peas if we dipped the pods briefly in boiling water. This softened the husks enough to let the rollers push the peas out unmashed.

But still, there we were in the kitchen half the night, feeding pea pods into a rubber-rollered maw—one or two pods at a time—while turning a crank designed for an elfin hand. In desperation, I reread the sheller's instruction sheet and discovered I could use an electric drill to turn the crank. Better living through gadgetry! I hooked a variable speed drill onto the sheller and, with Betsy feeding pods into the machine, let 'er rip.

Whizz! Peas shot out of the pods as fast as Betsy could shove the husks into the whirling rollers. Most of the peas actually landed in the bowl, though a lot shot across the room, splattering against the wall and ricocheting off the kitchen cabinets.

"Well, it's a lot faster, anyway!" I yelled over the roar of the drill.

"Yes," Betsy shouted back, as a stream of peas squirted into the living room, "Helen and Scott Nearing would be proud of us!"

April and May are incredibly busy months for me. The brunt of all garden crops go in now and I make no plans to be anywhere but in the garden for weeks on end. Beets, broccoli, carrots, chard, kohlrabies, onion plants, and parsnips go in first. I'll keep planting beets, carrots, lettuce and kohlrabies every two weeks throughout the season for continuous harvest. Parsnips go in only once, a large planting, and we eat them all winter. (Parsnips are made flavorful only by freezing in the soil. The cold changes the starch to sugar. After the first freeze we mulch the parsnips heavily and dig them out all winter and early spring. We do the same with salsify and carrots, though the latter must not be allowed to freeze.)

The crush of work in April is only a dress rehearsal for May. Beans, melons, cucumbers, eggplant, peppers, tomatoes, summer and winter squash, pumpkins, corn, and sweet potatoes all go in then.

Tomatoes are a main crop for us. They're easy to grow, heavily productive, and pure ambrosia when eaten sun-warmed in July. I put in about 50 tomato plants, 25 each of full-size ones and the paste type. We harvest bushels of tomatoes and use virtually all we grow.

I grow about 15 pepper plants, a wonderful trouble-free crop in my garden. We eat peppers green and deep red and freeze about a bushel of them at season's end.

Sweet potatoes are another easy crop for us. They're sensitive to chills but resistant to drought and bugs. I grow them in the traditional ridges (though I dig in plenty of compost) and harvest them just before frost. We produce about two bushels and eat them all winter.

Sweet corn is another staple, though it takes up more room than it's worth nutritionally. But who cares about vitamins and minerals when the corn is ripe and you bite into the season's first ear, the milky juice squirting back on your cheeks? We grow yellow and white varieties, staggering the plantings so we're corn-fed until frost. We also freeze as much as we can, using a stainless steel gimmick to cut the kernels from the cobs. Freezing whole cobs takes up too much room in our freezer.

I put in enough winter squash—Waltham butternut usually—and pumpkins to store all winter. Twenty-five or more butternuts and a dozen or more pumpkins keep us in baked squash and pies until spring.

And what's a garden without cucumbers? We don't grow as many as we used to when we made pickles, but we produce several crops for salads all season. Betsy used to spend a lot of kitchen time making sweet, sour, and dilled pickles, but gave it up when we realized the time spent was too much for what is essentially a high-salt nonfood.

We grow a lot of beans. Here I lean toward the bush type rather than pole beans. Bush beans only bear for a short time, while the pole types yield until they're killed by frost. But bush beans have advantages. They come to harvest faster (by as much as two weeks in some cases) and they can be used as a succession crop following early cabbage or lettuce.

We've relied on an unusual bean for almost a decade, the purple-pod bush bean. The beans are really purple. They turn green when you drop them in boiling water—an excellent indicator of cooking time. But the real value of purple-pods, other than their delicious taste, is twofold: purple-pods can be planted earlier than most beans. They don't rot easily in cold soil. And they are less attractive to bean beetles, the nemesis of every gardener. Perhaps the purple color has something to do with it, but we've managed to avoid heavy beetle infestations by harvesting large, early crops of purple-pods. And we put up several dozen quarts of them for the winter.

June is an easier month. We're eating out of the garden by now—salads and fresh peas, baby carrots, kohlrabies, and the first of the bush beans by the end of the month.

I'm still planting seeds, though not as heavily as I was in May. Mostly I'm putting in succession crops of beans, lettuce, carrots, and summer squash to keep the garden productive all season.

When July comes summer is over. Well, not really, as far as the brutally hot weather is concerned, but there is a subtle shift in the quality of the light. And I begin thinking about planting for the fall and early winter.

More of the same goes in as succession crops—more sweet corn, late cucumbers and squash—but now I begin seeding carrots and peas for the fall.

This is one of the most difficult tasks of our garden season. Not the actual work, but the challenge of getting cool-weather seeds to germinate in junglelike heat and humidity. I failed most years trying to bring in late crops of cabbage, peas, carrots, and broccoli. The calendar is willing but the heat is unforgiving.

Now I know it takes constant attention and daily watering. Using burlap bags and old aluminum siding to cover the plots helps too. Anything that cools the soil gives the seeds a chance. This is a crucial time. If I'm successful, it guarantees that we'll be eating fresh vegetables until the first killing frost and beyond.

As July passes into the first weeks of August, I continue planting seeds of Chinese cabbage, kohlrabi, and kale. Any leftover seedlings of cabbage, broccoli, and brussels sprouts go in now too. Chinese cabbage and kale are especially important crops for us. All of us enjoy eating them, but best of all, they are frost-resistant plants. The cabbage is less so than the kale, but it endures well enough to keep us in delicious salads and stir-fried meals until past Christmas.

Kale is amazing in its ability to withstand cold. Many winters we have pulled crisp kale leaves from under the snow, steaming them lightly in only the moisture from the melted ice. Kale is a gold mine of nutrients and minerals and our children love it.

Broccoli is another nutritional powerhouse everyone in the family enjoys. We try for both a spring and a fall harvest, putting at least two dozen quarts of the tender shoots into the freezer.

We always produce more vegetables than we can eat or preserve for winter, and we enjoy giving our surplus to friends. Once a friend dropped by to pick up some vegetables we'd offered, and he brought with him a woman who expressed interest in our gardening techniques. We walked down to the garden, but before I could start giving her my two-dollar tour she said, "And you claim to grow all this without pesticides?"

The word "claim" instantly got under my skin. She wasn't asking me a question, she was accusing me of something. "I'm an organic gardener, yes," I said.

"And how," she said archly, the prosecuting attorney, "do you define 'organically grown'?"

"The standard definition is the growing of plants without using harmful pesticides or chemical fertilizers, with regular soil-building based on the use of compost and natural soil conditioners," I said in one breath. "I guess I like to think of organic gardening as harmonizing with nature instead of trying to dominate it."

"I'm not a believer," she said, forcing a smile.

"It's not a religion," I said.

"I work for a company that makes agricultural chemicals," she explained.

"I'd never have guessed. What are you doing here? Spying on the competition? Or are you going to defect?" She laughed at this and we both relaxed.

"I just find it hard to believe you don't use any pesticides. The bugs must devastate your crops."

"Look around," I said. "There's some damage, but there's plenty to eat for all of us. Bugs included."

"Well, I'm sure you're getting some help from your neighbors."

"What do you mean?"

"Drift. When they spray their gardens you get some of the pesticide drifting over onto your garden. Obviously, that controls a lot of your problems with bugs."

"You've been reading too many of your own advertisements," I said. "Look around. My nearest neighbor is almost a quarter-mile away. And he's an organic gardener too."

"But. . ." She stopped, searching for words as she looked around. It was early June, the perfect time of year to bring a skeptic into the garden. Everything was lush and brilliantly green. Huge heads of lettuce seemed to burst out of the ground. The pea vines were festooned with hundreds of swollen pods. The tomato plants were deep green, wild with thick stems and leaves, covered with blossoms.

"I think you'd better take a shower when you get home," I said.

"I beg your pardon?"

"To wash off all the pesticide. From the invisible cloud that's swirling around us," I laughed. She laughed too, a little sheepishly. We walked back up to the house. She was silent. What she saw, an organic garden, didn't make sense to her. It wasn't supposed to work, not according to her grasp of the facts.

Those "facts," unfortunately, are produced by a lot of companies like the one she worked for, organizations determined to sell products to us whether we need them or not.

Some years ago I saw a magazine advertisement for a popular garden pesticide. It showed a big, juicy tomato. All around the tomato were white arrows shooting off with words attached: HORNWORMS, EARLY

BLIGHT, VERTICILLIUM WILT, MAGGOTS, WEEVILS, and a dozen other potential ills tomatoes are heir to.

The idea was to scare the hell out of you, to convince you that the only way to save your tomatoes was to run right out and buy this powerful systemic pesticide. (A systemic pesticide actually enters the plant's tissues, poisoning insects from the inside out.)

The problem is that a lot of people have been fooled by this propaganda. They've come from their TV sets and newspapers convinced that insects are our mortal enemies and that only a liberal use of pesticides will ensure a productive garden. Even with all the inroads made by the environmental movement, people still tend to zap their gardens with sprays, believing that to be their only choice.

I wonder what would happen if we used the same approach to having babies? What if a company that wanted to sell drugs distributed pictures of a cute baby with arrows tagged with all the ills threatening humans: CANCER, HEART DISEASE, INFLUENZA. That would boost drug and vaccine sales, I bet. It would also probably discourage a lot of people from ever having children, especially if the picture added a few more threats to our welfare: BORING CONVERSATIONS, POLITICIANS, PLASTIC FLOWERS.

If you envision only the horrors awaiting your plants, then a bottle of pesticide might seem like your only ally. But that's what I like about being an organic gardener; it allows me to accept both the risks and the benefits, giving me one season each year in which to work for a balance.

This involves a struggle to understand various forces of nature and subtle interactions between soil chemistry, weather, and the life cycles of insects and other predators. And the struggle allows *me,* as well as the garden, to grow. Each season gives me a harvest of new ideas and insights as well as vegetables. I couldn't get that out of a bottle or a spray can.

It took me a long time to understand that natural gardening *is* a struggle. When I first started I thought "organic" meant just letting nature take its course. Now I realize that the struggle is one to understand nature, not merely a battle against bugs.

So how do I manage my organic garden? How do Betsy and I manage to feed ourselves all year without spending a penny on artificial fertilizer or pesticides? The first thing to do is relax and accept the fact that it's impossible to have a garden without some insect damage. At least it's impossible to have a healthy garden without insects at work.

As predators and scavengers, insects play a key role in the balance of life. "Wiping out" insects, as many pesticides promise to do, is like burning your barn down to rid it of horseflies.

Gardens are like people: a healthy organism resists disease and attack better than a weak one. And a garden, though seemingly a random collection of varied elements, is actually a single organism of which we are part. The earth in microcosm. So the first thing we work for is a healthy ecosystem.

We continually build up our soil with regular applications of compost. All our kitchen wastes are returned to the soil. All plant wastes are composted at the end of the season and returned to the ground. (The exceptions are any residues showing evidence of plant diseases. These are burned.)

We transplant only healthy seedlings. We thin carefully, removing all plants that lack vigor. And we plant disease-resistant varieties whenever possible, sometimes saving our own seed from year to year if the plants are nonhybrids.

We also work hard to maintain a healthy and varied garden environment by encouraging bird and animal life. The brushline all around the garden is allowed to flourish. This is a haven for birds and insects and it helps cut down on the effect of hot summer winds that dry out the soil.

Nor do we weed as carefully as we once did. We weed the growing areas, of course, but the perimeter of the garden is left alone. Clear ground is unnatural. Nature always strives to produce greenery as food and shelter for a variety of life. A mixed environment is our goal both in and out of the garden.

One of the more important aspects of organic gardening—and one that comes only with time and experience—is the understanding of insect cycles. Almost all insects adhere to a natural cycle of birth, mating, and dormancy or gestation. If we are able to determine these cycles, we can actually plan our crops and harvests to fall between the cracks—when specific insects are at their lowest activity level.

Bean beetles in our area, for example, don't begin serious activity until mid or late June. Knowing this, I plant bush beans in late April. The beans mature and bear before the beetles are strong enough to do much damage. I plant again in late summer, harvesting beans in the fall after the beetles have reached their peak of activity.

I've planted corn in much the same way, timing the placing of seeds to miss the peak of earworm activity. Corn planted past June 15 in this area is only slightly bothered by worms. This doesn't mean I don't plant corn earlier, however. What would summer be without that first delicious ear of sweet corn? But I do plan my main crop to come to harvest as the earworms move into a less ferocious cycle.

Corn earworms are a good example of "sustainable damage," a

concept I think is crucial to good garden management. Some damage is unavoidable and normal. The notion of having a pest-free 100 percent productive garden is an invention of the advertising business—much like the dreams of having the whitest teeth, the sweetest breath, and the thickest, most manageable hair: dreams that keep 'em coming back to the drugstore.

Corn earworms only eat about the top 2 inches of a given ear, hardly enough to justify wreaking chemical doom on every crawling or flying thing in your garden. I figure an ear of corn is a good 10 to 12 inches of eating. If a worm eats 10 percent of that and leaves the rest for me, well, it's not worth getting worked up about. Worms have to live too.

I am not as affable about Japanese beetles. Though they too, have a discernible cycle, and I'm able to time some crop plantings to miss their ravages, they are ferocious attackers of pole beans. Left alone, they will eat the beans and use the poles as toothpicks.

We handpick Japanese beetles, a gruesome activity, dropping them into a mixture of kerosene and hot water. This is the least enjoyable garden procedure for me. I don't like killing anything if I have an alternative. With Japanese beetles, unfortunately, the only alternative is no beans at all. So we kill thousands of the squat creatures—drowning them and trapping them in special beetle canisters—all the while feeling guilty and creepy.

I meet the threat of other insects more peacefully. Flea beetles, the scourge of most young plants, have a passion for mustard greens. So I purposely plant mustard as a "trap crop." Even when young cabbage plants are nearby, the beetles will flock to the mustard instead, controlling themselves in the process. When I must control flea beetles directly, I use a little rotenone, a safe, biodegradable insect control made from the powdered roots of a tropical plant.

Rotenone is technically an insecticide, but organic gardeners have used it for years because it breaks down rapidly—within hours—when exposed to air and sunlight. It surprises some people that natural gardeners use any sprays or powders at all. But "we," speaking for most organic gardeners, have never been opposed to insect controls that were no threat to the environment. We object to poisons that kill indiscriminately or persist in the ecosystem.

Organic gardeners also like to concoct their own sprays from household or garden ingredients. When necessary I've used sprays made from hot peppers, garlic, onions, and a dash of liquid soap (for a wetting agent). I've read of other gardeners using horseradish, cayenne pepper, paprika, and chives. Whatever is used, it's mixed with plain water and whizzed in a blender. The mess is left to steep overnight, strained, and sprayed on the afflicted plants.

The value of such solutions is that they're cheap or free, limited in effectiveness, and harmless to the rest of the garden. Homemade sprays let a gardener deal with a specific bug problem without burning down the barn.

My favorite method of insect control—it's the simplest and most effective—has ended the problem of squash bugs for me and for all I've shared the idea with. Squash bugs used to destroy all the summer squash and muskmelon I dared to plant. I used homemade sprays, rotenone, and handpicking, but nothing helped.

I'd plant the seeds, watch healthy plants develop, harvest some squash, then come out one morning to see all the plants in a hill slumped over dead. The spittle of squash bugs spreads a bacterial wilt that eventually kills the plant.

Ah, I thought. If only I could figure out a way to give squash bugs a dry mouth. Make them guilty, perhaps. Another recourse was to plant a dozen plants at once, a friend's suggestion. "That way the bugs get some, but I always have enough squash for us," she explained. This seemed like an awful waste of garden space.

An article by Gene Logsdon in *Organic Gardening* magazine came to my rescue, solving the squash bug problem once and for all. Logsdon's suggestion was to protect the young squash plants at their most vulnerable time—another example of foiling insects—by interrupting their habits or breeding cycles.

Now, just before I plant squash seeds or transplant seedlings, I stop by the nearest grocery store for some cardboard boxes. I prepare the soil by digging a hole 12 inches deep by 18 inches or more wide. I mix compost with the topsoil I've removed. Then I shovel the loose mixture back in. The box comes next. I use a razor or matte knife to cut the flaps off, leaving a bottomless and topless frame of cardboard. I set this around the hole, heap dirt against the sides, and plant the seeds or transplants inside the framed area. (I usually plant five seeds to the hill, thinning to the best two plants.)

After watering-in the seeds or plants, I cover the frame with an old window screen. This stays in place until the growing plants literally push against it. When the plants are this large, I remove the screen and cardboard and mulch heavily with rotten hay or compost.

The squash bugs are foiled by these procedures because they are unable to get to the plants at their most vulnerable stage. The bugs can't lay their eggs beneath the plants or on the leaves. Nor can they do much damage once the screens are removed for good. By that time the plant stems are too thick for easy penetration.

Leaving nothing to chance, I also plant some radish seeds in with the squash plants to deter any really persistant bugs once the plants are unprotected. I taught this method to my friend who plants a dozen zucchinis, by the way, and I got a mixed reaction. This time *all* her plants survived. That made her happy, she said, "But what am I supposed to do with 25 zucchinis every week?" She stacked them up like cordwood.

Another natural insect and disease control we use is crop rotation. We keep this simple: never plant the same crop in the same place in successive years. Insects and plant diseases are like relatives. Given optimum conditions—enough food and shelter—they'll move in to stay. By shifting plants around from one garden spot to another, you prevent the population of any given bug from getting out of hand. Conversely, by using the same space over and over again for the same crop, you end up actually sowing your seeds right on top of eggs laid by the plant's enemies.

Crop rotation also helps balance out the demands made on the soil. Different plants use different nutrients and minerals at different soil levels. Some plants are heavy feeders—cabbages and sweet corn are examples. Other crops are light feeders—beets, carrots, and onions. Still others are soil builders—beans and peas put nitrogen back in the soil as they grow.

Here again, we keep it simple: we follow heavy feeders with either light feeders or soil builders. And we try to alternate leaf crops with root crops as the season progresses, following early crops of lettuce with late plantings of carrots or turnips. This takes planning. We keep a garden diary and spend many a winter evening charting the location of what we plan to grow.

Other garden pests are easier to deal with than insects or plant diseases. Birds, stray dogs, rabbits, woodchucks, and our cats, who can't resist using the superloose soil in the beds as their latrine, are all threats to growing things.

Birds are the most difficult to handle because I have no wish to banish them from the garden forever, which would probably be impossible anyway. I have trouble with birds at two times: just after I've seeded or transplanted, and for certain produce, at harvest time.

To stop them from digging up freshly planted seeds, I use that old stand-by, the fake snake. A lot of gardeners use pieces of cut-up garden hose, but I use some remarkably realistic rubber snakes I bought at a trick and joke shop. Other gardeners report mixed success in frightening birds off with these imitation enemies (birds are supposed to have an instinctive fear of snakes), but I've been thoroughly happy with the results.

I lay the fake snakes out alongside or across the beds, changing their position every day or so to keep the birds guessing. The snakes also scare the hell out of a lot of human visitors to the garden, something Noah and Rachel get a big kick out of.

When the corn has fully developed, I drag out a big bag of Styrofoam cups, the same ones I use for starting seeds. I place one cup over each maturing ear of corn. This simple measure totally foils the attacks of starlings and crows who would otherwise strip each ear to the cob. (The cups stay put on the ears; only a strong wind will dislodge them.)

We also get a lot of birds in the sour cherry trees and the mulberry trees, but there is always enough fruit for all of us, so I never bother to scare them off.

I've never had much luck using scarecrows. The birds always seem to catch on in a few minutes. I've seen them use a scarecrow's shoulder as a place to sit and enjoy their purloined goodies. Besides the snakes, I've had success with shiny discs, aluminum pie plates, and strings of inflated balloons. Very festive.

Mammals present more problems than birds. I used to have all kinds of trouble with dogs, rabbits, and woodchucks until I put in a solid fence. I was so inexperienced my first few years that I bought snow fencing, thinking it was a cheap barrier. It is. For snow. But the rabbits walked through the wide openings as though they were private entrances.

Now the fence is made of one- and two-inch mesh poultry wire (the smaller hole is near the fence bottom) stretched tight, about four feet high, with six inches buried along the fence row. This stops anything from burrowing in.

But one year, even with the fence in place, I had devastating damage night after night. Every morning I'd walk into the garden to find whole broccoli florets sheared off, cabbage heads shredded into cole slaw, and lettuce plants torn to pieces.

I tried every repellent I could think of: a portable radio left on in the garden overnight (my vegetables were destroyed to a musical accompaniment), moth balls, dried blood, flickering kerosene lamps (dinner by lamplight), and the most potent trick of all—human urine. Now *that* worked!

I'd read about this method being used by a fellow in northern Canada who successfully repelled moose and elk from his garden. The urine doesn't go directly on the vegetables, you'll be relieved—ah—happy to know, but only around the garden's borders.

Still, the prospect of anointing the garden every evening in ever greater amounts taxed my patience as well as my kidneys. Besides, I thought, it set a bad example for the children.

Finally, at my wits' end, ready to camp out in the garden with a shotgun, I discovered the culprit. A tiny rabbit had been sneaking in through a rusted-out hole in the fence. The hole was only about the size of a tennis ball, hidden by some weeds near a fence post. The only reason I saw the hole at all was because the surprised rabbit, who had grown bold enough to attack my plants in daylight, escaped through the opening when I yelled. Now I make regular fence patrols throughout the season.

My simple fence even stops woodchucks, which surprised me once I saw how resourceful they are. We have a whole family of 'chucks living under an old outbuilding. They have been living and breeding there ever since we moved in and will be there after we're gone, I'm sure.

Several of my older, nonecologically minded friends told me I should shoot the 'chucks. "Ain't good for nothing," snorted a neighbor. But we enjoy *seeing* the creatures, knowing they are there. And, no matter what the old-timers think, the 'chucks do serve a purpose, however obscure.

If nothing else they keep the mulberry bushes and wild plum trees harvested. Once I heard a strange chattering, almost like the sound of monkeys arguing. I followed the noise and discovered a mother woodchuck and her baby ten feet up in a plum tree, fighting over the ripe fruit. (I didn't know they could climb trees either.)

After that I saw 'chucks in mulberry bushes, stripping the mushy berries off in great gobbles. Why a creature that can climb like that—one with a voracious appetite for almost anything—hasn't vaulted my garden fence, I don't know. I suspect it's because the chicken wire is springy, too wobbly for a good foothold. Whatever the reason, I'm thankful. I've seen what determined 'chucks can do in a garden. They don't seem to eat any single crop, but they take a bite out of almost everything.

Another part of our garden design is the creation of a mixed environment. I've already mentioned letting the perimeter of the garden remain as wild as possible, the better to promote natural interactions. We also try to create a natural setting in the growing beds. Look at a meadow. All manner of plants grow in profusion, at random, wherever their seeds fall and conditions are right. Planting a single crop, or acres of single crops, is an invitation to insects who specialize in eating that plant.

So we alternate plantings of herbs and flowers and vegetables. A few feet of carrots here, followed by several feet of lettuce, followed by a dozen cabbage plants, followed by onions and so on throughout the garden. We also alternate especially aromatic plants like garlic, onions, and dill with members of the cabbage family. This is supposed to help protect them against insect attack by scrambling the biological clues used as homing beacons by various insects.

Does it work? Called "companion planting," the mixing of a variety of plants does seem to exert a protective influence on some plants under some conditions. I'm hedging here because too many people have been misled into thinking companion planting is a sure cure for bugs. It's not. Companioning is a tool that has only recently been studied. You can't merely "just plant a lot of marigolds" as someone once told me, and expect to create an insect barrier. But companion plantings do mimic the natural environment found in woods and fields. And if nothing else, the mixture of colors, textures, and odors should be a delight for the gardener. It is for me.

The truth is that home gardeners can do quite well without resorting to pesticides. There are many vegetables that are virtually without serious enemies—most of them, in my experience. While I have to battle the bugs on eggplants, beans, and cabbage, I've never had trouble with lettuce, onions, carrots, turnips, or tomatoes—not a single hornworm in ten years. And what troubles I've had were easier to deal with by organic or natural methods than by fooling with poisons so powerful even the cans they come in can't be "disposed of in landfills, or in streams, or by burning, or any other method that would bring its residues into contact with human or animal life." Talk about a pact with the Devil!

Another reason I don't want pesticides in my garden is because children and poisons don't mix. Obviously, we don't want Noah and Rachel exposed to toxic chemicals, but there's also a philosophical principle at work: we want them to grow up realizing that nature is a process to be understood, not a collection of enemies to be conquered. Relying on natural controls—the insect traps, barriers, homemade sprays, and other controls I've mentioned—means we never have to worry that the kids (or we) will breathe in something harmful or suffer skin irritation. Nor do we have to banish the children while we douse the garden with poison. The world is dangerous enough as it is. Shouldn't the garden be a safe haven, a place where children can learn the benefits of cooperation and harmony?

Noah and Rachel have their own gardens, actually a small section set aside in the main plot. They started young, both of them clamoring to plant seeds and hoe and water—*especially* to water—when they were two or three.

When Noah was a toddler he loved to sit in the garden playing with dirt and worms while Betsy and I worked at cultivating or planting. Rachel did the same, only she loved to sit chatting incessantly in baby talk, babbling on, whether anyone listened or not. She also ate a little dirt now and then.

I marked off special plots for the children, giving each a 4-by-8-foot bed. I thought that might be too much for children so young, but they took pride in having a part of the garden to call their own.

Of course, I do most of the work in their gardens. They plant their own seeds, pat the dirt down over the furrows, water, do some carefully supervised weeding, and harvest. But it's Dad who keeps the plots carefully weeded and cultivated.

Each child is allowed to raise only a few simple-to-grow crops; peas, carrots, beans, and a tomato plant are plenty for them (and me) to look after. They're also encouraged to help plant other crops when Betsy and I are seeding or transplanting. So they're really involved thoroughly in the entire garden process.

I've known some parents who use the garden to teach responsibility, taking a stern "no work, no food" approach. If weeds overwhelm the garden, so be it. That may be appropriate for teenagers, but small children need to have fun, to grow into gardening slowly. (I wonder how long I would have remained a gardener if someone had led me through the paces like a drill sergeant or demolished my childlike notion that gardening was a snap?)

Besides, a young child's attention span is usually so short that his gardening experiences come and go in spurts. Noah used to get all fired up about helping me cultivate the beds. I'd give him a pint-sized hoe and turn him loose on a vacant plot. He'd start off in a burst, chopping diligently and saying things like, "Boy, Dad—I'm a real farmer now, aren't I?" I'd say, "Yes, you certainly look like one" but before I even finished the sentence, Noah had a new thought:

"Whew," he'd say, leaning on the little hoe like a hired hand, "this sure is hard work, isn't it, Dad?"

"Sure is."

"I think maybe I'll take a rest. That okay?"

"Sure, take a break," I'd say, figuring he'd worked maybe a full five minutes. Then he'd flop down between the growing beds and find a worm or a bug and get distracted. And that would be all the gardening for that day.

The mixture of children and gardening isn't always so idyllic, however. One year I gave Noah and Rachel adjoining plots, to make it easier on me, I hoped, but their closeness often produced a harvest of tantrums.

Rachel decided to weed one day and accidentally pulled up Noah's cucumber seedling, one he and I had carefully planted together. Noah burst into tears and punched Rachel on the arm. She hit back and flopped down in sobs. Suddenly I had both of them rolling around in the dirt, wailing away, and kicking at each other. Sometimes children in the garden come under the heading of "pest."

And why is it that whenever I drag the hose out, they appear, each clamoring for a chance to "help" me water.

"Me first! Me first!"

"You can *share* the hose," I say.

"She's had the hose long enough!" Noah yells.

"I just got it," Rachel screams.

"Gimmee!" Noah says, grabbing the nozzle. Rachel turns toward me for help, watering my shoes, then turns back and sprays Noah full in the face.

"Arrgh!" he yells and bends the nozzle back on Rachel, drenching her. She shoves him back and he falls flat on his bottom in the middle of the newly transplanted cabbage seedlings we were supposed to be watering.

"That's it! That's it!" I scream, the blood pounding in my head, "Everybody out! Off limits! Go home! Betsy, help! Somebody call Cesar Chavez! Out! Out! Out!"

Rachel and Noah run for their lives, their sneakers squishing water as they race for the house.

"You're barred from the garden *for life!* " I yell after them.

Until tomorrow, anyway.

Later harvests are more joyful. The carrots Noah plants all germinate and grow to delicious maturity. We enjoy munching on them through most of the fall. Every time a carrot appears on the table, Noah almost bursts with pride. "That's one of *my* carrots!" he says, puffing out his chest. "And they're wonderful!"

Rachel's garden produced some particularly good Chinese cabbage, a food we ate daily at Rachel's insistence. She was so proud of her "cab-batches" that she dragged everyone who visited down to the garden to see. And she began making plans for "my next year's garden," counting off a dozen vegetables she wanted to grow.

One night we were having winter squash, particularly tasty Waltham butternuts. Noah hadn't eaten any since the winter before. He wrinkled his nose. "I *hate* winter squash!" he said. "When was the last time you had any?" Betsy asked.

"I don't know. I hate it."

"That's interesting," I said. "I don't remember you telling me that when you helped me plant the seeds."

"What?" he said.

"Don't you remember? Last May you and I planted these seeds together. You asked me what the seeds were and I said winter squash. And you said, 'Oh, boy, I can't wait.' Well, here it is."

I should have been a politician.

Noah stared at the golden squash half steaming in front of him, a pat of butter slowly melting and glistening as it trickled onto the plate. "I guess

I'll taste it." He took a birdlike peck with his fork. Then his eyes brightened. "Hey, this is really good!"

"No kidding?" I said. "I guess you really know how to grow this stuff."

"Yeah," he chuckled, enjoying the joke on himself.

Several days later we had some friends over who noticed the box of butternuts stored in a cool hallway. "What are these?" our visitor asked.

"Oh," said Noah nonchalantly, "those are winter squash. I grew 'em. We love 'em."

Our garden has grown considerably over the years. The 50-by-50-foot plot is still our main garden site, but we also have plots 40-by-40 feet and 25-by-30 feet. They total 4,850 square feet, enough to grow most of our food the year round.

But all that produce has to be handled correctly according to a schedule. The hardest part of producing our own food, we found, was getting experienced and getting organized. You must have a plan when the garden starts producing vegetables or you'll be swamped with bushels of overripe and rotted produce.

We divide our harvest into four categories: canning, freezing, drying, and storing. Some people can everything, but we can only tomatoes and fruits, not low-acid foods, which are risky to can unless you use a pressure canner.

Using the open-kettle method (heating a pot of beans, for example, then hot-packing them into jars) or a hot water bath (processing jars filled with produce in boiling water) for low-acid foods is an invitation to botulism, an almost always fatal type of food poisoning. (The incidence of death from botulism has actually increased in the United States with the renewed interest in home canning.)

Only a pressure canner capable of generating 240 degrees F. can kill botulism spores. It's *possible* to do it with a boiling water bath, but it means processing jars for as long as three hours. So much for the good old days.

We freeze most of what we grow. There is no danger whatever of botulism in frozen foods, and the process is much faster than canning, especially if there are only two of you with a mountain of produce piled by. Most fresh-picked foods need only a two-minute blanching in boiling water or steam, an equally long cooling period, followed by packing and freezing. The blanching process is important. It destroys enzymes that might hasten vitamin loss and color changes in the food.

The disadvantage of freezing is the cost of electricity in running the freezer and having all your food in one basket—subject to freezer malfunction or a power loss. We keep our energy costs low by using a chest-type freezer with manual defrost. A lot of the cold air mass in an upright freezer actually falls on the floor every time you open the door. And automatic defrost relies on a 600-watt heating element that may double the freezer's electric consumption.

We keep our freezer on an enclosed porch where the temperature stays cool but never freezing. We also make sure the freezer has plenty of space to vent its warm air. These steps reduce the freezer's workload and the amount of electricity it uses. We also keep the freezer as full as possible and defrost it annually, just before canning and freezing time. (A buildup of ice can act as insulation, causing the unit to work overtime. On the other hand, defrosting too often wastes a lot of power too.)

As for power failures, a well-stocked freezer left unopened will keep its cool for up to 48 hours. We've never had an "outrage," as the power company quaintly calls a blackout, that lasted more than a day. If power failures were more frequent or of longer duration in our area, I'd consider buying a back-up generator. (Or maybe we'd get a pressure canner and junk the freezer.)

The only malfunction we've had in a decade of freezer use was a slow leak in the system. We lost no food because of the trouble, and the manufacturer honored the warranty, giving us a new freezer in exchange.

Some people might criticize us for relying on a freezer at all. Here we've attempted to simplify our lives and we're relying on this piece of high-tech, if that's what a freezer is. But, as I've said, we never set out to return to the old days, only to find a blend between traditional values and appropriate technology. I think a freezer filled with organic homegrown food is appropriate in every way. But I guess we could argue about it.

"If I ever see another tomato, I'll SCREAM!"

That's Betsy in late August, tomato canning time. We grow a lot of tomatoes, a staple in our diet as whole fruits fresh in season, canned in winter, and the basis of all the things we make from tomatoes—paste, sauce, catsup, and juice. We like tomatoes because they're easy to grow, tasty, and their use enhances many other foods and food combinations.

Sometime in July the tomatoes begin bearing in earnest. Then they bear with a vengenance. By August they are producing fruit in an uncontrollable frenzy. This has a lot to do with how I grow them, I like to think. I dig a foot-deep trench for each plant, fill it with compost and topsoil and a dash of granular seaweed, rich in trace minerals. Then I lay each plant on its side and bend about three inches of the top up. I cover the stem with two inches of dirt, leaving the three-inch vertical stem standing straight up.

Arranging the stem horizontally with only two inches of dirt atop it allows the full length to absorb heat from early spring sunshine. In time the stem will put down collateral roots, creating a strong, drought-resistant root system. I water-in each plant with a quart of manure or compost tea. I give the plants a heavy soaking a week later. Then I mulch them heavily in mid-June and don't do anything after that except harvest. And harvest.

We haul tomatoes into the house by the bushelful. We've learned over the years that we need about 150 quarts of canned tomatoes to last us through the winter. There are two ways to do this: either we can a dozen or so quarts daily until we accumulate 150 quarts, or we can as many as possible every day until we're done. We do the latter.

Because we use the boiling water bath to can tomatoes, we must endure a constantly steaming kitchen, a horrible way to spend the day when the outside temperature and humidity are in the 90's.

A subtle transformation overtakes Betsy during canning season. Is this the same fresh-faced woman who, in May, complained that her mouth ached for the taste of a ripe tomato? Is this the same woman who checked the green fruits on each plant in June, wondering aloud when they'd turn crimson and edible?

Now we have a cranky drudge who snaps at the children, wisps of hair matted to her sweaty forehead. She wipes her nose on the back of her hand and snarls. Looking like the cook in *Alice in Wonderland,* Betsy is ready to boil the baby. And in the unkindest cut, she blames *me,* the innocent tiller of the soil, for even growing the damned tomatoes in the first place.

"How about a divorce?" I ask.

"No," she says, dissecting a swollen Big Boy with the dexterity of a surgeon. "I would prefer to be done with this, to never see another tomato."

"Ah, but isn't the simple life great?"

"Have you considered open heart surgery?" she asks, flicking the blade in my direction. She's been up since five in the morning, washing jars, sterilizing them, boiling water, slicing tomatoes, stuffing them into jars, processing them in a large kettle of boiling water. The wallpaper is starting to peel off the walls. And Betsy is wondering if she can learn to love TV dinners.

Her record is 55 quarts of tomatoes in one nine-hour day. With both of us working, doing little else but attending to tomatoes, we can put up a year's supply of whole fruit in a week, depending on the course of the harvest. Then we use the rest of the tomatoes to make paste, sauce, catsup, and juice.

By September, we have eaten enough fresh tomatoes and had enough of them pass through our hands to wish fervently for the first frost. When it doesn't come and the tomato plants are still robust and pumping fruit out like an assembly line, we have our annual tomatocide conversation:

"How about if I go down to the garden tonight and beat them all to death with a stick?" I suggest.

"No," says Betsy, "you got to do it last year. Now it's my turn."

"Okay. You kill 25 and I'll kill 25."

But all we do, as always, is keep harvesting. We could simply let the fruit rot where it falls, but it's a sin to let food go to waste. So we keep on harvesting, keep on canning, and give tomatoes away to all comers. And six months later, we know, we'll be eagerly looking forward again to the first ripe tomato.

We also can peaches (we buy several bushels of drops or culls from an orchard), pears (from our own trees), and apples (we have no trees of our own, but more about that later). Like tomatoes, each of these involves a lot of jar washing, sterilizing, boiling water, and dissection of fruits at the kitchen counter. Our tempers get short and we warn each other and the children to stay out of the way until the job is done.

The summer kitchen is where you pay your dues for self-reliance. Any notions of homesteading as a romantic life rise and disappear with the steam. But we never have any doubts about the worth of what we're doing.

Freezing vegetables is a lot easier, though still tedious toward the end of the season. Each crop must be harvested at the peak of flavor and processed as soon as possible. The vegetables must be washed, cut into manageable pieces, blanched, cooled, and packed into freezer bags or boxes. This goes on for weeks and weeks.

We also dry some foods—apple and pear slices, herbs, zucchini (makes wonderful "chips"), and green peppers. I built a solar food dryer some years ago, but sun-drying is difficult in our humid climate. We use a homemade dryer that uses light bulbs as a heat source. A low-wattage fan helps push moist air out of the dryer box, and a thermostat keeps the temperature in the proper drying range.

The better commercial food dryers use nichrome wire heating elements, superior to light bulbs (which are designed for light, not heat), but our jerry-rigged setup works well enough.

There's some talk that dried food is better than canned or frozen produce, but that demands some explanation.

Drying food at temperatures that range from 95 to 145 degrees F. causes the destruction of vitamin C. Cutting the food into small pieces increases the effect of oxygen and light, so vitamins A, E, and some of the B-complex are also destroyed. The heat also works to intensify the destructive effect of oxygen on other vitamins.

On the other hand, dried food is higher in minerals and fruit sugar than fresh food, but only because it's been reduced in bulk.

The best thing about drying food is that it's a simple, energy-efficient means of food preservation—the oldest known to humanity. Drying removes 80 to 90 percent of the water, so spoilage bacteria cannot form and the food keeps well at cool room temperature for a long time. Dried food saves space in the pantry or kitchen. Four pounds of fresh produce, when dried, weighs only one pound. We think a well-stocked kitchen should contain a range of stored foods, including, but not limited to, dried foods.

Our family loves dried apple slices, banana chips, zucchini chips, and pear slices. All make great snacks, trail food, and lunchbox additions. We also enjoy preparing our own dried vegetable soup ingredients and having dried basil, dill, and parsley for seasoning; and chamomile for tea.

Herbs are the easiest to dry. We put bunches of them in paper bags and hang them in our hot attic. We dry chamomile and other blossoms by simply spreading them out on a screen or tray in a hot, dry place.

By the time late summer and early fall arrive, we're harvesting sweet potatoes, white potatoes, winter squash, and apples. The books say sweet potatoes should be cured by keeping them at 85 degrees F. for ten days. When we first grew them we thought of setting up a room or a tent with a heater. But we never got organized enough to do that and ended up with uncured sweet potatoes that tasted great.

White potatoes we simply harvest and store in bushel baskets on a cool, enclosed porch. Winter squash—butternuts and pumpkins—are equally worry free. Kept in a cool room, they stay firm until February, if we haven't eaten them all as baked squash and pumpkin pies by then.

Other crops, as I mentioned earlier—carrots, parsnips, salsify, and Jerusalem artichokes—we leave in the ground. A heavy mulch keeps them fresh all winter and we dig them up as needed.

The first hard freeze signals the end of the growing season, but not the end of gardening chores. There is still much to do. The soil must be put to bed, a task (on the east coast) usually left until the first two weeks in November. Bare soil is subject to wind and water erosion, so I try to lay a heavy mulch on my raised beds to insulate them against the winter. (The mulch must be pulled away in the early spring to speed the warming of the soil.) Other gardeners prepare their gardens by sowing a cover crop of rye or winter wheat. The green blanket holds the soil in place and becomes a green manure the following spring.

Other chores include making up the last of the compost piles and covering them for the winter. Not much microbial activity will go on during winter's cold, but the pile will be waiting for you when the snows melt—one less thing you'll have to do at the start of a busy season.

All crop residues should go on the compost pile now. Plant stalks often harbor insect eggs or larvae that would otherwise winter-over and emerge to plague your crops in spring. Any diseased crop residues should be burned. (The heat of composting will destroy the insect eggs and larvae.)

All the vegetables to be stored for the winter—potatoes, carrots, cabbages, squash and the like—should now be in their proper place. All garden tools and equipment should also be put away, under cover, oiled, and safe from the elements.

Having attended to these final tasks, the gardener or small farmer can, as the last days of November arrive, finally have the chance to look back over the season and realize, "I'm done."

How appropriate then, that Thanksgiving arrives at the same time. Thanksgiving never meant much to me before I became a gardener. I always thought of it as an excuse for gluttony and a time when Alka Seltzer stock jumped ten points. But raising our own food has shown me the real meaning of Thanksgiving. Just this: thanks-giving.

Of course, as vegetarians we take some kidding on that day. A lot of people still have difficulty imagining a vegetarian Thanksgiving.

"Gee, what do you eat instead of a turkey?"

"Would you believe a 15-pound soybean?"

So we began working out our own Thanksgiving tradition after our first few harvests. Beyond the symbolism of the Pilgrims and turkeys (a lively combination), Thanksgiving is really a harvest festival. It's a time to relax and enjoy the bounty that our labors and the earth's rhythms have yielded.

We started out with a simple idea: to put on the Thanksgiving table foods we grew ourselves or foods that came from friends.

There wasn't much the first few years. Tomatoes, of course, and corn, salad, beans, and bread Betsy had baked. That alone doesn't make much of a meal, so we added whatever store-bought items we needed. Our Thanksgivings were small in those years anyway because our children were small and it's hard to dwell on thoughts of gratitude when one of your children is putting creamed corn in her ear and the other is screaming for his dessert first. But as our knowledge of gardening and food production increased, so did our array of foods on the Thanksgiving table.

Thanksgiving of 1979 was probably the culmination of all we'd set out to do. But the road to that dinner had been so long that the moment itself had no special quality. Only on reflection did Betsy and I realize how thankful we were.

We ate mashed potatoes, peas, broccoli, and a fresh salad of Chinese cabbage picked an hour before. We ate crescent rolls hot from the oven with cherry jam and had a fruit salad of wineberries and peaches. Dessert was a choice of pumpkin or apple pie.

Once everything was spread out, the food looking vividly beautiful as only fresh vegetables can, did we realize we had finally kept a promise made almost ten years before; almost everything on the table had come from our own labors. Only the wheat in the rolls and pie crusts had come from the store. The eggs came from a friend's chickens, we picked wild wineberries and sour cherries, and gleaned the apples from a neighbor's orchard.

But best of all were Noah's and Rachel's reactions. For the first time they recognized their place in this drama.

"That's *my* Chinese cabbage," Rachel piped up. "I grew that in *my* garden!"

"And those are *my* peas," Noah said, a little too loudly. "I planted the seeds!"

A bit competitive, I guess, but they got the point: life is made richer by self-reliance and the luxury of sitting down to food you've grown yourself.

Later, after the children had retreated to their rooms for an especially raucous game, Betsy and I shared a special moment. We enjoyed a glass of homemade wine.

As we sipped the wine and talked, the dinner dishes spread in disarray between us, Betsy and I realized how fortunate we were. All of us healthy, all together, with almost a year's supply of food we'd produced and stored.

Thanksgiving isn't the only time we realize this good fortune, of course. One snowy evening last winter as I was sitting in the kitchen listening to the news on the radio, Betsy walked in with an armload of kale she'd just picked. She stood smiling, her cheeks flushed from the cold and from the wood stove's heat. This was our annual vote of confidence—the harvest of fresh vegetables even as the snow fell. Each blue-green kale leaf, every carrot or parsnip dug from its mulch of maple leaves, was witness to our progress.

She started to speak as she put the kale down on the oak table but the radio intruded. We stopped to listen. An agriculture department official was being interviewed. He was talking about preserving the standard of living in the United States. And then he said, with obvious pride, "It's no small triumph that American technology and industry have finally freed 98 percent of the American people from the drudgery of raising their own food." A pause. And then we laughed.

From late July until the first frost is apple picking time. Notice how neatly it overlaps tomato-and-everything-else picking time, canning time, freezing time, and firewood cutting time? The simple life. I don't know how many apples Betsy and I pick during a season—we lost track one year at well past 50 bushels—but it's enough to form calluses on the tip of my thumb and the outside tip of my index finger. That's from rolling a thousand apple stems away from their branches.

We press 70 gallons or more of cider each season, make about 100 quarts of applesauce, dry apples, apple pies, and apple butter, and eat at least one fresh apple every day. Not bad, considering we don't own a single apple tree.

We're apple foragers, harvesting from trees owned by friends and acquaintances who either don't want the apples or can't do all the picking by themselves.

We do the harvesting, usually returning a percentage of the apples to the owner. Sometimes, when fortune smiles, we get all the apples to ourselves. Occasionally we'll hear of an abandoned farm with an old orchard and ripe apples about to go to waste. We rush in like locusts, thrilled at the booty, though saddened to see another farm being swallowed by the suburban real estate market. The apple trees we pick from one year may be bulldozed the next to make way for a tennis court or lawn.

No one sprays or really looks after the trees we pick from, so I'd have to describe them as more wild than organically grown. What always surprises us, though, is how good the fruit looks and tastes. The apples aren't perfect, blemish free, as in the supermarket, but that's an expensive illusion anyway.

Growers have to spray and work like crazy to produce the uniform fruits you see in the produce section. What happens to the not-so-pretty fruits—the ones with harmless bumps or scars? They're sent off to make juice, applesauce, and other products, while the public pays a premium for the cosmetically appealing apples.

There's a saying about wild apples: don't eat them in the dark. (You can't see the worms.) But we've seen little serious insect or worm damage over many years of picking. My experience with these unkempt trees convinces me that chemical companies have oversold the need for poison sprays.

Apple trees *do* have insect and fungal problems, but organic orchardists have successfully used safe controls for decades. And other environmentally minded growers have significantly reduced their dependence on poison sprays. Just think how much money and petrochemicals could be saved if the American public could be convinced that apples and other produce didn't have to look like wax fruit to taste good.

Picking apples day after day throughout the summer is hard, satisfying work. Everything seems to reek of apples, our backs hurt from lugging bushels of the fruit around, and I even dream about apples. If nothing else, picking all that fruit makes me thankful—not just for the bounty, but for the fact that I don't have to do this for a living.

I remember once picking strawberries at a pick-it-yourself farm. One of the employees was supervising the crowds, walking among us, keeping us in our respective rows, and showing us which rows to harvest next. He marked the various picked and unpicked rows with two-foot-long pine stakes that he shoved into the ground.

I was squatting, picking berries left and right, shoving a few in my mouth as I picked, when I looked up to see this fellow wandering through the rows holding one of those sticks in his hand. He towered over the several dozen pickers. Most were women in from the city and suburbs. They were laughing and chatting as they worked. All very benign.

But the sight of this man, stick in hand, striding amongst all those kneeling figures, was too much for my imagination. Suddenly I was Paul Muni on a chain gang. Tom Joad in *The Grapes of Wrath.* The Man with a Hoe. The farmhand had become a field boss, the row marker (which he rhythmically slapped against his thigh) a swagger stick or truncheon. The kneeling suburbanites were suddenly families of migrants struggling to fill their berry boxes.

I swallowed hard, I'll tell you, and the vision stabbed a chill through the sweat stains on my back.

I've had other, less painful experiences during our apple harvesting—and have learned the importance of good tools. When we first started we knew nothing, not even the best way to get the apples down. We used to shake the branches until apples came thudding to the ground. Then we'd pick them up, though many were shattered or badly bruised by the fall.

This was an awful way to harvest. We ended up with a lot of rotten apples and swarms of yellow jackets attracted by the damaged fruit. Next we tried a variety of stepladders. We picked the apples and put them in buckets and boxes balanced precariously on the ladder's shelf.

But the buckets filled up too fast or fell off with a sickening crash; and we seemed to be forever going up and down the ladders, which were too short anyway.

Then one year we looked ahead to what was to be our biggest apple harvest yet. We had 11 trees lined up, and the thought of our annual clumsy bucket brigade was too wearying to contemplate. Up to then we had tried to save money by keeping our equipment simple, but we paid for that with inefficiency.

So that year we bought professional apple harvesting bags. These look like knapsacks, only you wear them on your chest. The mouth of the sack is held open by a stiff wire hoop that frees you to pick hand over hand if the ladder is sturdy.

When the bag is full, you climb down and unsnap a clasp on the bag's bottom, letting the apples spill into a box. Our bags hold a half-bushel, which is all you'd want hanging around your neck at one time, especially when you're perched on a ladder.

Climbing down the ladder with that heavy bag hanging in front always gives me a hint of what being pregnant must feel like. And when I reach the ground and have to walk to the bushel baskets, feeling ungainly and off balance, my heavy load swaying and bouncing out in front, I can empathize with every woman in her ninth month. Then I squat over a basket, unsnap the bag's bottom, and the apples pour out, rumbling and clicking against each other. Ah. The joy of birth.

Another piece of apple harvesting equipment we use is a friend's 26-foot orchard ladder, or, in a pinch, an aluminum extension ladder. Green apple wood is fairly resilient, so we can lean either type ladder against the outside branches, climb up to the treetop, and pick all the way down. When we've done one section we move the ladder a few feet sideways, turning it around itself—actually flipping it around the tree—and we begin again.

A 26-foot ladder, all one piece, is no easy tool to handle. Just standing it upright is dangerous. We start with the ladder flat on the ground. Betsy holds the bottom rungs down while I lift the top end and begin "walking" the ladder into a vertical position.

And there we stand, the two of us with more than 20 feet of heavy wooden ladder swaying overhead, delicately balanced.

"Have you ever thought of a life in the circus?" I ask Betsy. If the wind kicks up even a hair, or if the ladder's weight shifts slightly, everything comes unglued. We laugh nervously. This is an object lesson in physics: how do you control 26 feet of heavy lumber by hanging on to the bottom 6 feet?

Sometimes you don't. The ladder shifts, we scream at each other, at the ladder, looking up, holding down, afraid to hang on, afraid to let go.

"Let go!"

"Hang on!"

"Get out of the way!"

"Timber!"

The ladder falls flat, making less noise than we do, its crash blowing dry leaves and grass to the side. And we begin again, struggling to stand the monster up. Next year we'll be ready for Ringling Brothers.

The aluminum extension ladder is much easier to stand up, but it's harder to handle in the trees. Twigs and branches snag easily in the aluminum channels. And the metal tends to scrape more bark off the tree than does the wood ladder. Besides, an extension ladder just doesn't feel right up there in the tree. The metal is too cold to the touch. And it clanks when you move it.

The funny thing is that we never end up hating apples the way we do tomatoes at season's end. Maybe it's because picking apples keeps us outside, high up in the trees, instead of in a steaming kitchen.

Once I was almost at the top of the 26-foot ladder, wedged in among branches heavy with fruit. Twenty-six feet above ground doesn't seem that high until you're up there swaying in the breeze. I felt a sense of danger mixed with exhilaration. The sun was bright, the air mild, and there were so many apples in front of me I didn't know which one to pick first.

I heard a noise below me, looked down between the leaves, and saw Rachel wandering around singing to herself. She makes up her own operas, running long strings of her observations together in wonderful atonal songs:

> "Oh here we are picking apples and I love apples every day 'cause my Momma's up a tree and Daddy is too and brother's over there and I see a horse 'way across the field . . ."

I chuckled, watching her from my aerie. Suddenly, the wind gusted and the ladder lurched sharply, making me lose my balance. My heart leaped into my throat as I grabbed at the rungs to steady myself. I hugged the ladder, taking a deep breath, relieved that I hadn't tumbled.

Then the most incredible apple aroma enveloped me, distracting me like a magical vapor. Several branches had been scraped in the jostling and the torn bark emitted an overwhelming scent. And below me, Rachel was singing:

> ". . . apples, apples, apples oh we love those apples you and me my brother and my Momma and my Daddy uppa tree uppa tree . . ."

About a century ago, apple cider was the national drink in our country, and it remained so until the introduction and popularizing of soft drinks. (Cider is what comes straight from the apple; apple juice is cider that's been pasteurized or otherwise treated.) Every farm with an orchard produced its own cider or hauled apples to a local cider mill. Such mills were once fixtures in our country.

Laying up several barrels of cider was as common as storing potatoes. The cider didn't stay fresh all winter, of course, but as folks said then, it had "a lovely way of turning."

So when Betsy and I and the children are making cider from the apples we've foraged, we aren't just making something to drink, I like to philosophize; we're making a connection to part of our past.

When we first started making cider, we used an electric juicer at the kitchen counter. But once we got heavily into apple foraging we started thinking about doing some serious cider making. I couldn't find much in the library or bookstores on how to make cider on a large scale. So I went to see Merle Ketchum, an old farmer we know.

Merle's a disappearing breed. His farm land is 35 miles north of downtown Washington, hard on the edge of the advancing suburbs. Already from his porch you can see tract houses on half-acre lots that were once the pastures and gardens of other local farmers.

His land is already worth a million as potential building sites, but Merle wants to stay a farmer. "I'm doing all right," he'll tell you, but rising property taxes eat into whatever profits he makes. "What'll I do with all that money?" he asks the real estate agents who make him offers. "What'll I do? Go down to Florida and sit on some goddamn park bench and read my bankbooks?"

Merle was out by his pig sty, fussing with a coil of tangled rope, cursing under his breath. He's in his seventies, though you'd never guess. He's not in what you'd call excellent condition—he's got a belly that overhangs his belt like a sack of corn drooping off the end of a loading platform—but he endures. And he puts in a day's work that would kill a mule.

"Hi, Merle," I said. "Do you know anything about . . ."

"Mah goddamn teeth's killing me," he roared back. Merle always started a conversation in the middle.

"I'm sorry to hear that, Merle."

"Got a cow down with what the vet says is milk fever, a pig that looks punky, and mah fool dentist put these fool teeth in upside down, I think."

"Gee, Merle, I'm sorry to hear . . . "

"Do I know anything about *what?*"

"Huh?" I'd lost track of the conversation. "Oh," I said, "what do you know about making apple cider?"

"Hell. You just get your apples together and bring 'em on up to Westminster to the mill. Fellow there has a hydraulic press. He'll press 'em for you for 'bout forty cents a gallon."

"Well, Merle, Betsy and I wanted to do it ourselves."

"Lord, you two are doing all the chores that made me run away from home. You're living in the past, Boy!"

"We try, Merle."

"Well," he said, spitting tobacco juice off to the side—actually making the sound "p-tui"—"I guess I got an old cider press 'round here somewheres."

Merle hung the tangled rope on a fence post and took me with him into one of the many ramshackle outbuildings that dot his farm. He rummaged around for several minutes, cursing his dentist, kicking rusted buckets and milk pails aside, tripping over bound copies of old *National Geographics*. Then, "Here 'tis!" he shouted, pulling some moldy boxes away.

He'd found an old screw-type cider press. Next to it was a motor-driven apple shredder complete with a plywood hopper. Merle and I dragged the equipment out and he helped me load it in my truck.

"Thanks a lot, Merle. We appreciate the loan."

"Oh, well, there's one more thing you oughta know 'bout that machine."

"What's that?"

"Don't forget to put a bucket under that hole there or the juice'll run all over the ground." He leered at me, enjoying his wit.

"I'll remember, Merle," I said, shaking my head. "What would we do without all your old-time wisdom?"

We learned a lot about making apple cider that first year, the hard way, as usual. There was a little more to it than simply chopping apples and squeezing them, the way Merle had told us to. The press was the classic cider press design: a solid hardwood frame held a cylinder of closely spaced hardwood slats (the basket). We lined this with a coarse cloth (pressing sack), filled it with shredded apples (pomace or "pummice"), put a circular top (the follower) into the cylinder, and screwed down the threaded rod. Merle was right about one thing: the cider did come out of the little hole in the bottom. Praise the Lord.

Our first pressing was a time of great excitement. When a thick torrent of cider came coursing out of the press—it sounded like someone had turned a faucet on full—we cheered like wildcatters striking oil.

Noah and Rachel got the first tastes, holding their cups under the stream of golden cider, giggling with anticipation. But the old press was a mixed blessing. We got cider, all right, but the work we had to do for it made us wonder if we shouldn't forget the whole thing and head for that commercial mill in Westminster.

The key to efficient pressing, we discovered, is the shredder. Apples are tough. The cider is tightly locked in the fibrous cells. Just chopping apples into bits does nothing. The liquid stays trapped unless you can shred the fruit into a mush. Merle's old shredder used a motorized drum studded with stubby projections. It did a reasonable job, but much of the juice stayed in the pulp.

Screwing the threaded rod down was good arm exercise, but frustrating. The cylinder held about a bushel and a half of pomace, but the pressure had to be applied slowly. We'd wait now and then for the pulp to settle before turning the rod again.

When the pulp no longer produced enough to make it worthwhile, we'd unscrew the rod and empty the pulp onto the compost pile. All this was done amidst hordes of yellow jackets, hornets, white-faced wasps, and bumblebees drawn by the sweet juice. I can't remember anyone ever getting stung, though. I think the bugs were too happy to get angry.

But after the novelty had worn off, Betsy and I often lost our tempers with Merle's clumsy press. It was hard to fill, harder to empty, and pressing down on a solid cylinder of pomace meant that the juice had to pass through almost a foot of pulp.

It's all very well to "make a connection" with the past, as I've said, but how far backward do you go in search of authentic experience and the satisfaction of doing it yourself? Would our ancestors have stayed with a crosscut saw if the chain saw had been invented? Should we stay with this primitive cider press for old time's sake? There's a delicate balance to be struck somewhere between the extremes of using a quaint unproductive press and buying processed cider made with sprayed apples and preservatives. We began sending away for information on modern cider presses.

"Look at this brochure," Betsy said one morning. "It says their press will squeeze three gallons of cider per bushel."

"Three gallons? We'd have to work half a day with Merle's press for that. How much does it cost?"

"Oh," said Betsy in a low voice, swallowing as she read the price. "Have you considered a second mortgage?"

"That much?"

"Close enough, on our budget. Figure on a thousand bucks with shipping."

"My God!"

"A thousand dollars would buy a lot of cider," Betsy said.

"We'd have to get a loan to swing it. I don't know . . . "

"The simple life, huh?"

"It would probably pay for itself in our grandchildren's time," I said.

"I like the way you plan for the future."

The issue was resolved when Merle broke the news to us at the start of the next year's apple season. "Can't lend my press no more, I'm afraid," he said, kicking at a pebble.

"Why not?" I asked.

"Stolen."

Merle suspected the thief was a Georgetown woman who boarded her horse with him and had earlier admired the antique press and said it would make a great lamp.

"Hell, I'm sorry, Merle."

"Well, so am I. I know how you liked it. Bet she's got that goddamn thing all wired up in her living room by now."

"It's what you call a conversation piece, Merle."

So we got a loan, entered the wonderful world of credit, and bought a modern cider press. Were we a little guilty, prattling about the simple life with the wave of one hand and signing a chit for a thousand rat-race dollars with the other? A little. But it passes if you lie down with a cool cloth on your head.

The new press was a welded steel frame using a three-ton hydraulic jack to expel the cider. Unlike Merle's cylinder-type arrangement, this press used flat lattice-work pressing boards.

We laid a board out on the press base, covered it with a coarse pressing cloth, dumped some pomace on it, and shaped the pulp into an inch-thick "cheese." Then we'd fold the edges of the cloth over, lay another pressing board on top, cover with another cloth, and continue building cheeses one on top of the other.

When all the cheeses were stacked, we lowered a heavy pressing-plate down, locked it in place, and jacked the cheeses up, squeezing them between the plate and the press base. What a difference! The cider came gushing out all at once, swirling in a golden torrent into a five-gallon pot we'd put under the press. And we filled that pot on the first pressing! The press held 2½ bushels of apples, yielding, as the maker claimed, between two and three gallons per bushel.

The high price we paid included a motorized shredder with a remarkably effective design. Instead of crushing or merely shredding the apples, this device—a stainless steel drum fitted with a thin blade—actually shaved the apples into a coarse applesauce. A hopper over the drum housing allowed us to dump a bushel of apples in all at once, with the whole mess reduced to a pulp in a minute.

The press's overall design was, as I had hoped, a combination of the traditional and the modern. The building of cheeses, for example, goes back more than a century to the old cider mill designs. (And stacking cheeses means the cider need only pass through an inch of pomace at one time.) In the old mills, pomace was ground between huge granite grinding wheels. Our electric shredder was simply an extension of that technology.

And while the initial cost of the press was high, the energy costs were almost nil. The shredder used a half-horsepower electric motor, but so efficient was the cutting action that each bushel of apples needed only a

60-second burst of electricity to be converted to pulp. The press itself was manual, using a standard auto jack.

The entire design was a prime example of how an ancient skill or craft can be sensibly modernized without losing its human scale.

Suddenly, we were awash in cider. We'd pick apples for days on end, then devote a single Saturday to pressing. Starting in the morning, we'd wash apples and trim off any bad spots. Then I'd shred all the apples at once, packing the pomace into a clean garbage can lined with a special food-grade polyethylene liner. With shredding done, we'd spend the rest of the day pressing.

On a typical Saturday, we'd work ten hours straight, getting 25 to 27 gallons of cider for the day. That was a problem at first because we ran out of jugs. Then I bought new plastic milk jugs from a local dairy. We filled these and froze them because frozen cider tastes like fresh. (Earlier we'd pasteurized jars of juice in a hot water bath, keeping the temperature at 185 degrees F. to preserve the taste.)

And one year we decided to try another one of those romantic old ways. Why not, we thought, store some cider in a barrel? How quaint. We bought a barrel from a cider mill, having been assured by the owner that the barrel had been washed thoroughly and had never held anything but apple cider.

We put the barrel on the back porch and filled it with about 25 gallons of fresh-pressed cider. Thoughts of going out on crisp winter days to draw off mugs of sparkling hard cider flashed through our minds. And mulled cider. Ah.

But the first time we siphoned off a quart we got a shock.

"I think this stuff has gone hard already," I told Betsy, smacking my lips. "It's sort of tart."

"Let me taste," she said. A sip, then she wrinkled her nose. "It's tart, all right. It's going to vinegar!"

"What?" I tasted again. She was right. I didn't know whether to laugh or cry. "Twenty-five gallons of vinegar," I moaned, staggered by Mother Nature's crazy sense of humor.

"I thought he said this barrel only had cider in it before."

"He did. And it probably did. But once those vinegar bacteria get into the pores of the wood, you can't wash them out."

"You're not angry?" Betsy asked, smiling.

"Naw. Good cider vinegar is hard to find. *Organic* cider vinegar, indeed."

"But 25 gallons of the stuff?"

"Think of it as a lifetime supply of salad dressing."

We still have plenty left, by the way. Aged-in-the-wood organic apple-cider vinegar. All our accidents should be as profitable. Aside from salad dressing, we use it to make an old Vermont drink. Put one tablespoon of cider vinegar in eight ounces of water, add a dash of honey, and enjoy. And we make herbed vinegar for Christmas presents. Just put a sprig of basil, tarragon, or mint into a bottle of vinegar and let it sit until the flavors mingle.

We ask ourselves whether cider making is really worth the work many times during the fall. After all, cider sells here for less than $2 a gallon in season. But the answer, so far, is always yes. Yes, for the same reason Betsy bakes bread, that we grow as much of our food as we can, that we like to cut our own wood. Apple foraging and pressing keep us outdoors, working together, sharing the pleasure each time that golden stream pours into our cups.

Our kitchen is the center of the household. That's as it should be for us. Not only is food the cornerstone of our drive for self-reliance, but we really enjoy eating. This wasn't always so in my case. I was a junk food junkie and a meat-and-potatoes guy most of my life. To me, food was merely fuel for the furnace, a biological necessity like breathing, nothing to get excited about. And I ate as though I was stoking a furnace: I just shoveled it in.

Getting interested in natural foods and healthful living changed my attitude, as did gardening and raising my own food, but the essential catalyst was Betsy's culinary skills. She's a wonderful cook, inventive, adventurous, and proud of her ability to consistently come up with delicious meals made from fresh ingredients. She's skilled at many things, but the kitchen is her studio and canvas—although none of her masterpieces survives long enough to muse over, except as leftovers.

Of course, there are also times when the kitchen is an anvil on which Betsy is pounded out of shape. Summer food preservation, the tension between homestead chores and Betsy's desire to "make something special," and struggling with the rapidly changing likes and dislikes of small children can make the fast-food industry seem like a mother's salvation.

Betsy likes to cook and experiment, but the children usually prefer simple fare: sliced apples, pears, or oranges; fresh peas in the pod; lightly steamed broccoli; sliced raw carrots or kohlrabi from their own gardens; and yogurt, fruit, and whole grain cereal. These are all wonderfully wholesome foods, but a dinner of sliced apples isn't exactly a balanced meal. So Betsy strains her patience and originality to the breaking point, trying to match her imagination to the children's changeable tastes.

"What's this stuff?" says Noah, holding his nose.

"Stuffed cabbage and rice," Betsy says. "And why the face?"

"Yuck," says Noah.

"Yickety-poo," says Rachel.

"I hate it. I won't eat it," Noah protests.

"Me too," says Rachel.

"You haven't even tasted it," Betsy says in desperation. "You *like* cabbage, don't you? It's our cabbage, right from the garden. And you like rice? And you like cheese? Well, that's what this is, a mixture of. . ."

"Yeah," says Noah, "but I don't like them all mixed up on the same plate."

"How 'bout a peenie butter samwich, Ma?" asks Rachel.

Times like this and our kitchen resembles a behavior modification laboratory. The trick, when children announce their undying hatred of a food they've never tasted, is to help them past the first bite. Like most parents faced with this challenge, we employ only the most rational, compassionate methods of persuasion: we use reasoned suggestions ("Taste this or I'll kill you!"); the carrot-and-the-stick method ("Eat those carrots or I'll hit you with a stick!"); and reward for positive behavior ("I'll pay you a penny a taste.").

I'm joking, of course. (Sort of.) We don't really try to force our kids to eat for the simple reason that it can't be done. We don't believe in the old methods of encouraging to "Eat! Eat!" as though they'd die of malnutrition before morning. Both Betsy and I have too many memories of those classic dinner table exchanges:

"You eat like a bird!"

"The starving children in (pick one: Europe, India, Armenia) would be happy to have what's on your plate."

"Don't you want to grow up big and strong like your father?"

But, on the other hand, there's a price to pay for merely letting children eat whenever and whatever they want, the Open Kitchen Policy. The Child's First Law of Sustenance is: a child will always become ravenously hungry immediately after the kitchen has been cleaned and the food put away.

So we try to walk a thin line between respecting a child's right to not be hungry on schedule and the obvious need for a well-balanced diet and an orderly household.

We are helped enormously in our efforts by the fact that we don't have a TV. The constant bombardment of junk food commercials would make dealing with juvenile tastes a far more excruciating ordeal than it already is. We never hear demands in our house for candy, soft drinks, chocolate-covered breakfast cereals, or similar nonfoods. The children aren't exposed to TV, nor do Betsy and I set a negative example by eating such food ourselves. Peer pressure is another matter, but its influence isn't nearly as great or its management as difficult as dealing with the incessant reinforcement of the Tube.

So Betsy puts up with the difficulties of matching her cooking to Noah's and Rachel's often perverse desires by constantly exposing them to good, unfabricated food—everything from hearty vegetable soup and homemade pasta to whole wheat pizza and fresh potato blintzes. We don't rule with an iron hand, of course. There are occasional treats of ice cream, flavored yogurt, or store-bought cookies. But these are in the realm of special treats, not regular fare. The snacks available (and the food the children usually ask for) are those I've mentioned—fruit, fresh vegetables, and whole grain bread.

Aha! you say. That's all very well and good now, when the children are young and manageable. But what happens as they mature? Won't they one day be sneaking out behind the barn to eat hamburgers and slosh down milk shakes?

A woman asked me once how you could really control what your children ate. She had teenagers she was trying to "convert" to a natural-foods-vegetarian diet, but they were always breaking training. You can't convert anybody to a new diet, I suggested, unless you lock them up in the attic and slide each day's offering through a slot in the door. We have it easier with small children, yet even then who knows if the "tree's inclined as the twig is bent"? Once I teased Noah, "You'll probably grow up and live in an apartment and eat junk food and watch TV all day long."

"Oh no!" he said, shocked at the suggestion, "I'd *never* live in an apartment."

Once the demands of the summer garden are met, we enjoy producing our own basic foods, turning our kitchen into a small factory. First on the list is bread, Betsy's domain. Years of experimenting have made her a superb baker, always ready to invent a new recipe or adapt an old one. The breads she bakes, everything from whole wheat, sourdough, rye, and cornbread, to muffins, biscuits, French bread, English muffins, and bagels, contain no white sugar (and little sugar at all; she uses no more than ½ cup of honey to six loaves of bread), no salt, and only a little oil. Betsy also adds nutritional yeast, eggs, milk, and powdered kelp, so a slice or two of her bread is almost a meal in itself.

As she got more serious about baking (she normally produces six to eight loaves every two weeks, with other baking in between) we decided to buy a grain mill to make our own flour. We agonized about the expense—$200—but now regard the price as a small one in comparison to the overall value of a home mill, a true investment. Our mill began paying for itself from the first time we used it.

Seeds are amazing packages, impervious to the damaging effects of oxidation and spoilage as long as their hard shells are unbroken. But once that barrier is cracked by milling, spoilage begins immediately, though slowly. As soon as the oil in wheat, for example, is exposed to the air, rancidity begins. How rapidly this happens is still open to question, but numerous studies have shown that rancidity itself increases our risk of cancer.

When you buy flour in a store, even a trustworthy co-op like the one we rely on, you have no way of knowing when the flour was milled or how long it sat in a truck or warehouse. A grain mill allows us to buy organically grown wheat berries (kernels) in bulk, 50 pounds or more at a time, and keep the sack stored in a cool, dry place until just before baking time.

Now we make flour and bread in one operation. Is there a difference between the taste of bread made with store-bought flour and that made from fresh-milled grains? We think so. The flavor seems more pronounced, heartier, though our reactions may be psychological, induced by the knowledge that what we're eating is as fresh as possible.

Milling flour at home, beyond the obvious aesthetic pleasures, is also an appropriate use of technology and energy. The mill uses only a few cent's worth of electricity while enabling us to sidestep all the industrialized steps that normally go into the production of flour: factory milling, packaging, storage, delivery, retailing.

Equally important, we're able to buy grains from a reputable source who guarantees the pesticide-free qualities of the foods he sells. (He also keeps his grains refrigerated until shipment.)

There are a variety of grain mills on the market, everything from hand-cranked steel-burr models to fancy electric types with stone wheels and fine wood cabinets. We bought a mill that operates with either electricity or a hand crank. This mill is a plain-looking workhorse with no cabinet or other "design qualities." (A cabinet may look nice but it traps flour in its crevices, a breeding ground for mold.)

What we were looking for in a mill—and what we found—was the most important feature: the slowness with which the burrs or stones turn. A fast grind heats the flour up, hastening oxidation and rancidity. A slow grind takes more time, but the flour comes out cooler. Our mill turns at only 90 revolutions per minute. The flour comes out at about 100 degrees F. or cooler, just right for the introduction of baking yeast.

We had another, long-term reason for buying a grain mill. We plan to grow our own grain soon, wheat or buckwheat to start with. Not much land is needed for this. A plot only 40-by-130 feet can yield a bushel of wheat, according to Gene Logsdon's book, *Small-Scale Grain Raising.* A bushel of wheat will keep our family of four in bread and other baked goods for a year. I really look forward to the work involved in producing our own grain—the planting, scything, hand-threshing, and drying of the grains. Think how *that* bread will taste!

Here are some of Betsy's favorite bread recipes:

BETSY'S FAVORITE WHOLE WHEAT BREAD

Makes 4 to 6 loaves depending on size of loaf pan

4 cups potato water (left from cooking potatoes)
¼ cup oil
¼– ½ cup honey or molasses
4 eggs
4 scant tablespoons yeast
9– 10 cups whole wheat flour
1 teaspoon kelp

Warm the potato water to about 100° F. and add oil, honey, and eggs. Beat well. When mixture is lukewarm, add yeast and allow it to work. Then add

4 cups flour along with the kelp and beat again. Let this sit about one-half hour until yeast is bubbly again. Add about 5 cups flour, a cup or two at a time, until you can no longer stir. Dump onto a well-floured board and knead, adding small amounts of flour until mix is smooth and only very slightly sticky. Allow dough to rise, doubling in size. Punch down and allow to rise again. Form into loaves or rolls and let rise double again. Bake in a 350° F. oven for about one hour. (You'd better check the bread's progress after 30-45 minutes. All ovens are different.) This may seem like a lot of rising but it makes for a lighter, better-textured bread.

BAKING POWDER BISCUITS

Makes 1 dozen

2 cups whole wheat flour
3 teaspoons baking powder (aluminum free)
3 tablespoons oil
¼ cup honey or molasses or maple syrup
enough liquid to make a very stiff dough
2 eggs (optional)
1 teaspoon kelp (optional)

Mix all dry ingredients in a bowl. Make a well in the center. Put all other ingredients in the well and add a small amount of liquid (this can be milk, water, fruit juice, or yogurt with water). Keep adding liquid until all the flour is moist and batter is quite stiff.

Drop by spoonfuls onto a greased sheet and bake at 350° F. for about 15 minutes or until golden. Recipe doubles well.

Optional ingredients to add, alone or in combination:

raisins
oatmeal
fresh fruit, chopped
sesame seeds
sunflower seeds
nuts
anything else you can think of.

Another food we make from grain is pasta—homemade noodles and spaghetti. Pasta can be made by hand with a rolling pin and a knife, but we use a noodle machine with evenly spaced rollers and cutters. Our machine is hand cranked, not electric. Power tools, whether in the workshop or kitchen, should help us speed up essentially routine, mundane tasks, not rob us of the chance to get involved with a creative process.

But then, there's a narrow border between the creative and the monotonous. Grinding grain in small amounts can be meditative and fulfilling. But grinding more than ten pounds each week or so, as we do, becomes tedious. On the other hand, Betsy wouldn't use an electric dough hook to make bread because this would cheat her out of the pleasure of kneading the dough.

I admire those people who have the time and inclination to do *everything* by hand, making every task a sacrament or a spiritual exercise. But on a homestead where there is much to be done besides earning a living, and where there are children making demands for attention, and only two adults to handle the work, *some* power tools are a blessing. The trick is to pick those that use little energy in return for a thorough job. (Food processors and blenders are in this category; each uses about five cents' worth of electricity in a year.)

Anyway, back to the noodles. Making pasta is easy, but the payoff comes with the taste. Freshly rolled pasta dropped into boiling water, drained, and heaped on a plate is dramatically different in taste from store-bought dried noodles. And *this* taste difference is the real thing, not psychological.

We don't consider pasta a great nutritional treasure, however, certainly not the equal of bread. But the way we make it, with whole wheat flour, yields a good complex carbohydrate food and a nice dish to smother with tomato sauce, garlic, and a light topping of cheese. (Betsy adds nutritional yeast to the tomato sauce.) We enjoy making pasta because it tastes so good and because its manufacture becomes a family affair.

Here's how we do it:

WHOLE WHEAT PASTA

Makes about 1 pound of noodles

3 cups whole wheat flour
3 eggs
5 tablespoons milk (more may be necessary)
3 tablespoons oil

Form the flour into a hill and scoop out a well in the center. Crack the eggs into the well and beat with a wooden spoon. Add the milk and oil, mixing until you've made a moist ball of dough. Add enough milk to ensure that the ball can be worked with your hands. Knead thoroughly to mix all the ingredients.

Make a tube from the dough, about ten inches long. (Add more milk if the dough is too dry to form properly.) Cut the tube into sections one inch long. Dust a cutting board or countertop with flour and flatten the sections into disc shapes.

Set the noodle machine to a setting that produces a thick noodle roll. Feed the dough through four times. Flour the dough to stop it from sticking and feed it through on a medium-thick noodle setting. Separate the dough into three sections and feed through the second smallest noodle setting twice. After this, put each dough piece through the cutting blade.

We hang these long ribbons on dowel rods and let them dry. (You can also spread them out on waxed paper.) Be sure the noodles are separated so they'll dry thoroughly. This takes about 12 hours on dry days. When the pasta is completely dried it may be stored in tightly sealed plastic bags. You can also break the noodles into convenient lengths and store them in half-gallon mason jars. Homemade noodles make a wonderful gift.

The noodles needn't be dry to cook. Drop fresh ones into rapidly boiling water and cook for only two or three minutes. Smother them in a topping of your choice. This recipe, by the way, makes enough noodles to feed a family of four for several meals with the noodles as a main dish.

If you don't have a noodle machine you can still make good pasta, of course, though it will take longer. Roll the one-inch pieces of dough out until they are paper thin. Then cut them into whatever width you desire. Dry or cook them as above.

One of the most important staples we make at home is tofu—soybean curd. This is my province, a job I love as much as Betsy enjoys making bread. I first started making tofu out of necessity. Bean curd was impossible to find except in a few Asian grocery stores in the city, and even though it was locally made, the quality varied.

My guide to tofu making was (and still is) a great book published in 1975, *The Book of Tofu,* by William Shurtleff and Akiko Aoyagi. This book almost single-handedly created a tofu revolution, with tofu shops and factories springing up across the country. But even now, with tofu available in my local supermarket and food co-op, I still make tofu for the sheer pleasure of it. Besides, homemade tofu, like almost everything else homemade, tastes better than store-bought.

Tofu, as most people are learning, is a superfood. High in protein, low in calories, inexpensive, and adaptable to an infinite number of recipes—everything from the main course to dessert and snacks—this simple food has become a basic item in our family's diet.

One of Rachel's first words was "tofu." As a toddler, she'd sit and watch me in the kitchen as I went through the tofu-making steps. Then, as she saw me ladling the slippery curds into the settling box, she'd shout, "Tofu, Daddy! Tofu-me!" She couldn't eat it fast enough and still loves to eat it plain, by the handful.

Tofu making is simple, though when everyone in a family of four loves to eat it, the problem becomes how to make enough. When I first started making tofu I followed the standard recipes. These generally yielded about two pounds of tofu, which we consumed at one sitting. Yet to make that much tofu took about an hour and a half. I enjoyed the work, but it seemed like a lot of kitchen time for only one meal.

Then I began carefully studying the commercial tofu-making process, trying to adapt factory techniques to my needs. Tofu making is the same whether you make a little or a lot. Beans are soaked overnight, drained and pureed, and brought to a boil. The puree is then poured into a pressing sack of cotton or similar coarse material and the remaining pulp is pressed to expel all the soy milk. (Tofu is made by coagulating the soy milk. The leftover pulp, okara, can be used as a versatile food in itself.)

Pressing the pulp is what takes all the time. For small yields of tofu—two pounds or so—it's easy to press the pulp with the bottom of a bottle or jar, mashing the sack against the sides of a colander. But as you increase the recipe and the amount of pulp grows (and remember, it's boiling hot!) the pressing becomes tedious and less efficient.

When tofu is made on a large scale in factories, the milk is squeezed out using hydraulic presses or large screw jacks. I began fiddling around in my workshop and came up with a simple frame made of 2-by-4s. I sat the pressing sack on the frame bottom, put a cover plate of white pine over the sack, and used a small hydraulic auto jack to expel the milk. This worked fine, cutting my tofu-making time by more than 30 minutes.

Still, using a greasy auto jack in the kitchen left a lot to be desired. I knew it was only a matter of time until somebody complained that the tofu tasted funny.

Fortunately, Keith Marks, a machinist with Rodale Resources, was also working on a design for a home tofu press. Keith's idea was to come up with a small unit something like an apple-cider press. His design was simple and effective: two uprights fastened to a horizontal base and top. A threaded rod ran through the top piece, acting as a miniature screw jack. To use it, you screwed the rod down against a wood plate atop the pressing sack.

I took Keith's design and adapted it further, brazing some scrap

¾-inch conduit to two horizontal pieces of 1-by-2-by-$^{3}/_{16}$-inch steel bars. I burned a hole in the top bar, welded a nut into place, and fitted a threaded rod into the nut. Now I have an overbuilt tofu press, destined to last for centuries at least, and I'm making tofu five and more pounds at a time, enough for dinner and plenty left over.

We use tofu as a main course. Though it can be deep fried, pan fried, or baked, we prefer it broiled. We also eat it as agé pouches. These are delicious chunks of baked tofu, hollowed out and stuffed with chopped vegetables, rice, and soft tofu. (Tofu's outstanding quality is a subtle, almost bland taste that easily takes on any flavor asked for. It's the philosopher's stone of foods.)

We make tofu salad dressing, tofu mayonnaise, sandwich spreads and even desserts of whipped tofu and fruit. We also enjoy making freeze-dried tofu, using the long-keeping result in soups and sandwiches. There's no end to the wonders you can work with tofu, but the best part, for me, is the joy of making it.

Tofu making involves craft, art, and mystery. You begin with dried beans, inert pellets that only alchemy can convert to subtle tofu. When the bean puree is first cooked, the odor is strong, almost paintlike. But as the transformation ensues, the odor sweetens and pervades the kitchen. By the end of an hour the aroma rising from the steaming pot is tantalizing, much like egg drop soup.

More than the beans change. As I make tofu I find myself changing, becoming more reflective, at peace. Such feelings aren't unique to me, either. Shurtleff and Aoyagi say that many professional tofu makers seem to have the inner peace usually found in monks. Why is this so? What is it about tofu making that encourages a feeling of calm? Why don't I feel the same way when I rotate my tires, change my underwear, or make yogurt? I don't know. Making tofu is special. The manual preparation of the beans somehow involves one's hands and spirit in a unique way.

The most exciting moment comes after the beans are converted to soy milk and brought to their final stage. A precipitating agent is added to the milk—lemon juice, vinegar, a magnesium sulfate or calcium sulfate solution, or the traditional agent, nigari, a component of sea salt. Once a solidifying agent is added, a little at a time by the spoonful, a beautiful transformation takes place.

The solids of tofu begin breaking away from the whey or clear yellow liquid. The tofu maker must be careful now, adding the solidifier slowly. Too much or too little will change the character of the tofu. (Even so, the curds are forgiving. Too much or too little won't ruin the batch, only affect the yield.)

Looking down into the pot is like looking at clouds or eddies of sea water swirling in the sand or smoke twisting into a quiet summer sky. Soon the solids are floating free and thick on the pot's surface. I move the pot to the sink and begin ladling the fragile curds into a wood settling box.

From here on the process is much like cheese making. (Tofu is often erroneously called "soy cheese.") The curds are slowly transferred into the settling box, weighted down to expel the last of the whey, and left to form into a solid, off-white block.

Yet even as I go through the steps of making tofu, other possibilities reveal themselves. As the puree cooks, a skin forms on the liquid's surface much the way a membrane forms over heated milk. This film is called "yuba" by the Japanese, and it's a special food in itself. I skim the yuba off with a chopstick, sprinkle with a few drops of tamari, and eat it warm from the pot. Yuba can also be hung up to dry, formed into jelly-roll-like shapes, and used as an addition to soups and stews. I also make kunigoshi, silken tofu, not solid or in cake form like regular tofu, but smooth and custardlike.

And at the end of making tofu, there is no waste. The pulp or okara can be dried for use as a granola base or addition to bread dough. Even the whey can be used to wash off the utensils. Still warm, it makes a pleasant shampoo.

There is the answer to the question I asked a moment ago: why is making tofu so special? Because in making tofu I find keys to doors I never knew existed. The tofu process leads and follows at the same time. It yields, contracts and expands, and fills the kitchen with good cheer.

I can't think of any more important food in the self-reliant household than a sack of soybeans and the easily acquired skill of tofu making. Best of all, tofu will feed your spirit as well as your body. No food gives as much. As Shurtleff and Aoyagi say so eloquently:

> Like water that flows through the worlds, serving as it moves along, tofu joyfully surrenders itself to the endless plays of transformation . . . . Holding to simplicity, it remains in harmony with all things, and people never tire of its presence. Through understatement and nuance, it reveals its finest qualities.

TOFU STUFFED POTATOES

Serves 4

4 baked potatoes
1 cup chopped or crumbled tofu

½ cup grated cheese (your choice: cheddar, mozzarella, Parmesan)
¼ cup oil, tub margarine, or melted butter
1 tablespoon shredded onion
herbs, pepper, garlic to taste

Slice off the top few inches of the baked potatoes and scoop out the insides from both sections. Put shells to one side. Blend potato and other ingredients, adding milk if necessary to create a mash of stiff but light consistency.

Stuff the potato skins with the mixture. Place potatoes on baking pan, sprinkling with more grated cheese if you wish. Bake in a 350° F. oven until skins are well browned. Serve with chilled applesauce.

BROILED TOFU

Slice tofu into ½-inch-thick slices. (Pressed tofu makes a chewier meal, but soft tofu will broil as well.) Arrange tofu pieces on a baking pan. If using pressed tofu, pour water into pan to a ¼-inch depth. Set oven broiler to its highest setting and place pan very close to flames. Broil tofu until speckled brown. Turn pieces with a spatula and broil again.

Serve hot with brown rice and mixed vegetables or use in sandwiches and soups. Leftover broiled tofu makes a tasty chilled snack and a great addition to lunchboxes.

ALL-PURPOSE TOFU WHIP

Makes 1 cup

6–8 ounces tofu
2 tablespoons oil
2 tablespoons apple cider vinegar or lemon juice
½ teaspoon powdered kelp
herbs and dash of pepper to taste
other optional ingredients: mustard, chopped garlic, onion, parsley, celery

Blend until smooth. Use as a dip, sandwich spread, or salad dressing.

Another soy food we make regularly is tempeh, an Indonesian food—a staple in that country—still largely unknown in the United States, though its day, like tofu's, is just beginning to dawn. Tempeh is much easier to make than tofu. The process is so straightforward that, while it results in a delicious food, it's hard to rhapsodize about making tempeh as I have about making tofu. But this hardly means tempeh is any less valuable or tasty.

To make tempeh you cook cracked soybeans and inoculate them with the spores of *Rhizopus oligosporous.* (This is available from The Farm, Summertown, Tennessee 38483, and from natural foods stores.) The inoculated beans, like yogurt, are then left to incubate in a warm spot (88 to 92 degrees F. is the optimum range) for 22 to 24 hours. At the end of that time the beans are covered with a beautiful layer of brilliant white mold.

Hold the phone.

"Mold? You eat a moldy food?"

It's all a matter of perspective. If you think of tempeh as a "moldy food" the appeal certainly vanishes. But so would yogurt's charms be lost if you regarded it as "bacteria-laden sour milk." And who would eat cheese if we called it "microbe-coagulated milk"? And what about bleu cheese—a *really* moldy cheese, or mushrooms—a *fungus.* What about wine and vinegar and beer and all the other products made with the assistance of microbes?

Too many of us were subjected to those Health 101 classes that reduced the microbial world to good guys and bad guys. Remember those "educational" films? The good guys were our heroic antibodies; the bad guys—cartoon germs with scowls and fangs—were always invading our innocent teenage bodies with loathsome diseases. No wonder so many of us automatically react with fear when we hear the words "bacteria," "mold," or "germs."

Don't start off thinking of tempeh as a "moldy food." Regard it as just another healthful product—like bread or sauerkraut—produced by microbial activity.

Tempeh is a superior food. Like tofu, it's a low-calorie, high-protein food. (Tempeh contains about 157 calories per 100-gram portion; its net protein utilization of 76 percent ranks it with cottage cheese and fish.) Tempeh is also extraordinarily inexpensive considering what you get in return. Soybeans are widely available and are cheap in bulk. The tempeh culture costs only about $1, though if you'll check with *The Book of Tempeh* or *The Farm Cook Book* (revised edition) you'll learn how to extend the life of tempeh culture indefinitely. That way, all you'll ever pay for is the beans.

The only other thing you need for tempeh making is a simple incubator, anything that will maintain a temperature of 88 to 92 degrees F. for 22 hours. Even an electric frying pan set on low works, as does an electric warming tray, or a warm area near a wood stove. Both of the books mentioned above give clear directions for making an incubator out of a Styrofoam picnic cooler and a 7½-watt light bulb. (You can find similar directions for an incubator in the March, 1980 *Organic Gardening.*)

Both tempeh and tofu are usable in an infinite variety of preparations. Both tend to take on the flavor of the foods they're combined with. But unlike bland tofu, tempeh has a unique flavor. Some people have compared it to veal or fried chicken. I've been a vegetarian too long to vouch for that. But tempeh does have a crispy, chewy taste that most people find appealing.

After incubation, the *Rhizopus oligosporous* (one of the good guys) binds the beans into a firm, white cake. To use tempeh, slice the cake into smaller cakes and deep fry or pan fry. Tempeh can also be baked, broiled, dried, or cooked directly in soups.

We like to make sandwiches of pan-fried tempeh with a little homemade mayonnaise or catsup. My favorite is a slab of hot tempeh on a whole wheat bun with lettuce, tomato, and catsup—watch out McDonald's!

Both tempeh and tofu taste so good in all their various incarnations that I often feel guilty when I eat them, as though I was digging into a hot fudge sundae. But both foods are delights you can enjoy daily. Their nutritional contributions are all good, important to normal health, and inexpensive.

DAGWOOD BUMSTEAD'S TEMPEH SANDWICH

2–3 slices whole grain bread
3 or 4 squares tempeh (amount and size depend on your appetite)
lettuce, thin slices of tomato, onion, and cucumber
mayonnaise or tofu whip
anything else you like on a sandwich

Pan fry tempeh until light brown on both sides. Slather bread with mayonnaise or tofu spread. Lay on the fixings, alternating with hot tempeh slices. Put on a bib and enjoy!

TOMATO-TEMPEH SOUP

Makes 4 cups

1 onion, chopped
1 tablespoon oil

1 tomato, chopped
2 cups milk (cow, goat, or soy)
6–8 ounces tempeh, chopped
herbs (marjoram, oregano, etc.) or pepper to taste
2 tablespoons chopped parsley

Sauté onions until they become clear. Add tomato and sauté for several minutes. Add milk, tempeh, and seasoning and bring to a boil. Cover pot and cook 20–30 minutes. Remove pot from stove and let soup cool. Blend until smooth. Serve immediately, chilled or rewarmed. Top with parsley.

CREAMED TEMPEH ON TOAST

4 cups tempeh slices, 2 inches long by ½ inch wide
1½ cups water
4–5 tablespoons oil
5 tablespoons tub margarine or butter
5 tablespoons whole wheat flour
2½ cups milk (dairy or soy)
herbs, pepper to taste

Arrange tempeh slices in frying pan. Add water. Cover and steam until water boils off. Add oil and fry over medium heat until golden brown.

To make white sauce: Melt margarine or butter. Work flour in with a whisk to make a smooth paste. Add milk and seasonings. Cook for 3–5 minutes at a low boil.

Add tempeh slices to white sauce and serve over whole wheat toast or brown rice.

Sprouting seeds for food is a lot like working with soy foods. In both cases you begin with inexpensive seeds that go through a simple process and result in a vastly improved end product. Sprouts also have the distinction of being one of the few foods to actually double or triple in bulk, while dramatically increasing in nutritional value.

The vitamin C content of soybeans, for example, increases by more than 500 percent by the third day of sprouting. Sprouted seeds also show increased levels of B vitamins and vitamin E, with a correspondingly high protein value. Considerable research has been done on sprouts over the years and no one has come up with anything but good news about this simple food.

We've tried all kinds of sprouting techniques including plastic trays, clay dishes, and "wonder sprouters," arcane gizmos that are supposed to make sprouting easier than it already is. We've settled on plain old mason jars as the best bet. Whole books have been written about sprouting, but the process couldn't be more fundamental: put the seeds in a jar of water, soak overnight, and drain in the morning (use the soak water to feed your house plants).

Leave the seeds in the jar and rinse thoroughly at least three times daily. Germination produces heat and waste matter that must be washed away to avoid mold formation. You can't over rinse.

Eat the fresh sprouts when the sprouted part is as long as the seed. This, for most seeds, is when the nutritional value is at its peak, though you can continue eating the sprouts when they've grown longer if you enjoy a slightly changed flavor. We often let our sprouts grow quite long, putting them on a sunny windowsill to develop green leaves and chlorophyll.

Our favorite sprouts are alfalfa, lentils, and chickpeas. Soybeans are harder to sprout than most seeds and the raw beans, we've found, taste best when mixed with stir-fried vegetables. We've also enjoyed sprouted radish, buckwheat, fenugreek, sunflowers, and corn seeds. Just make sure the seeds you buy are intended for human consumption. Many seeds destined for planting have been treated with fungicides.

We've also had success sprouting seeds in dirt, using shallow trays. Aluminum baking trays about 18-by-26 inches by 1 inch deep work well, though almost any flat container will suffice. We put a layer of peat moss on the tray bottom to absorb moisture, then cover it with a layer of good potting soil or sifted, weed-free garden soil.

Soak seeds overnight. Wet the soil and sprinkle the seeds across the surface. Don't let the seeds clump into piles. Then cover them with eight to ten sheets of newspaper (black and white print only; the colored inks contain heavy metals) and cover again with plastic sheeting to hold the moisture. After about three days you should notice the sprouts lifting the newspaper. Remove the coverings and place the trays either in direct or indirect sunlight.

Water these sprouts occasionally, keeping the thin layer of soil moist but not waterlogged. Wheatgrass will take about seven days to grow 6 to 12 inches high. Harvest with a pair of scissors and use the grass in salads and soups. Wheatgrass is a chewy, juicy green. You should get about two harvests from one planting.

Trying sprouting sunflower seeds this way. Buy them unhusked and soak them overnight. Sunflower sprouts are thick and succulent and make delicious additions to sandwiches. Harvest with scissors. Only one harvest is possible.

Sprouting gives us fresh salads all winter. We like to dig some carrots out of the garden (they keep well under a heavy mulch), shred them, and mix with sprouts and some tofu salad dressing. We also use sprouts to complement main dishes, for snacks, and in soups and stews. The children love eating sprouts by the handful and it's a pleasure to watch them enjoying something so good for them.

Sprouts are a real inflation-fighting food, though they'd taste good no matter the state of the economy. Seeds can be purchased in bulk and stored for a long time in a cool, dry place. Sprouts yield nothing but first-class fresh food. No high calories, no excessive fat, no bones, and no plastic wrappers to worry about.

Handling the daily output of milk our goats produce is a lot more difficult than sprouting seeds, of course, especially because no one in our family *drinks* milk. We convert all our milk into yogurt, kefir, or cheese. Yogurt is a growth industry in the United States and has been since the late 1960's. Unfortunately, most people eat yogurt as a snack food laced with sugar, corn syrup, thickeners, stabilizers, and preserves. Other people think of yogurt as a "diet food," though a pint of flavored yogurt has about 250 calories, as much as a slice of apple pie.

Homemade yogurt is a wholesome food, however, with no more or less calories than the milk it's made from. All kinds of claims have been made for yogurt over the centuries—that it will cure disease or prolong life—and some of these claims have been scientifically studied in recent years. It now appears, in fact, that yogurt and other fermented milks like kefir do have some special qualities.

One researcher found that subjects eating large amounts of whole-milk yogurt actually showed a decrease in serum cholesterol levels rather than the rise that might have been expected. Another scientist has suggested that, based on his studies with rats, yogurt may contain an X-factor that is a positive growth stimulant. And there is evidence that the variety of bacteria found in fermented milk cultures (much like the flora found naturally in the human gut) have antipathogenic properties that may possibly strengthen one's disease resistance.

We've had some first hand experience with this. An acquaintance who suffered from a mouthful of painful canker sores cured himself with nothing more than regular ingestion of the active bacterias, *L. Bulgaricus* and *L. Acidophilus,* found in fermented milk. He bought these active cultures in freeze-dried form at a drugstore, mixed the powder with yogurt, and ate a cupful several times a day. The sores cleared up within three days.

This isn't a folk remedy, by the way. The same freeze-dried bacteria are regularly prescribed by physicians as an antidiarrheal. These microbes implant themselves in the gut (*L. Acidophilus* does, though *L. Bulgaricus* may not survive long after ingestion) and somehow neutralize the bacteria responsible for the upset. The same bacteria are used to help people who've been on antibiotics. Eating yogurt and kefir has been shown to aid in the reestablishment of intestinal flora killed off by the antibiotics.

Whether the current research will prove fermented milk to be a genuine "miracle food," I don't know. Even if none of the claims were true—and some obviously are—fermented milk would still be a good food because of the ease with which it is digested (even those allergic to milk can eat yogurt or kefir) and its refreshing flavor.

Making yogurt is easy. To make the first or "starter" quart we first pasteurize the milk, heating it to 160 degrees F. Milk must be pasteurized before culturing to destroy certain naturally occurring enzymes that would overpower the yogurt cultures. We cool the milk to 105 to 110 degrees F. and add a packet of freeze-dried yogurt culture (available at most natural foods shops).

Many people make yogurt by merely adding a couple of spoonfuls of store-bought yogurt. Starting with a pure freeze-dried culture makes the yogurt more consistent and better tasting.

The first, or starter quart, is held at 105 to 110 degrees F. for six to ten hours, until it's obviously thickened. The next day we pasteurize a gallon or more of milk and use the first quart as a starter. All batches of yogurt after the starter quart take only about two hours to thicken.

Holding the milk at 105 to 110 degrees F. isn't difficult. (Some recipes tell you to hold the milk at 115 to 118 degrees F., but better-flavored yogurt results from the lower range. Besides, yogurt bacteria are killed off at 120 degrees F.) Our friend, Annie Kelley, who has six milking cows, simply wraps her milk-filled jars in an old fleece and lets them sit overnight in a bucket. So much for those fancy plastic deluxe yogurt makers you see for sale.

We culture our yogurt in winter by putting the jars in a pot of 110 degree F. water and nestling it next to the wood stove. In summer, we use the oven set on its lowest heat.

The original culture lasts about 30 days. After that, it gets invaded by various bacilli that cause changes in flavor and consistency. We don't use the calendar as a guide for changing yogurt culture, however, but rely on our taste buds. We begin with a new culture whenever the yogurt looks different—runny or thin—or when the taste becomes unpleasant.

Some people claim to be using yogurt cultures that are years or decades old. I'm dubious. Bacterial cultures, like any community, constantly change in composition. The specific cultures that result in yogurt, for instance, are particularly sensitive to variations in pH. As yogurt ages, it becomes more acidic, causing some bacilli—notably *L. Acidophilus*—to die. Other bacilli may respond favorably to the decreased pH level. That's why yogurt changes in taste and texture as time passes.

Those stories of 100-year-old yogurt cultures handed down through the family remind me of the fellow who owned an ancient axe. "Been in my family 125 years and it's still sharp and true. 'Course now, we've had to replace the handle and the axe head from time to time, but. . . ."

Kefir is similar to yogurt though not as well known. We make both types of fermented milk because the children prefer yogurt, while Betsy and I like kefir. Unlike yogurt, kefir is a semiliquid. Its flavor is tarter than yogurt's and it has a pronounced fizziness. The lid gives a healthy "pop!" when we uncap the jar. This is because the microbes that make kefir produce some carbon dioxide during fermentation. Kefir, which originated in Central Asia, has been called "the champagne of milks" (probably by a Mongol PR man).

Kefir is the easiest product to make. The freeze-dried culture is added directly to unpasteurized or pasteurized warm (75 to 100 degrees F.) milk and left to culture at room temperature. Kefir will even culture in the refrigerator, though it may take a week.

If using unpasteurized or "raw" milk worries you, consider this: the microbes in fermented milk have been shown to exert definite antipathogenic qualities. This has been of enormous importance to people around the world who use fermented milk. (And every society that has used milk has used it largely as fermented milk. Only when refrigeration appeared did drinking milk become popular—though it was the dairy industry and advertising more than refrigeration that contributed to this in our country.) Studies have shown that a wide variety of pathogenic bacteria cannot survive in fermented milk. The acidic nature of the milk discourages their growth, while certain lactobacilli actually act as bacteriocides and bacteriostats, respectively killing or retarding bacterial growth. This doesn't mean that fermented milks cannot go bad, but they announce their deviation by an obvious aroma, color changes, and textural variations. The appearance of mold is more common than any other sign of spoilage.

Succeeding batches of kefir are made the same way as yogurt, by seeding milk with several tablespoons of previously made kefir. We use both fermented milks the same way: for breakfast with whole grain cereals and fruit; in baking or cooking where plain milk would be used; as a snack or light meal; and—in the case of kefir—as a refreshing, tart drink.

I said yogurt and kefir were staples in our diet, but we don't consume either with abandon. Our milk, straight from the goats, is whole milk. And since neither Betsy nor I like to eat much fat or consume excess calories, we limit our use of dairy products in any form. As vegetarians, we eat little fat from other sources, so our daily portion of whole milk hardly boosts our overall consumption of fat.

KEFIR FRUIT DRINK

Serves 2

1 cup kefir (or plain yogurt)
1 cup fruit juice (orange, pineapple, apple, etc.)
1 or 2 bananas
¼ teaspoon nutmeg or cinnamon
honey to taste
ice cubes

Blend all ingredients at medium to high speed, adding the ice cubes slowly until the beverage is smooth. Add more ice if you prefer a thinner consistency.

YOGURT SALAD DRESSING

Makes 1 cup

1 cup plain yogurt
2 cloves garlic, chopped or crushed
1 tablespoon chopped chives
2–3 tablespoons fresh, chopped parsley
1–2 teaspoons apple cider vinegar or lemon juice
powdered kelp, herbs, or pepper to taste

Blend at high speed until creamy smooth.

YOGURT CHEESE

Equipment:

large square (2-foot-by-2-foot) cheesecloth or coarse towel
colander
large pot
1 gallon yogurt (low-fat or regular)

Line colander with cloth and, if you wish to save the whey, place in large pot. Pour yogurt into cloth, gather up corners, and hang sack over pot.

The recaptured whey is a nutritious liquid that can be used in soup stocks and bread dough.

Let the sack hang several hours or overnight until solids form a cream cheese. Chill and use as a sandwich or cracker spread.

(Note: Yogurt cheese made with whole milk is a *very* high-fat food. Use sparingly or choose low-fat yogurt. A nondairy "cheese" can also be made in a similar fashion with soy milk.)

A few years ago I was doing a lot of research on fermented foods, their production and health benefits. Because I try to do both objective and subjective research, I get thoroughly involved in whatever it is I'm investigating. My enthusiasm usually affects the whole family.

At one point during this research, I was making a study of beer, particularly home brew, and its nutritional value, if any. For several days Betsy and I had a lot of conversations about beer. I brought home various types of imported beers and she and I sampled one or two each evening and discussed the taste and merits of each. Very scientific, of course.

One night, just before dinner, Betsy asked Noah if there was anything he'd like to eat in particular.

"Bread and butter."

"You can't have just bread and butter for dinner."

"Why not?"

"Because that's not a meal. How about some nice soup?"

"Naw."

"How about noodles, broccoli, and . . ."

"Naw."

"Well," Betsy said, her exasperation rising, "what *do* you want?"

"Aww," Noah said, his exasperation matching hers, "just gimme some eggs and a glass of beer."

Noah got the eggs, anyway. I continued my research on fermented foods, and eventually got involved in one of our more exciting kitchen adventures: wine making.

Betsy and I aren't big drinkers, except of fruit juice. Hard liquor has never had any appeal for us, and more than a glass of wine or beer makes us sleepy. We don't drink beer, with any regularity anyway, unless it's a hearty home brew. Most domestic beers taste like they've been brewed by accountants searching for the common denominator. But wine is something else.

Wine has been part of human culture for 10,000 years, a fact not lost on us, as concerned about tradition as we are. Wine has some mystery to it, some class, and a little romance. Unfortunately, my palate is more finely attuned and worldly than my checkbook. I find it difficult to afford good wine and impossible to buy fine wine. So for a long time I drank cheap wine.

Betsy and I started making jokes about keeping the paper bag wrapped around the bottle or drinking the wine while lying down in the doorway to get the full effect.

"What vintage is that wine?"

"Let's see, what time is it now?"

Then we met John and Lee Paul, homesteaders and managers of a small Maryland winery. John persuaded me to have a try at home wine making, sold me a few bushels of grapes he'd grown himself, and gave me detailed instructions. That, plus some books and some basic equipment, got me started.

Making wine is easy. Making *good* wine is difficult at best, but the essential steps in wine making are simple and can involve the whole family. And what fun! Crushing the grapes is the first step, and this is where everybody literally jumps in with both feet. I suppose I could have crushed the grapes with a 2-by-4 in a tub as several books suggested, but I hated to let a chance pass to have us share in an ancient tradition.

I called Noah and Rachel into the house. This was October, a beautifully crisp day, and they had been out playing in the fallen leaves. They were delighted when I told them I needed their help to make the wine. I don't think they really understood all that I said about tradition and the past and how we were going to do something people had been doing for thousands of years. They just knew it sounded like crazy fun.

"Are you joking, Daddy?" Noah asked.

"No," I said. "This is the traditional way of crushing the grapes. You trample them with your feet. Do you want to help do it?" (Come to think of it, it did sound a little nutty.)

"Yes! Yes!" they squealed, clapping their hands and leaping up and down.

I would have preferred to celebrate our wine festival outdoors, but the day was already waning and turning cooler. Grapes don't sit well for long—their weight while piled causes them to break down and begin fermenting on the spot. We pulled the grapes and a ten-gallon crock into the house and began our first vintage.

"It's *cold!*" Noah screamed as he climbed into the crock.

"Me next! Me next!" yelled Rachel, tossing her shoes and socks in all directions.

The children and I took turns. And the grapes *were* cold! They had been sitting on the porch overnight and had been chilled thoroughly. What a slippery mess! Just the thing to delight a child, squishing around in a tub of grapes. Betsy looked in and laughed at our trousers rolled up to our knees, our feet and ankles purple with grape juice, and Noah and Rachel pink with laughter, giggling and sliding in the pulp.

The rest of the wine-making process was more mundane. I took a sample of juice and tested its sugar content with a hydrometer. It was okay; otherwise I would have added sugar to boost the level or water to lower it. Then, using an inexpensive acid titration kit, I checked the "must" (crushed grapes and juice) for acidity. This was also within the correct range. If it wasn't I would have added an acid blend (tartaric, citric, and malic acids) to raise the acidity or water to lower it.

I added the yeast next, a special wine yeast, not bakers' yeast. Some people make wine using a cake or package of yeast from the supermarket, but a purified wine yeast produces the best results.

I covered the crock with a large sheet of plastic, tying it in place tightly enough to keep the air out, but not so tight as to stop the carbon dioxide produced from escaping. The must then went through its first fermentation, a period of about five days.

The must bubbles vigorously during this time as the yeast cells multiply, feeding on the sugar and producing carbon dioxide and alcohol. Noah and Rachel took an active interest in this process, checking the crock with me every day as I stirred the must to distribute the yeast and break the "cap," or thick layer of grape skins. The children had countless questions about the bubbling and the yeast cells ("I can't see anything, Daddy") and I answered their queries with child-sized microbiology lessons.

By this time the whole house reeked with a rich, yeasty aroma. We were picking apples then, and making cider and hauling in the last of the tender vegetables from the garden. All the odors and activities blended and the house seemed wonderfully alive and active, bubbling with creativity and potential, like the wine crock.

When the first fermentation was finished I racked (siphoned) the juice off into a five-gallon carboy, fitted it with a fermentation lock (which lets carbon dioxide escape but allows no air in) and left it to go through the second fermentation, about ten days.

The wine is racked again after that, leaving a heavy deposit of dead yeast cells and sediment in the jug bottom. This time the carboy sits in a cool, dark place for about two months. Then comes a third racking and storage for six months or more. This racking is a thrill because you can't help getting a mouthful of the liquid as you work the siphon. And damned if it doesn't taste like wine! This doesn't mean that the whole batch won't change to vinegar before you're through, nor can you really enjoy the taste of this green (young) fermentation, but it *is* wine. Miraculous.

The wine is ready for bottling any time after six months. There's no rush. Red wine improves with age, up to a point, so except for a taste, we didn't drink the red until it was almost two years old. We let most of it get even older than that. John Paul, my wine tutor, bet me I couldn't wait that long, that like most first-time wine makers I'd get impatient and guzzle my premier vintage no matter how green it was. But fortunately we made five gallons of white wine shortly after making the red. White can be consumed (and should be) while young, only a year old, so we could afford to forget about the red aging slowly in the crawl space.

John was right about one thing, however; it *is* hard to wait out the year while the wine goes through its mysterious metamorphosis. But the day finally arrived when I could uncork a bottle of white. Was it wine, I wondered, or had the bad guys triumphed, turning my efforts into vinegar? I didn't need any more salad dressing.

"Hey!" said Noah, "that's the wine we helped make!" His comment struck me. A year had passed. Not much time to an adult but a lifetime to children only six and three. The wonder was that both of them clearly remembered the fun we'd had as though it was yesterday. Rachel started giggling all over again about her purple feet and how cold the grapes were. I joked with Noah about the wine smelling like his feet, just the sort of gross humor every six-year-old loves to roll around on the floor over.

We tasted the wine. Rachel and Noah each had a sip and made the appropriate nose-wrinklings. "This is *good,*" Betsy said, half in surprise.

"Well," I said, in my most oenological manner, "it's rather assertive, even a trifle presumptuous for its age, but I find the boldness . . ."

Betsy threw a cork at me.

The foods I've described make up only part of our diet. I hate calling what we eat a "diet," by the way. It sounds so medicinal and regimented. Just because we avoid eating fabricated foods doesn't mean our food choices are bland or monotonous. If they were, we would have made some changes over the past ten years. Neither Betsy nor I are interested in doing nutritional penance. We enjoy good food and that's what our family eats. Of course, we do get a bit reckless now and then, maybe once a month, and actually eat an ice-cream cone or some cheap doughnuts. (Boy, what a *fun* couple!)

What people forget is that most of the world does without fabricated or high-fat foods. Most people don't even eat the large amount of flesh foods consumed in the United States. Vegetarian recipes and food combinations, therefore, should be imaginative and diverse, reflecting the enormous range of options open to us. Unfortunately, many people still think of vegetarian fare as limited. It isn't. When people ask, "What *do* you eat?" I answer, "*everything* but meat, fowl, and fish."

That's a whole lot of food to choose from. For more on the nutritional and health aspects of vegetarianism see my previous book, *The Vegetarian Alternative*. But now, here are some of our favorite recipes:

VEGETABLE QUICHE

Pastry for one 9-inch crust:
2/3 cup butter
1 cup whole wheat flour
¼ cup water, approximately

Work butter into flour until it's the texture of cornmeal. Add water and mix until dough holds together. Roll out on a floured board. Put in a pie plate and prick with a fork.

Filling:
½ cup grated cheddar cheese
½ cup grated Parmesan cheese
2 eggs
1½ cups milk or yogurt
1 teaspoon sweet basil
¼ teaspoon pepper
1 large potato
1 cup peas, approximately
1 onion, chopped
1 cup corn, approximately
1 cup whole wheat bread crumbs (optional)

Mix the cheeses together and set aside. Beat the eggs, milk, basil, and pepper together and set aside. Put a layer of thinly sliced potato on the bottom of the pie shell. Sprinkle lightly with cheese. Next put a layer of peas in and again sprinkle with cheese. Add enough of the egg mixture to just cover peas. Next do a layer of onions, then cheese, then corn. Now add the rest of egg mix or enough to fill crust. Top with bread crumbs and remaining cheese. (Any combination of vegetables can be used as filling.)

Bake at 350° F. for one hour or until a knife comes out clean. I usually put a cookie sheet under the pie plate to catch drips. Let cool 10–15 minutes before cutting, or serve cold.

LIMA BEAN CASSEROLE

Serves 4-6

2 large tomatoes, sliced, or 1 quart canned tomatoes
2 cups cooked lima beans
1 large onion, chopped and sautéed
1 clove garlic, minced
basil
pepper
1 cup grated cheese

Line the bottom of a casserole with half of the sliced tomatoes. Combine the beans, onion, garlic, seasonings, and ¾ cup cheese. Pour over the tomatoes. Add a layer of tomatoes on top and sprinkle with the remaining cheese. (You could use bread crumbs or bran with the cheese.) Bake at 350° F. for 20–30 minutes or until golden and bubbly. Serve hot with noodles or rice.

BLINTZES

Batter:
3 eggs
1 cup milk (or just enough more to achieve consistency thinner than pancake batter)
¾ cup whole wheat flour
2 tablespoons oil

Beat everything together by hand or in a blender. Use enough butter (you can use oil if you prefer but I've found butter works best) to lightly coat a frying pan. (An iron omelet pan is great but any frying pan will work. It's a little harder to get the blintz out of a regular pan but with a few mistakes you'll learn.)

When the pan is hot, pour about ¼ cup batter onto the center. Then turn the pan until the batter coats the bottom of the pan. (Again, adjust to suit you and your pan.) Cook until the batter is no longer liquid. Then slip the blintz onto a plate. Continue stacking them up until you've used all the batter.

Filling #1

2 cups cottage cheese
2 eggs
honey to taste
½ teaspoon cinnamon
1 cup raisins
1 cup chopped nuts

Mix all ingredients together. Place a tablespoonful in the center of a blintz and fold first top and bottom over, then the sides. Fry these in a little butter until they are golden, or place on greased pan and cover. Bake in 350° F. oven about 20 minutes.

Filling #2

½ cup milk
2 eggs
2 cups mashed potatoes
1 large onion, chopped and sautéed
optional: chopped cooked spinach or broccoli, or whatever you may have

Mix everything together and proceed as in filling #1. Serve both fillings with either applesauce or yogurt.

How does our vegetarian diet fit in with the idea of self-sufficiency? The classic picture of the homestead includes a chicken house, pigpen, beef cattle, and perhaps a rabbit hutch. True self-sufficiency is supposed to mean raising your own meat. We don't eat animals, though we use milk and eggs, so how can we aspire to self-reliance?

I think the idea of raising your own meat as a necessary link to self-sufficiency has been overdone. If you raise animals you have to feed them. And if you have to *buy* the grain or hay to do this you're obviously not self-sufficient. If you raise your own grain and breed and slaughter your own animals you're a step closer to the ideal of total independence, but there are still some unanswered questions: Knowing what we do today, that a nonflesh diet is an inexpensive, healthful, and preventive diet (a low-fat, high-fiber diet appears to work against the development of cardiovascular disease and certain diet-related cancers), does it make sense to feed grain to animals in order to fatten them so you can eat them in return?

Consider also the feed-to-meat conversion ratios for any animals you might raise: you have to feed a steer 16 pounds of grain and soy; a hog 6 pounds; turkeys 4 pounds; and chickens 3 pounds to get back 1 pound of edible meat. Milk production is far more efficient, needing only 1 pound of grain for each pint of milk returned. (Of course, you don't get milk from cows or goats endlessly. Females have to be bred annually and their offspring have to be fed and disposed of, either a good or bad thing depending on your orientation.)

Whether you buy grain or raise it yourself, doesn't it make the most sense to use the grain as efficiently as possible? Putting 16 pounds of grain into a steer and getting back 1 pound of meat is a poor bargain, what Frances Moore Lappé calls "a protein factory in reverse." Look at it this way: it takes an acre of land to support a single steer. When the steer is slaughtered the carcass will supply a human male with a little more than an eight-month supply of dietary protein. But the same acre used to grow soybeans will yield enough protein for one person for *six years!*

The evidence is now clear that humans don't need to eat meat, given wholesome and nourishing alternatives. Perhaps the old notion of the self-sufficient homestead relying on animal protein needs some adjustment. And there's another factor to be considered: the unpleasantness of slaughter.

Open any book on homesteading or animal husbandry, and you'll find identical observations on the act of killing another creature. Everyone agrees that "it's unpleasant, but you'll get used to it." The gory mess and the guilt about killing an innocent creature are glossed over by presenting slaughter as a repulsive but necessary task, a "them-or-us" proposition.

This is nonsense. If you don't like killing animals, you don't have to do it. Nor do you have to cop out by having someone else do it for you. You can, if you choose, become a truly self-reliant homesteader like Helen and Scott Nearing. The grandparents of the current back-to-the-land movement in America, the Nearings have supported themselves for 50 years on a vegetarian diet, without livestock, and even without using animal manure in their extensive gardening operation. But even as lacto-ovo vegetarians, as we are, you still sharply reduce your dependence on animals and the systems needed to support them.

Animal husbandry, as I've pointed out, involves a prodigious amount of labor, time, expense and responsibility, not to mention its moral burden. On this basis, then, the vegetarian homesteader or urbanite does have a simpler life.

I realize I'm offering a heretical picture. Instead of a farm with hams hanging in the smokehouse, roast beef in the oven, and headless chickens flapping wildly outside the kitchen door, I'm suggesting wheatgrass salads, tofu burgers, and tempeh pizza. Hardly the stuff of Norman Rockwell paintings.

But while the argument over which is best, the traditional or vegetarian homestead, will go on endlessly, each of us intent on simplifying our lives must ultimately face the issues involved and make a decision.

It was a cold, bright day in January and the goats were dozing in their yard. The temperature was only in the 20's but the winter sunshine was intense and wonderfully warming. The goats were sprawled out, their faces turned toward the sky, moaning in pleasure. I knelt down to stroke an ear, felt the sun on my neck, then sat down, my back against a stump. "I'll just sit here for a moment," I explained to the goats. Then I closed my eyes and turned my face up to the sun. And I fell asleep.

A wood stove has the same effect. Flames unlock the woody cells, releasing decades' worth of photosynthetic energy, stored sunshine, with its deeply comforting natural radiance.

But never sit near the stove with ambitious plans, a briefcase full of work, or a book that absolutely must be read. Never ease into a comfortable chair within the stove's zone of comfort, thinking, "just for a moment." Not if you have important things to do.

The stove is a siren, its hissing and crackling a song that unravels knotted ganglia, melts contracted muscles, and postpones all dreams of conquest. Your blood turns to old wine, thoroughly mulled, your bones to hand-rubbed teak. Your consciousness slips into a delicious ooze.

You awake refreshed and mellow, your tensions consumed in the belly of the stove. This is what winter is for, I think, especially for the homesteader and gardener who wrestles with earth's coquettish timing and moods through summer and spring. Winter, croons the wood stove, is a time to let go, to reflect, to renew by dormancy.

But these effects seem limited to adults and cats. The cats come close to hibernation once the stove is burning steadily. They sleep under it until their fur becomes hot to the touch and we fear they might burst into flames. Often they'll stretch out on the floor beside the stove, occasionally lying full length on their backs, hind legs limp with pleasure, mouths slightly open, eyes glazed.

The children stay as lively as ever, their exuberance having no off-season. They run on like waterfalls, leaping and dancing all day until their headwaters run low. Then we pour them into their beds, where a single night is enough to refill their reservoirs of enthusiasm.

Yet the stove does have an effect on the children, subtle as it is. A wood stove, unless it's quartered in the basement like a furnace, acts as a magnet. Like the sun, the stove becomes the center of our family's universe in winter. After dinner we're often like a scene from *The Little House on the Prairie* books. Noah lies on his stomach near the stove, reading a book or drawing pictures. Betsy and Rachel sit on the couch, snuggled tightly together, Rachel looking scrubbed and pink after a bath. They're reading a last book before Rachel's bedtime. And I'm in an easy chair dozing off, an open book on my lap.

The oil truck came lumbering up our driveway, inching slowly in reverse, the warning signal in the wheels ding-dinging its arrival. A January wind was ripping through the trees from the west-northwest and the driver had to lean into it, squinting and hunching over as he climbed down from the cab. He walked to the back of his truck and began unhitching the thick black hose. He was just pulling it off the reel when Betsy came out.

"Hi," she said brightly.

" 'Lo," he mumbled, looking up briefly, then back down at the hose again, yanking it toward the oil tank.

"Ahh," Betsy said, feeling strangely embarrassed at what she was about to say, hugging herself, her hands in her armpits, shivering in the cold. "We don't need any oil today."

"Whuh?" he said. His job wasn't made easier by helpful homeowners. Just lemme alone and let me do my job, his face said.

"We don't need any oil today," Betsy repeated, smiling as much from the cut of the wind as from her message. "Or any day. We called the company. I guess the dispatcher didn't get the message."

"You goin' with another awl company?"

"No. We put in a wood stove. We don't use the oil burner anymore."

"Huh," he said. "Well." He lowered the nozzle and dropped his shoulders a bit. "How 'bout that," he said, erasing the trace of a smile as he wiped his nose on the back of his glove. "Guess I won't be coming here no more, huh?"

"Guess not," said Betsy. He moved past her and began reeling the hose back up. Then he turned and smiled broadly. "Y'all really warm in there? This Jan-yoo-airy weather can tear you up."

"We're warm. Toasty."

"Yeah." He looked at the horizon. "I grew up with a wood stove, y'know. Nothin' like it for heat. Beats the heck outta buying awl, don't it?" he grinned.

"Yes," Betsy said, now dancing a little, shivering in the wind. And then, because she couldn't think of anything else to say, "Thanks for delivering oil all these years."

"Yeah," he said, looking at his shoes. "You burnin' oak?"

"Mostly," Betsy said, her teeth chattering.

"Yeah. Don't burn no pine nor poplar. Punky wood. Burn oak and maple if you can get it. Thass best, y'know?"

"We're learning," Betsy said.

"Well," he said, glowing in the warmth of his remembered stove, "well, good luck and take care o' yourselves, hear?"

"We will. You too."

He got back into the truck and eased it down the driveway, touching the brake slightly so he could take a look as he passed our woodpile. Then he turned right out of the drive and we heard him shifting gears all the way around the bend.

We've heated with wood for ten years now. I can't imagine heating our home any other way unless it would be with passive solar heat. Even then I'd like wood heat as a backup. No other method of heating is so comfortable and satisfying to body and soul.

"The radiant heat streaming from the surface of a hot wood stove," explains writer John Cole, "pushes right through clothing and skin. It warms the inner person. That's why, when you are chilled through, nothing—not anything—will make you feel better or warm you faster than a working wood stove."

I put the emphasis on wood because not just any fire speaks to us in the same way. Coal, charcoal, and newspaper logs don't really entrance us in the same way that a November bonfire or a campfire on the beach does. Nothing replaces the feel and sight of logs dancing with flames. We know, having lived with the imitations.

Our rented city house had a fireplace fitted with a gas log, which is no log at all. It's a ceramic or metal fake with molded "bark" and tiny gas jets spaced around the sides and edges. Twist a valve, strike a match, and poof! Instant eternal blazing log. Sort of.

We tried to get into the spirit with our ersatz blaze but we couldn't keep up the charade. We pulled easy chairs up to the hearth, turned the lights down, sipped mulled cider (warmed on the kitchen stove), and dutifully stared into the flames. Gas flames. Blue with a little yellow. Monotonous, mechanically flickering, lacking embers and character and charm. A gas log is the incendiary equivalent of Muzak.

When we found the Potomac house and saw it had a Franklin stove in the pine-paneled upstairs room, we were delighted. Its presence blinded us to all the defects we should have seen in the house. Had the real estate agent recognized our weakened condition, and known about our reverie of glowing coals and moonlit, snowy evenings, she could have sold us the Statue of Liberty along with the house.

We turned the upstairs into a large living room with a couch and easy chairs arranged around the stove. And because our bedroom, a 8-by-10-foot cubicle, opened onto this room, we had the luxury of falling asleep while watching the dappled firelight on the walls. The house was poorly insulated and drafty then, so we needed no coaxing to spend our indoor time upstairs near the stove. And though we hadn't planned on it, we started heating with wood that first winter.

There was no energy shortage or wild inflation in 1969, and fuel oil sold for less than 50 cents a gallon. But it seemed silly and wasteful to have the oil burner heating the whole house when we preferred staying upstairs. We kept the thermostat at 55 degrees F. and carried logs upstairs.

Come to think of it, we carried a *lot* of logs upstairs. The Franklin isn't a terribly efficient stove, though it's better than most fireplaces. As long as we kept a blaze going constantly, however, our Franklin produced plenty of heat. When the fire waned or went out, as it did each morning, the room got cold fast. But I don't recall either of us complaining, though we did have a constant battle of wits to see who would get out of bed first in the morning to light the fire. If, when we lived in the city, a landlord had denied us heat we would have been outraged. Yet here we were shivering out of a warm bed, seeing our breath come out in puffs of steam, as we padded along an icy floor, happily attending to the ritual of the hearth.

When Noah was born we set his crib up in an alcove just outside our bedroom. A south-facing window let in warm winter sunlight. And the stove was nearby.

Betsy nursed him while rocking near the flames, resting her feet on the brick platform that supported the stove. Noah's first bath was set up in front of the hearth. When he was able to sit up he enjoyed watching the changing pattern of the flames, occasionally pointing a finger and babbling in discovery.

Overly helpful friends and relatives worried out loud that this tender infant was living without much central heating or, in their view, much heating of any kind. They warned of pneumonia and frostbite unless we came to our senses and kept the house at a respectable 72 degrees F. Noah himself was the best rebuttal. Ruddy-cheeked and cheerful, he stayed free of colds and sniffles.

But as little as we used the oil burner, it was still a constant drain on our resources. Hidden beneath the house like a dragon in its lair, the stolid machinery served us less than we it.

Is it sick to hate a machine? Every time the squirrel-cage fan roared to life and blew hot kerosene-tainted air through the house, I seethed. Every time the oil burner quit or faltered, I gnashed my teeth. And I paid for the privilege.

We were on what the oil company laughingly calls a budget plan. To satisfy our monster's oily appetite we paid $40 a month for ten months each year. This basic fee entitled us to regular oil deliveries and certain repairs specifically—*very* specifically—outlined in the service contract: "Fan, motor, and nozzle will be repaired at no charge provided said mechanical abnormalities occur on the second Tuesday of months ending in 'R' or during the passage of Halley's comet, whichever comes first. Otherwise customer will assume all charges for parts, labor, acts of God, and the orthodontic work of the serviceman's minor children."

The day of the $40-a-month budget plan is long gone, of course, gone the way of $2-a-barrel oil and 10¢ phone calls. But back in the innocent days of the mid-1970's, we were, by strict conservation, several sweaters, and the Franklin stove, able to keep our heating costs down to about $500 per year.

Yet the one thing we couldn't control or conserve was the mechanical health of the oil burner. These infernal devices operate according to arcane laws. Test your knowledge of them with this simple two-question quiz:

1. Oil burners break down:

A. On Christmas, New Year's, or Thanksgiving night, whichever is coldest.
B. During blizzards or freezing rain, whichever closes the highway first.
C. When you're out of town or sick with whatever is going around.

2. Oil burner repairs will always:

A. Be expensive enough to make you suck your teeth and simple enough to make you feel like a fool.
B. Be to some part of the machine for which they no longer make parts.
C. Be cyclical: the incidence of breakdowns will increase as your bank balance decreases.

The correct answers to both questions are, as you guessed, all of the above.

We lived with this sort of thing for years. I tried to beat the machine at its own game by scouring the library for books on oil burner service techniques. I did, after long research and fumbling in a dirty crawl space, manage to learn about minor maintenance. I could clean the flue and repack the joints with stove cement. But my efforts saved no money. I never learned how to do the heavy-duty tune-ups and maintenance. Oil burner manuals are written in language only slightly less difficult than treatises on tensor physics. And the servicemen I questioned about procedures were as tight lipped as secret agents.

The worst of it was that all my efforts came to nothing because of the service contract. I paid for a total maintenance package. So unless I could somehow do all of the maintenance and cancel the contract, I paid for everything whether I did it myself or not.

So, the oil burner men would always arrive in spring to tune and clean the system. For years I simply showed the fellows in (it always takes two able-bodied men to properly service the machine) and let them go about their work. "They know more about it than I do." I'd mumble. The homeowner's classic cop-out. I treated them like doctors, assuming what they did was beyond my ken. And of course they never did anything to convince me otherwise.

Oil burner servicemen are a mysterious lot. No doubt they're good family men and stalwarts at the local VFW hall, but on the job they present an air as occult as the devices they minister to. And their appearance adds to the mystery. All oil burner servicemen of my acquaintance carry a thin coating of oil on their skin, that gives them a sheen, almost a patina. With the soot and grease they pick up they take on a Moorish swarthiness that makes the otherwise confident men and women they deal with falter in speech and fall back.

And because their appearance always coincides with disaster in our homes, we welcome them too effusively, embarrassing them with our gushing thanks. They brush this away with a grunt, and, toolbox in hand, head for the patient. There, like Saracens armed with wrenches and a flashlight, they perform secret clanking rites in solitude, muttering their incantations in guttural tones.

Ask them what was wrong with the machine and their answers are always abstract: "She's okay now, just a clogged jet." Or "Her points were corroded." If, armed with some knowledge, you protest that the points were new two months ago, you get a standard reply: "Yeah. Can't get good parts anymore."

Our deliverance from all this came when we added three bedrooms downstairs (tying the addition to the south wall), and installed an efficient wood stove in the downstairs living room. We ran a double-walled stainless steel chimney through the room above out to the roof. Actually, we only expected to partially heat with wood. We planned to continue relying on the oil burner as the same kind of backup it had been for the Franklin, expecting the wood stove to provide only localized warmth.

The north wall of the kitchen was virtually uninsulated and was destined to stay that way. We couldn't blow insulation in, and we couldn't fit batts between the studs without ripping out the kitchen cabinets, the sink, and the wall. That's one of those jobs whose cost and immensity make it easy to put off forever. Besides, the kitchen warmed up enough when there was cooking in progress and when the oil burner kicked in. Having hot air forced through two vents seemed the only practical way to keep the chill off.

The addition presented another problem. The bedrooms were at the end of a long hallway. I didn't think heat from the wood stove would be enough or could travel far enough to raise the bedroom and kitchen temperatures significantly without simultaneously roasting anyone in the living room. So we figured we'd use a little oil and a little wood to even things out.

Fortunately, we were completely wrong.

In the first winter of using the downstairs stove, we went from burning about 1,000 gallons of heating oil to burning *none.* And all the rooms, including the kitchen, stayed comfortable.

Our experiences have convinced us that the heating systems in most homes are grossly overbuilt. They heat the house, all right, the *entire* house. Every nook and cranny is warm and cozy whether a human body is there or not. A house needs a minimum temperature to keep pipes from freezing, but why warm unused areas? More recently built homes have zoned heating or thermostats strategically placed in various parts of the house, but the majority of modern houses and buildings in the United States are little more than overheated boxes—with much of the heat escaping to the outside.

We did a lot to insure that the heat our stove produced stayed in the house and warmed us directly. Old houses usually have severe problems with cold air blowing in through window and door frames and minute openings in walls and floors. Several studies show that the amount of cold air infiltrating an average house is equal to having a one-foot-square hole in the wall.

We weather-stripped windows and doors, caulked even the smallest cracks, and put masking tape over unused electrical outlets on outside walls. (An extraordinary volume of cold air blows through these outlets unless insulation was carefully applied when they were installed.)

We already had outside storm windows, but I made additional inside storm windows to give us triple glazing. These were simple frames made of pine and covered with 4-mil polyethylene. I measured the frames so they would press-fit into each window. Then we sealed them in place with clear plastic weather-strip tape.

They are not pretty. The next time I make a set of these I'll spend more money for a better grade of glass-clear plastic instead of cheaper, cloudy polyethylene. And I'll paint the frames to match the window trim. But the money is well spent on simple frames, no matter how fancy you get. The plastic isn't subjected to extremes of cold or ultraviolet light, so the windows should last indefinitely. And the investment, in our case, paid off immediately. Room temperatures jumped five to ten degrees within hours after we installed the frames.

We also insulated ourselves. We wear wool sweaters, wool socks, and insulated vests and booties around the house. I work upstairs in the coolest part of the house, and if it's a particularly cold morning and the heat has yet to percolate to my room, I'll wear a wool cap. Very stylish. I draw the line at typing with mittens, however.

This may sound very bulky and chilly, but we enjoy it, preferring cooler temperatures. The house actually has several temperature zones, so we can always warm up or cool off as we desire. The warmest room is the living room-dining room-kitchen area in which the stove sits and where our family spends most of its time. Temperatures there stay in the mid to upper 60's, though the immediate area around the stove is considerably warmer.

The bedrooms stay at about 63 degrees F. by day, dropping to the upper 50's by night and sometimes more toward morning as the fire ebbs. Our room is a little bracing first thing on a cold morning. Sometimes I feel like taking my pajamas off with an ice pick.

The downstairs bathroom—an older part of the house that sits over an uninsulated concrete slab—holds a special terror until the stove's heat has worked its way down the hall. The children never complain, but whenever Betsy or I hit that icy seat, a loud "WHOOO-HA!" echoes through the downstairs, announcing our descent.

I've said that we prefer cooler temperatures, but there's a difference between indoor and outdoor comfort zones. Temperatures in the low 60's indoors wouldn't be comfortable to us if they were produced by the oil burner because forced air is an inefficient heating method. Hot air blown through living spaces literally bakes the moisture out of the air. Your house becomes a gigantic blow-drier. A thermostat only adds to your misery by clicking on and off, letting the room temperature rise and fall. You can add a furnace humidifier to this welter of equipment but this only increases the complexity you must live with, tend, and pay for.

Humidifiers come with screens and filters that must be cleaned regularly. When they're not cleaned—and most homeowners have probably never checked theirs—bacteria and mold can flourish in ideal conditions of warmth and moisture. Then the humidifier blows these microbes and spores through your home and lungs, helping to pay for your allergist's new yacht. Several studies have shown humidifiers as a source of pneumonialike illnesses caused by mold spores.

We used to have a furnace humidifier that I kept as clean as possible (though who knows without a microscope?). The instructions said to change the filters annually, which I faithfully did, replacing the aluminum filters at ten bucks a pop. The acidity of our well water regularly corroded the humidifier's water outlet, giving us a long, expensive history of clogs and corroded filters, and as a result, most of the humidity stayed under my collar as I struggled with the mechanical delights of the machine. The worst of it was that even when the humidifier was working properly, the indoor relative humidity never got above 20 percent. The house felt cold even when the temperature was within a reasonable range.

We have a new humidifier now. This one fits right on the wood stove. Amazing device. It's called a pot of water. We fill it several times daily and it never fails. On some cold days the pot steams five gallons or more of water back into the air. Our oil burner meant a winter of cracked lips, dry noses, and parched throats. No more. The pot keeps the air at 40 percent humidity all winter. No filters, fans, electricity, mold spores, or bills to pay.

We did have to replace a pot once when we forgot to refill it. Betsy yanked it off just before it melted. Now Betsy tosses a handful of spices into the pot to serve as an early-warning pot-saving system. Spices produce a minor fragrance as the water vaporizes, but as the water level drops and they dry out, they hiss, pop, and emit a strong odor noticeable anywhere in the house. We haven't lost a pot since.

But even beyond its usefulness as a house warmer and humidifier, a wood stove is a wonderfully utilitarian device offering many hidden delights. For instance, you can't dry your socks on an oil burner or electric baseboard panel. Well, you can, but you can't really *enjoy* the sight in the same way as you do with a stove. We dry more than our socks, though. We load our home-built laundry rack at night with freshly washed clothes and collect them dry in the morning. They're stiff, lacking the slow-motion fluffiness of TV-hyped fabric-softened garments that seem to float in the air, but the shirts and towels smell almost as good as they do when dried outdoors. And the price is right.

Betsy uses the space beneath the stove to raise bread dough or culture yogurt or kefir in half-gallon mason jars. And always in winter the children's snowsuits, mittens, hats, boots, mufflers are laid out before the stove, a cheering and curiously moving sight. The melting snowflakes caught in the wool fibers of a mitten or scarf always catch my eye. They glisten like dewdrops, then vanish quickly.

I doubt that our living room will ever be featured as an example of fashionable interior design. Yet for us the clutter of wood, animals, laundry, children, books, mittens, and rising dough is evidence of a truly "living" room, with the wood stove as its heart and soul. And once, I remember, the stove even took an active role in redecorating our home.

We were standing in the kitchen one winter evening when everything happened at once. There was a muffled explosion in the living room. WHUMMPF! The dog yelped and ran down the hall, the smoke detector screamed EEEEEEEEeeeeee in outrage at the clouds of smoke filling the room, and children and grown-ups ran around bumping into each other, all talking at once and asking, what happened? What's wrong?

What happened was that Betsy had put a can of frozen orange juice on the wood stove, to defrost it faster, then forgot about it. The can defrosted all right, then boiled and blew its top.

We found Ozma, our blonde Afghan hound, cowering in one of the bedrooms. Wide-eyed and sticky with globs of orange juice matted in her fur, she refused to come out. She'd endured flea spray, haircuts, nail clippings, and trips to the veterinarian. But this was too much.

Actually, Ozma had the right idea, staying in the bedroom, for the living room looked like an explosion in a citrus grove. Books, magazines, the children's toys, the walls, and furniture were glistening with goo. And whatever glop hadn't burst from the can in all directions had dripped all over the hot stove and vaporized into acrid smoke.

We opened doors and windows and got a fan going. This was bracing because the outside temperature was below freezing. The cold air kept us alert, anyway. Then we noticed the ceiling. The concentrated juice had spread across overhead in a giant starburst pattern. I suppose we should have cleaned the ceiling immediately, but we didn't. We put the job off until tomorrow. And tomorrow.

You do that around a homestead. You say, "We'll get to it one of these days." In time, nature helped out. Armies of fungi grew on the spattered juice, devouring its stickiness. The ceiling bloomed into a riot of subtle pastel fungal hues, giving us a new overhead mural: Jackson Pollock's Citrus Period.

Eventually, once the mold fully blossomed, we removed the display with a few swipes of a damp rag but frankly, we missed it. We didn't have to wait long for a new one. Betsy left a metal cup of honey and butter on the stove top, trying to liquefy it for some cooking project she was involved in. And she forgot about it.

Honey and butter don't explode. They foam and billow and hiss and make enough smoke to set the smoke detector wailing in outrage like an electronic *yenta.* And again we opened doors and started the fan going and ran around saying what's happening?

Advice from the homestead: don't try to clean a hot stove. The cleaning water and soap only vaporize, adding to the smoke and odor. We waited until spring to clean the stove. The honey, butter, and soap mixture baked on the stove's enamel, giving the whole thing an odd luster.

Another element that may not mix too well with a hot stove is children.

We've known of several people who've held off getting a wood stove because they feared for their children's safety. Having a toddler reeling about the room while a stove is blazing away seems almost inviting a tragedy. We worried about this when Noah first started walking and again when Rachel began toddling around the downstairs. But neither of the children was ever burned, a testament, I think, not to wood stove safety but to parental vigilance.

With children on the loose you begin with the premise that almost everything can be a source of trouble. We considered putting a fence of some kind around the stove, but this was never necessary. Actually, a hot wood stove is probably less dangerous than many devices in your kitchen, including exposed cooking range burners which a child can easily reach. A wood stove's heat is so intense it creates a zone of discomfort reaching several feet out from the stove surface. Few children will march through this heat without stopping, so the stove creates its own "fence."

Beyond this, it helps to visually and physically isolate the stove from the rest of the room. Our upstairs Franklin sits on a double layer of bricks. This creates an "island" effect that separates the stove from the rest of the room. The stove downstairs sits on 14-inch cast-iron legs on a large piece of slate that extends 6 to 18 inches out from the stove sides. All this creates a visual roadblock; you can't walk up to the stove without having your eyes caught by the protruding slate apron, which slows your approach.

None of this will prevent a bumptious child from tripping and falling against the stove. Children get burned by radiators, space heaters, and hot tub water in the same way.

I said neither of our children was ever burned by the stoves, but I'm hedging a bit. Rachel did burn herself once, though I couldn't call it an accident. She was about 18 months old and filled with curiosity about wood stoves and everything else. We pointed to the stove and said "Hot! Hot! Don't touch!" But she couldn't resist. As soon as we turned our backs she marched right up and touched the stove, and yowled in pain and anger. The burn was only a tiny red dot on her fingertip though it triggered three quarts of tears and many earsplitting screams. Betsy applied kisses and hugs and the pain was quickly allayed and forgotten. But the lesson, and the word "hot," stuck.

Of course, at a time like that I wished we were heating with a passive solar system. Not even curious Rachel could have burned herself on a sunbeam. But next to passive solar heat, heating with wood the modern way is probably the most efficient, comfortable, and inexpensive home heating system available.

Notice I said heating with wood the *modern* way. Our forebears right back to the caves heated with wood and they were happy to be done with it once the industrial age rescued them. Primitive fireplaces were smoky and warmed only as long as they held a roaring blaze. Even then your front was toasted while your back stayed chilled. Early wood stoves were some improvement but they also smoked, got choked with soot and creosote and easily roared into infernos.

The modern wood stove has changed all that. It's a perfect example of what happens when we apply a little science to a human-centered, low-technology device. Our stove is a cast-iron airtight model in which the only air entering the stove is controlled by a damper. This means we have control over the rate of burn and produce more heat with less wood.

Our chimney is double-walled stainless steel, with the space between the walls filled with fireproof insulation. The chimney sections are threaded and their ends lock tightly together. The pipe does get hot to the touch but needs only a minimum of two inches clearance from combustible surfaces. The insulation packed in the pipe also lessens creosote buildup caused by cold outside air condensing hot chimney gases.

Well-built masonry chimneys with flue liners work equally well, and have the advantage of absorbing heat and radiating it back for several hours after the fire has gone out.

None of this is cheap. Our colonial ancestors could have lived well for a year on what it costs for a new top-quality stove and metal chimney. And I could live well on what it'll cost you to have a masonry chimney installed. Still, even at its most expensive, wood heat is less costly in the long run than installing the ducts and equipment for oil or gas heat or paying the ever-increasing bills for fossil fuel or electricity.

Our entire wood-heat setup—stove, chimney and accessories—cost just under $1,000. We could have put a system together that was considerably cheaper, but we wanted to go first class. The climate in the Washington area is such that a wood stove stays cold six or more months out of the year. We wanted a stove that had some aesthetic appeal, something that would be nice to look at while it stood unused through spring, summer, and a long, mild fall. No converted oil drums or tin trash burners for us.

We bought a classy, efficient, enameled Danish airtight stove with bas-relief forest scenes on its sides and an arched and filigreed heat exchanger towering above the firebox. The price tag was over $600. That made us wince, too, but we thought it made more sense to put our money into something tangible rather than to mail a check out every month to the oil company.

The chimney wasn't cheap either. We needed 15 feet of double-walled stainless steel pipe—at $25 per 30 inches—to run through two floors to the roof, plus expensive accessories like a chimney cap and joist protectors. But damn the cost of the chimney; that was one item we refused to cut corners on. We wanted the best and safest chimney available.

We weren't rolling in cash then any more than now, but we believed that whatever we spent on wood heat we'd get back. This is an investment, we told ourselves when we borrowed the money. We'll get it all back in three or four years. Our new heating system was a one-time expense. Once purchased, the wood stove would only increase in value, its use unaffected by increased energy costs.

Of course, we were ahead of the times by about three years and we had to endure a lot of eyes rolled heavenward and tongue clucking from friends and family. One overly protective friend called in outrage when she learned of our conversion.

"You've gone too far, Sussman!" she shouted into the phone. "This is absolutely primitive! You've no right to subject Betsy and the children to such craziness!"

I got much the same reaction, though somewhat muted, from my in-laws and from a family physician. The doctor lectured me on fire safety, carbon monoxide poisoning, double pneumonia, and chilblains. He pursed his lips, pressed his fingertips together into a little steeple, and, rolling his eyes skyward, reminded me that wood stoves were quaint. Like my thinking.

We didn't have to wait long for vindication. Nature and economics converged to give us the last laugh. Shortly after we installed the stove, a coal strike made electricity prices jump. Utility companies passed the increased costs on to their customers and customers jumped even higher when they got their bills. Hardest hit were those living in that miracle of the modern age—the all-electric house. People we knew started getting monthly electric bills that matched what we'd spent on our stove.

People in oil- and gas-heated homes fared better but the prices of these fuels were rising too.

So many consumers were hit with astronomical bills during the coal strike that several states passed emergency legislation to give homeowners extra time to pay. Extra time? The doctors couldn't keep the patients from bleeding to death so they compromised by slowing the rate of hemorrhage.

But guess which primitive family stayed warm and financially secure all that winter? I don't know which benefit of wood heat I've enjoyed more, that the stove paid for itself in two years instead of three, that the stove has moved us another step away from dependence on threatened energy systems, or that our enemies looked sheepish. The family doctor said haltingly, clearing his throat, "Ah, well, um, yes, ahem . . . it seems you took the right path after all." And not a word about chilblains.

But you can't win. First I was accused of being a throwback. Now they tell me I'm too smug. That may be. But I've learned this much, at least:

Modern living lulls us into a false sense of security. Thermostats silently close circuits, power hums through lines buried in the walls, hot or cool air is generated. Everything is automatic. You do nothing but pay the bills. And when something breaks down or needs adjustment you make a phone call and pay more bills. You're safe and sound, all right, but at a price. Your security leaves you totally isolated from providing for yourself and dangerously vulnerable to breakdowns in unseen, ill-understood systems.

People click their tongues over the dangers of wood heat, but its risks are those you can see, at least, and can make adjustments for. I can protect myself by checking the chimney and cleaning the stove and pipes regularly. I can also use standard safety regulations and the fire code as a guide to proper wood-heat procedures. Given some diligence and caution, the risks of heating with wood are manageable.

Having said this, however, I must admit that the numbers of house fires linked to wood stoves have increased significantly over the past few years. These tragedies, according to fire officials, are largely the result of improper chimney installation or maintenance and—most especially—having the stove located too close to combustible surfaces. That is, most house fires can be traced to the homeowner rather than to any intrinsic dangers of a wood stove.

And let's not forget that modern heating systems also involve risks. Houses catch fire and people are killed when oil burners malfunction. Propane tanks and natural gas lines have been known to explode. And short circuits in electrical wiring have destroyed many lives. These incidents always shock us because they're "not supposed to happen." Perhaps that's a key to our relationship to technology. We never know it's there until it breaks down, blows up, or stops cold.

At least wood stoves keep you honest. Forget to tend them and the fire goes out. Forget to clean them or get careless and your house burns up. The risks and benefits are all up front where they belong.

I read an article recently that criticized wood stoves, calling them "only 40 to 60 percent efficient," nowhere near the 75 percent efficiency claimed for gas and oil, or the even higher efficiency of electric heat.

Am I kidding myself? Glorying, basking in the glow of my wood stove, am I really a victim of self-delusion? Wouldn't I really be better off with more conventional heating with its "proven" efficiency?

Let's examine this question of stove efficiency. When a furnace's efficiency is rated—usually by the manufacturer (or an equally biased trade association)—the percentages are based on the testing of a furnace operating under *laboratory conditions,* not in an actual home.

The 75 percent efficiency of a furnace means, on paper, that only

25 percent of the heat generated is lost up the chimney. But wait. The furnace in your house is connected to a thermostat, ductwork, and a blower. When the gas or oil is burned it heats a cast-iron heat exchanger. The fan kicks in at a preset temperature and blows air past the heat exchanger, into the ducts, and into the various rooms in your house.

That's quite a complex of parts. But again, the ratings of various conventional furnaces are based solely on the *furnace itself*—not the entire system as it actually operates in a home. Efficiency ratings are even more misleading when you realize that they're based on a furnace that's already warmed up and operating at an optimum temperature. (A cool furnace wastes fuel getting up to its normal heat.) But furnaces in homes are always on and off, hot and cool but not cold, throughout much of a 24-hour period, thanks to the thermostat. Also, when the thermostat cuts the furnace off, all the unused heat stored in the heat exchanger's mass goes up the flue, an expensive waste.

None of this is taken into account by the lab technicians rating the furnace. They simply measure how well an isolated furnace burns fuel. This is as sensible as determining a car's gasoline mileage by putting it up on blocks and shifting the gears by computer. You get lots of nice numbers with no relationship to reality.

Jay McGrew, a Denver civil and space engineer who worked on heating and cooling designs for the moon shots, made a study (as reported in *Soft Tech,* Penguin Books, 1978) of actual gas furnace efficiency based on the entire system in home operation. His company, Applied Science and Engineering, considered the heat loss and energy use in housing in the Denver area and came to the conclusion that gas furnaces are really only *20 to 30 percent efficient.* The implications are awesome if McGrew's figures are applied to the country as a whole because more than half of all space heating in the United States comes from natural gas burned in forced-air systems—systems based on the outdated premise that natural gas is cheap and abundant.

The efficiency of oil burners can't be much better than McGrew's findings for gas. Oil burners need regular tune-ups to burn economically. If we assume that homeowners, eager to save a buck, put off oil burner service the way they put off regular auto tune-ups, we can guess at the condition and effectiveness of most of the country's oil burners. Yet even given a well-maintained oil or gas burner, we still come back to McGrew's point: the true measure of efficiency is *how much heat actually gets into a room,* not how many Btu's the furnace produces.

Electric heating is more efficient than oil or gas, even when, according to some studies, you add in the costs of the "gross energy source," the full price of producing electrical energy. But what good is an efficient electric furnace if your energy bills exceed your mortgage payments?

Now look closely at my primitive wood stove, an anachronism that gas, oil, and electric industry lobbyists dismiss as inefficient.

One evening in October the outdoor temperatures dropped into the upper 40's. Not particularly cold, but cool enough to make the house chilly. We started a small fire in the stove just before dinner. By the time we sat down to eat, the room (kitchen, dining, and living area, all contiguous, unseparated by walls) was comfortable. The bedrooms down the hall were considerably cooler, but unoccupied, as was the rest of the house. When we did enter the bedrooms it was to sleep, so the temperature was of no great concern.

To heat roughly 1,000 square feet of living space from 5:00 P.M. until midnight took only three or four logs. These were 22 inches long by 4 inches in diameter, seasoned oak and "free," having been sawed by me from a lightning-killed tree the year before.

Had I been relying on the oil burner the story would have been much different: to heat *only* the room the family was in would have meant firing up the entire system, distributing heat to unoccupied rooms upstairs, to the empty bedrooms, to the crawl space under the house, and to all the joists and framing supporting several hundred feet of ductwork. Moreover, I would have burned several gallons of a nonrenewable resource, paying dearly for it, just to warm two children and two adults for a few hours.

This isn't to say a wood stove can't heat an entire house. Grates cut in ceilings do an admirable job of distributing heat by convection, depending on the design of the house. Low-wattage fans can also be used to move the warm air around. When we want to heat our upstairs, we build a fire in the stove up there or, on a particularly cold day, we build a bigger than usual fire in the downstairs stove and let the air rise up the stairwell. This naturally rising heat, we've found, is just as efficient and a lot easier to live with than the whirling fan and ductwork we used to rely on.

The irony is that as warm and efficient as our wood heat is, we're probably breaking the law. Ken Kern says in *The Owner-Builder and the Code* that both the Uniform Building Code (section 1410) and the Uniform Housing Code (section H701a) require houses to have heating units capable of maintaining 70 degrees F. "at a point three feet above the floor in all habitable rooms."

I've never gotten around to actually measuring the temperature three feet above the floor, but we do have two little people living with us who have lived entirely within the 36-inch zone for all their lives and have remained comfortable and healthy.

In fact, I lie awake many winter nights, wondering when the building inspector and his goons will come crashing through my door waving warrants and thermometers with their beefy hands, shoving flashlights into my terrified face, and barking in gravelly voices, "Okay, punk, what's the ambient temperature three feet off the floor?" Then they'll force me down into the crawl space to confront the final, damning, code-defying evidence: my furnace, dead these many years, a thoroughly incapable heating unit.

Because the catch in the code is this: while the bureaucracy can't really force you to live at a certain temperature (at this writing) it can, as the building code says, demand that you have a heating device capable of maintaining the official 70 degrees F. Like many wood heat advocates, I have no idea whether my moldering oil burner will do this, couldn't care less, and so I remain a code-breaker and scofflaw.

But what if you or I were about to build a new house, one designed for energy efficiency, simplicity, and low cost? We could go ahead and put in our stoves and passive solar heating systems but we'd still have to meet the code's demands. We'd still have to install an expensive gas, oil, or electric furnace complete with thermostats and ducts, even though we never planned to use it. (Wood stoves don't qualify as capable heating devices because, as Kern says, "a Btu rating cannot be established for wood heat." Or for free-falling sunshine, I guess.)

Consider also that wood stoves don't waste fuel turning on and off, don't get cool in regular winter use, and don't throw their excess heat up the flue when a thermostat, which they also don't have, shuts them down. Wood stoves in use are always warm or hot depending on the desires of the stove-tender. The heat they produce warms air and people directly. Nor are wood stoves affected by power failures, common in winter when ice or snow snaps transmission lines. Gas and oil furnaces depend on electricity to activate thermostats, fans, and igniters. But a wood stove keeps burning merrily no matter what.

The true measure of efficiency in a heating device should be based on total fuel costs, including the environmental impact of fuel production and delivery; costs of operation, including equipment maintenance and installation; and most importantly, *the ability of the device to directly warm human bodies,* not lumber, sheet metal, vacant rooms, or the clipboards of lab technicians.

I could throw in intangibles like a wood stove's contributions to well-being, the parameters of smug satisfaction, and economic security, but engineers and programmers would have trouble factoring these data in.

Violate the code if you like and the county or local jurisdiction will smother you with an avalanche of citations and summonses. But you won't even get that far if you plan on borrowing money for building. The odds are the bankers you traipse around to with your raggedy plans will sniff and wave you off.

Banks, only slightly less ossified than building codes, care about their investments and the resale value of the houses they finance. They rarely rush to support unconventional housing or unconventional builders.

What's the solution? In the long run we'll have to press for changes in the building code, a project not unlike rewriting the Bible. This will demand an enormous amount of lobbying, political clout, an informed public, and courageous politicians willing to question the sense of traditional building practices.

Bankers will also have to be convinced that simple, well-built, energy-efficient houses are better investments than traditional energy sinks. I suspect, in fact, that bankers will see the light faster than builders and bureaucrats. Simple economics can be appealing. What's the resale value of a conventional house if you can't heat it or cool it without printing money in the basement?

Our rapidly changing attitude toward energy will help speed changes in building codes and changes in the ways lending institutions view so-called "unconventional" housing. Until that day, however, we non-climate-controlled rebels will have to remain outlaws, choosing to build in areas that don't have building codes or skirting archaic regulations when necessary.

One set of regulations we do adhere to, however, are those concerned with safety.

John Vivian quotes an old saying in his book *Wood Heat:* "heat 'n' sleep scared." We've been guided by caution from the day we started our first fire.

Just as most automobile accidents are caused by the nut behind the wheel, most fires related to wood stoves can be traced to someone's carelessness, ignorance, or cavalier attitude toward the special character of wood heat.

Rarely is the fault in the stove itself. Virtually every modern stove on the market, even the least expensive, is quite capable of containing a fire safely.

Your first thoughts should be about stove placement. Our Franklin stove was already in place when we moved in and I was relieved to find its position a safe one. Fire codes call for a radiant stove to be 36 inches from a combustible surface, meaning anything but brick, stone, or block. Gypsum board or sheetrock isn't considered noncombustible—it can warm to the kindling point—nor can it safely protect the 2-by-4s that back it up.

The recommended three-foot distance can be reduced safely if necessary. We reduced it. While the Franklin was 12 inches away from a cinderblock wall, the downstairs living room was too small to allow for a 36-inch clearance. That would have put the stove almost in the middle of the room.

We put the stove 24 inches from the wall, reducing the fire risk by using a sheet metal insulator to protect the wall. We didn't use the sheet of asbestos board a local stove shop recommended because of its carcinogenic fibers.

Instead I went to a sheet metal shop and had a large panel made of 24-gauge steel with two inches along the vertical sides of the sheet bent at 90 degrees. This gave us a panel that hung behind the stove but didn't fit flush against the wall. The bent sides kept the sheet two inches from the wall, creating a chimney effect with cool air constantly rising and passing between the wall and the sheet metal. The side of the metal facing the stove gets hot but the heat is reflected and the wall stays cool to the touch. This panel is large enough to extend one foot beyond the sides and top of the stove to protect against heat radiated outward.

Given a choice, though, I'd prefer to have a brick or masonry wall behind my stove. It would act as a heat sink, radiating warmth back even as the fire burned low.

Next comes the chimney. We didn't have a masonry chimney to hook up to so we installed the stainless steel, double-walled model I mentioned. This is UL approved and safe if installed correctly. We followed the manufacturer's instructions to the letter, keeping the chimney itself a minimum of two inches from combustible surfaces, and securing it solidly as it passed through the floor and roof. Double-walled or not, the chimney *does* get hot and could start a fire if carelessly installed.

We were fortunate that we could run the chimney straight up through the roof with no bends or angles to restrict the smoke. The straighter the pipe the better the draft and the fewer potential creosote problems.

Outside chimneys can get dangerously choked with heavy creosote deposits when cool outside air condenses the resins in wood smoke. If enough creosote clogs your chimney, you're set up for a rip-roaring chimney fire—a blaze that sounds like a tornado and is just as deadly. All but 3 feet of our 15-foot chimney is inside the house. We get creosote only on the chimney cap, virtually none inside the pipe itself. This is due, in part, to a warm stack plus the way we maintain the stove's fire.

We clean our chimneys every spring or fall, pulling a weighted burlap bag up and down until the interior of the pipes is clean. This is a primitive but effective method, though I expect soon to begin using stiff chimney brushes made for the job. After scraping the pipes' interiors, we vacuum out the soot collected in the stoves' baffles and heat exchangers. Soot isn't a fire hazard, but it reduces the amount of heat radiated by the stoves.

None of these chores takes long. I can clean both chimneys, stoves, and stovepipes in an hour or two. Dirty work, and surely not something I look forward to as much as taking a swim, but the job always leaves me with a sense of accomplishment and confidence. The simple task of cleaning and maintaining the stoves and chimneys rewards us with another winter of inexpensive, safe heating and profound comfort. I never got such a sense of self-esteem from living with an oil burner.

Wood heat has another problem that concerns me: air pollution. There's plenty of evidence that various gases and particulate matter released by burning wood constitute a health hazard, especially in communities where a majority of houses rely on wood heat. What a paradox! To search for a simple, bucolic existence only to choke on a miasma produced by all your neighbors' cheery blazes.

But the problem isn't insoluble and certainly not as vexing as the dangers presented by other forms of space heating or power generation. Nobody is concerned about the half-life of wood wastes or whether terrorists will begin stealing ashes. Wood fires have been used since our beginnings as a race, but it's only in the past few years that modern science has started to analyze the problems and benefits of wood heat. One of its virtues, in fact, is that wood heat is so simple that very little technology need be applied to dramatically increase its efficiency. Research has already shown, for example, that pollution from wood fires can be significantly reduced or eliminated by following certain guidelines:

1. Burn hardwoods. Resinous softwoods like spruce, pine, hemlock, and cedar tend to release more particulate matter and potentially hazardous gases than oak, hickory, birch, or ash. We burn mostly red oak, maple, and hickory.

2. Burn dry, seasoned wood. Green wood, because of its high moisture content, tends to give off thicker smoke than properly seasoned wood. (We age our wood in loose stacks for six months to a year.)

3. Use an efficient woodburner efficiently. A stove beats a fireplace and some stoves are better than others, but even the best-made stove can be misused, forcing it to produce more pollution than it otherwise might.

Many people, for instance, pack their stoves with wood and keep the damper shut down. This gives them a long, slow burn with less frequent tending. It also results in considerably more air pollution and creosote problems because neither the firebox nor the stack gets hot enough to consume all the gases and particulates.

Complete combustion, a theoretical ideal resulting in no pollution, may be impossible. But an *optimum* burn can be achieved by keeping a hot stove. Betsy and I refuel our stove frequently, adding lots of small chunks and logs rather than stuffing the firebox and forgetting it. We enjoy tending the stove and our ministrations result in a constantly hot firebox. The only time we pack the stove and damp down is at night. In the morning we build a hot blaze to get the firebox and stack up to their optimum heat.

4. Maintaining a proper draft is related to firebox temperature, but getting the proper air-to-fire mixture is tricky. Closing down the draft supplies too little oxygen, creating a smoldering fire and letting excessive pollutants escape up the chimney. A wide-open draft and a roaring blaze, however, may actually suck in enough air to cool the firebox, resulting in similarly inefficient combustion. The goal is a draft setting that consistently produces a steady fire somewhere between a roar and a smolder.

In sum, then, the least air pollution is produced when dry hardwood is burned in an efficient stove that's refueled frequently and kept at a steady blaze. The rate of burn should be controlled *not* by restricting air intake, but by adding or withholding firewood.

We can also reduce wood smoke pollution by properly insulating our homes. Wood may indeed be renewable, but the less wood we burn the less smoke we produce, and the less we deplete the forests.

The problems created by wood stoves, as I said, are eminently fixable. There are already designs available for stoves and furnaces that actually approach complete combustion. So, if nothing else, wood burners can be cheered by the fact that the gross pollution and the social problems created by wood stoves are minor compared with those caused by oil, coal, and nuclear mishaps. When was the last time you heard about a "log spill" or a "loss of coolant" in a woodpile?

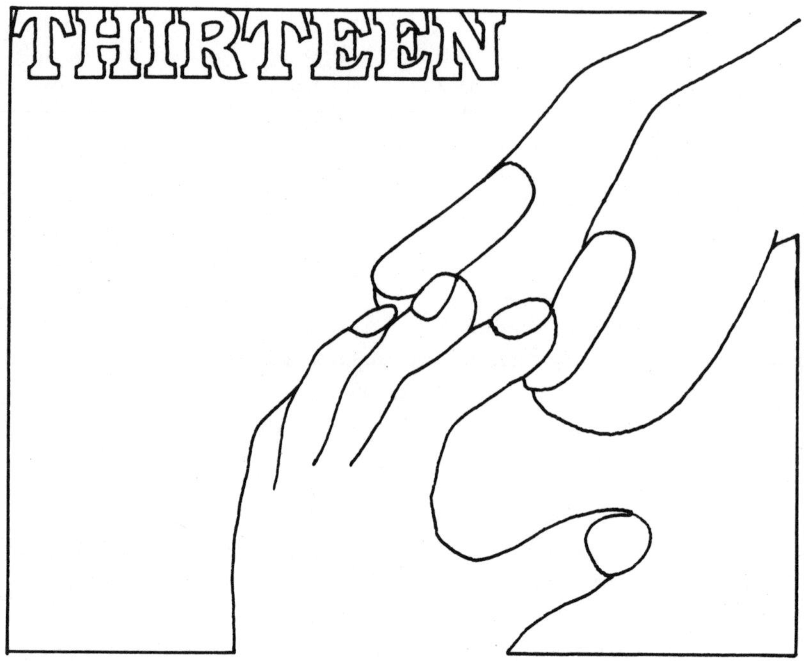

This was going to be our most ambitious do-it-yourself project. But we kept it to ourselves. We only told a few people that Betsy planned to have her baby at home.

"At *home?* You're very brave."

"At *home?* You're crazy."

"What are you trying to prove?"

And we didn't tell our families that Betsy was seeing a nurse-midwife instead of an obstetrician. Grandma, to put mildly, would have plotzed.

"A MIDWIFE? Why not a witch doctor?"

"What if something goes wrong?"

"I think you're carrying this back-to-nature thing too far."

We hadn't made the decision casually. The first time someone mentioned home birth as a logical extension of our philosophy, Betsy and I rejected it like a do-it-yourself appendectomy. Maybe we'd seen too many westerns, but home birth conjured up images of sputtering lanterns, boiling water, bedsheet bandages, and an old granny lady who stank of asafetida and snuff. The only kind of home delivery we approved of was when one of our goats gave birth out in the barn.

But the idea wouldn't go away. We kept hearing and reading about home birth and its benefits. We talked to knowledgeable friends and doctors. We read books and articles on the subject and remembered the problems we'd had with Noah's hospital birth. We began to think seriously about the alternatives.

By the start of Betsy's pregnancy—timed to end in the lull between spring seeding and late-summer harvesting—we realized that a lot of the negative stuff we'd heard about home birth was untrue. Home birth wasn't "going backward." It seemed to be a blend of the best of the modern world's advanced medical knowledge, and the best of the past.

Betsy called Maternity Center Associates in Bethesda, Maryland, the nation's first private nurse-midwife service for women who wanted home deliveries. She met with Janet Epstein, a registered, certified (by the American College of Nurse-Midwives) nurse-midwife and one of the founders of the Maternity Center.

"Well, what do you think?" I asked when Betsy got home.

"I want to do it," she said. "No doctor ever talked to me—talked *with* me—that way. Woman-to-woman. Jan said, 'Look, here are all the risks and benefits. Here's what you have to do and what we can do. If you're willing to accept your share of the responsibility and do your share of the work, we can do this together.' My God!" Betsy laughed. "The obstetrician we had with Noah told me not to worry my pretty little head—that he'd take care of everything!"

So Betsy began going to the Maternity Center for regular prenatal care. Her pregnancy was closely monitored. Home birth was an option for us only as long as the pregnancy remained normal, Jan told us. Any abnormality meant Betsy would have the baby in the hospital. "But we'll be there with you too," Jan said.

One day, Betsy came home all excited, "I saw my cervix today!" she said.

"I don't really know what to say—do I offer congratulations?" I said.

"You're a male," she said, "so you can't relate to that, but Jan did something no doctor ever did before. She held a mirror up and showed me my cervix! That's the first gynecological exam I ever had that made me feel like it was *my* body that was being examined."

There's nothing primitive about modern home birth, we learned. Registered certified nurse-midwives, specializing in the processes of normal pregnancy, labor, and delivery, are offering women the chance to actively participate in an intimate drug-free birth at home.

Nurse-midwives blend contemporary medical expertise and procedures with human sensitivity. They're committed to preserving the basic nature of normal childbirth as a woman's personal experience and a family event, rather than a medical emergency or trauma.

And there was something else that impressed us, something we read in Charlotte and Fred Ward's *The Home Birth Book:* "Those of us who believe in having our babies at home aren't being masochistic or foolish. Nobody wants it *exactly* the way it used to be. What we want is to preserve some of the old values that were lost with hospital deliveries. We want the *best* of the past: the shared moment, the intrinsic education for our other children, the personal dignity, the serenity."

Jan came in to check Betsy's cervix and to listen to the baby's heartbeat. We burst out laughing when she walked into the bedroom. She had changed into a sweat shirt that said, in huge letters:

HAPPY BABY HOME DELIVERY SERVICE

That's when the difference between having a baby at home and having one in the hospital struck us: at home with a nurse-midwife, Betsy would be able to endure the waiting and contractions in comfort and dignity. In the hospital, she just endured.

Betsy woke me at six that morning to tell me her contractions were five minutes apart. We had been preparing for this home birth for months, so I should have been blasé. But when she nudged me awake and said, "This is it. Today is the day," I shot up in bed, rubbing the sleep out of my eyes.

"W-what . . . who? Call Jan . . . uh . . . I'll get dressed," I stammered.

"Relax," Betsy laughed. "Go back to sleep if you want to. We aren't going anywhere, remember?"

Sleep? My wife is about to give birth to our second child and I should roll over and go back to sleep? That's sacrilegious. Un-American. But then I thought, why not?

This time there would be no Keystone Kops chase to the hospital, no worries about heavy traffic on the 20-mile drive across the suburbs.

This time I wouldn't have to mentally review the techniques for delivering a baby in the back seat of a car.

Betsy was right. I could relax.

The sunlight was just beginning to filter through the kitchen window as Betsy walked down the hall from the bedroom. The house was quiet. Noah, then three years old, was still asleep. Even our dogs hadn't yet stretched themselves awake.

"How nice it was to start this special day so quietly," Betsy said later. "I had no bags to pack, no last-minute preparations to make. I was in my own home and I was going to *stay* there."

Betsy telephoned Jan, who asked a few questions about the contractions and said she and Ruth Johnson—her birth assistant—would leave immediately.

Betsy called our neighbor, Kathy, and they talked excitedly about the big day finally arriving. Kathy was to come over with her youngest daughter, so Noah would be able to spend the day playing and cared for at home while the birth proceeded.

Then Betsy did something I think says a lot about the symbolic importance of home birth.

She set out a loaf of banana bread she'd baked the day before, some of her elderberry preserves, butter, and honey. She took down a package of Red Zinger Herb Tea and put water on to boil. "I feel like I'm preparing for a small party," she said. "A *real* birthday party!"

She got Noah dressed and fed that morning as always. We didn't want him overexcited, so we didn't make a point of telling him that today was "the big day." He knew Jan and Ruth, having been to their office many times with Betsy during her prenatal care, so we knew he wouldn't think it strange to see them in our living room.

We had prepared Noah for the impending birth by handling his questions and curiosity with equal amounts of empathy and information. We used picture books to explain how the baby grows and how it eventually comes to be born. We talked about *his* birth and how it was when he was born.

But no amount of information can really explain away a child's fears about acquiring a sibling. There is always the threat of displacement and abandonment.

Home birth helps to ease that transition. It softens the impact of events. Noah suffered no separation from his parents, no anguish at seeing his mother "go away for a few days," only to return with "somebody new" in her arms.

His life changed with our new arrival, but that change occurred gently, naturally, with no major disruption of his family life to complicate matters.

Jan and Ruth arrived a few minutes apart. They had a crisp, professional air that instilled confidence in us—there was more than a decade of obstetric experience between them—yet both of them greeted Betsy with genuine warmth, as friends, embracing her like a sister, enthusiastic about helping her have this baby at home.

Then Kathy swept in and hugged Betsy, her eyes shining with happiness. And Noah ran into the kitchen squealing with delight at seeing Kathy's daughter, his favorite playmate. Then I came in and introduced Jan and Ruth to Kathy. More hellos and congratulations and embraces and laughter. Then the dogs barked. And the phone rang.

Happy pandemonium.

Later that morning Betsy went out to milk the goats. People tease her about that (I do too), but being able to stick to her usual routine, caring for her goats, milking, feeding, and mucking out their shed while she was in labor, was important to her and confirmed the fact that this day belonged to her. "It's all your peasant blood," I said.

If we were "eccentric" or "radical" in our plans for a home birth, it was only because we lived in the United States. Most of the world's children are born at home, delivered by midwives.

In many countries, even hospital births are primarily attended by midwives. Obstetricians are generally called in only to deal with complications and abnormal deliveries.

In our country, the reverse is true. Home birth was common up to 1935, when about two-thirds of all babies were born at home. But by 1974, 95 percent of all births were occurring in hospitals.

Advances in medical science, reliance on anesthesia, the advent of medical insurance, and the rapid change in social values since the end of World War II, have all, unfortunately, made home birth and midwives seem hopelessly backward and potentially dangerous.

Yet for all its space-age technology and modern hospitals, the United States has for years had one of the highest infant death rates among developed nations. The figure has improved somewhat since Betsy and I first looked into the subject (infant mortality rates for the United States were 17 deaths per 1,000 births in 1976, 14 deaths per 1,000 in mid-1979) but more than a dozen nations have better records.

Sweden, with the lowest infant death rate (8 per 1,000), has an intensive national program of prenatal and postnatal care, coupled with natural childbirth classes. Almost all deliveries are made by midwives in hospitals.

Midwives are especially active in the Netherlands (10 deaths per 1,000) where *half* of all births take place at home. And 90 percent of Norway's babies are delivered by midwives. (Norway's infant mortality rate is 10 per 1,000.)

Supporters of hospital births in our country say our record just *looks* bad, that it results from statistical differences in the way various nations report their infant deaths. The United States also suffers in comparison, they argue, because it has so many urban poor, higher risks during childbirth.

Others in medicine believe our poor infant death rate stems in part from an overreliance on drugs and surgical procedures. Obstetricians agree that 90 to 95 percent of all labors are normal, yet many hospitals—as we discovered—still treat deliveries as though they were high-risk cases needing a full routine of medication, anesthesia, and operative procedures. Otherwise healthy women may be routinely dosed with an arsenal of hormones, anesthetics, analgesics, anticoagulants, diuretics, and barbiturates. And almost every substance introduced into the mother's system crosses the placenta and affects the fetus.

But we knew nothing of this when Betsy was pregnant the first time, with Noah. We assumed, like most people, that the only safe place to have a baby was in the hospital. The best we could do, in trying to share fully in our child's birth, was to prepare for natural childbirth in the hospital.

We enrolled in a six-week Lamaze course, read a dozen books on pregnancy and birth, and got our obstetrician's permission for me to remain with Betsy all the way through the delivery. Yet none of our training and planning prepared us for the cold edge of hospital rules and procedures.

The Lamaze natural childbirth techniques demand concentration and cooperation between husband and wife, but the drab, poorly lit labor room we were confined to soon resembled a bus station. Orderlies, interns, nurses, and doctors constantly wandered in and out, interrupting Betsy's breathing techniques, shattering her concentration, and repeatedly offering her painkillers.

That was our first surprise. Our obstetrician knew this was to be a Lamaze delivery. Wasn't that noted on Betsy's chart? Weren't any of the nurses notified? No. Ours was just another delivery. Routine.

Betsy resisted, explaining to the nurses that she wanted a natural, drugless childbirth. One nurse laughed at this and said, "Don't try to be a hero, Honey. Have a little Demerol." I suppose we shouldn't have been surprised at this. A lot of women we knew fully expected to be medicated at the onset of labor. Their attitude was "wake me when it's all over, Doctor."

A little later, Betsy called a nurse and told her she had to urinate. "Well," the nurse said, obviously annoyed, "you're all hooked up to that fetal heart monitor, Dear, and I can't disconnect everything just to let you go to the bathroom."

"Then can I please have a bedpan?" Betsy asked.

"I'm too busy now, Honey," she answered with a wave of her hand as she walked out. "Just do it right in the bed."

They wheeled Betsy down to the delivery room with me trailing behind, looking like a kid on Halloween in my cap, mask, and gown. I had never been in a delivery room before, so when we pushed through the doors I was startled by how huge and bright and *public* the room was.

I realized then that, except for me, Betsy was among strangers. She knew her doctor, but only in a formal, businesslike way. And though we had expected there would be several nurses, we were annoyed to see three interns standing off to one side of the room.

They were there, I suppose, to observe the procedure. But this particular "procedure" was Betsy's private experience. No one had even thought to ask her permission before issuing invitations.

"I felt so helpless," Betsy told me later. "They treated me like a side of beef." I felt helpless too. There I was, the proud father, "allowed" in the delivery room, Betsy's coach for the big event. But I was obviously a fifth wheel. All I could do was stand aside and watch as she was lifted and placed on a cold delivery table and covered with what seemed like a dozen surgical drapes. Her feet were fitted into stirrups and her legs and arms were strapped to the table.

Strapped down? My God, where did they think she was going? Flat on her back, strapped to a table, her splayed legs stuck up in the air, surrounded by strangers—this was the "natural" childbirth we had prepared for?

Betsy leaned back and looked at me. I was standing behind her, my hands on her shoulders. Beads of perspiration had popped out on her forehead. I murmured something about doing the breathing exercises. She gave me a weak smile and nodded.

"Push," the doctor said. Betsy pushed, straining against the metal stirrups. The leather straps pulled against her forearms.

"Push again," he said. That was the only thing anybody let her do all afternoon.

Betsy was fully conscious and pushed Noah out herself. That moment at least, was the one thing hospital procedures and technology didn't take away from her.

A nurse quickly wrapped Noah in a cloth, rinsed his eyes with silver nitrate, measured and weighed him, held him up for Betsy to see (no touching allowed) and briskly started out of the room for the nursery.

But we had planned for Betsy to handle her baby immediately, to nurse him right after birth, to fondle him, to feel his flesh against hers.

"Hold it," I said, stopping the nurse. "This baby stays with its mother. I cleared this two weeks ago with the chief neonatalogist."

Another nurse stepped between us. "The rules say all babies must be taken directly to the . . . " The nurse holding Noah started out of the room again. "Don't worry," she said, "we'll take good care of your baby."

"Like hell you will," Betsy said, pulling herself up on one elbow on the delivery table. "*I'll* take good care of him." She finally got her way *and* her baby, but only after a delivery-room shouting match, complete with Noah's screams, pointed fingers, and threats of lawsuits.

The tension didn't end there, either. Betsy spent another day and a half in the hospital, so the battles continued about her right to keep her baby with her 24 hours a day.

We had paid for a "rooming-in" facility in which mother and infant could remain together, but the maternity ward staff still expected to waltz off with Noah whenever their sacred routine demanded that he be removed to the nursery.

At one point, a nurse came in and was shocked to find Betsy and Noah blissfully asleep, with Noah stretched out on his mother's chest.

"Oh, no, no," the nurse said as she shook Betsy awake. "You can't sleep with your baby. You might roll over on him. Let me take him to the nursery if you want to sleep."

"Hands off!" Betsy growled.

So it went.

We were worn out when we finally left the hospital with Noah. The only thing they hadn't done was stamp his bottom, "Hospital Property."

Jan, Ruth, Kathy, Betsy, and I spent the morning talking, nibbling at the banana bread, and sipping herb tea. Noah was playing in the yard with his friend.

By midmorning the contractions were coming in waves. Betsy and I went into the bedroom and did the Lamaze breathing exercises. As we worked together, we heard Noah outside laughing as he played on his swings.

Hearing his voice was comforting. "Hey," Betsy said, listening to Noah playing, "look how fortunate I am. I'm giving birth to our second child while listening to the sound of our first child's laughter."

Home birth gives the father a new role, I discovered. Rather than biting his nails in a waiting room or feeling useless in the delivery room, though trying to comfort his partner, the home-birth father can take a more active and supportive role.

In my case that role turned out to be more active than I ever imagined. Shortly after Jan arrived, she turned to me and asked, "Do you want to catch the baby?"

"Do I . . . *what?*"

"Catch the baby. Assist in delivering it."

"Oh. Um. How? What do I do?" I said.

"You just stand next to me," Jan said. "When the time comes I'll tell you where to put your hands and what to do. Okay?"

"I . . . ah . . . uhh," I stammered, all my cultural conditioning hammering away at once, giving me a thousand reasons to say no.

Deliver my own child?

I'm not a doctor.

I'm just the husband.

The most I can do is hold Betsy's hand and coach the breathing exercises.

I'd get in the way.

I'm squeamish about blood.

I might drop it.

I said yes.

By one o'clock the pressure of the contractions was suddenly tremendous, overpowering. Betsy was ready. Jan directed everyone to their positions. Ruth was behind Betsy holding her shoulders, giving her support to push against. Betsy was sitting up, her hands locked behind her knees, in the position she'd learned in the Lamaze class.

Jan was in front of Betsy. I stood next to her. We were watching the baby's head starting to crown. "You're almost there, Betsy," Jan said. Her voice was even and composed. Betsy held on, breathing rapidly.

"Now PUSH."

She pushed, hard.

The head popped out.

Betsy gasped. She sobbed. She laughed. "All the waiting, the pain, the work—all the discomfort—vanished in that one fantastic moment," she told me later.

Then she sat there holding her knees, laughing and weeping and looking down at that marvelous, beautiful head poking out into the world.

When the baby's head crowned—a round, slightly hairy bulge—Jan told me to put two fingers on the head to stop the infant from coming out too quickly. I reached down with my right hand and put my index and middle fingers on the bulge.

What an electric feeling! I felt as though I had touched a source of power, as if in touching that tiny skull, my fingers had dipped into some mystic reservoir of energy. My body seemed to tingle, to glow. I was touching something that had never been touched before—part of Betsy, yet part of no one: independent, a new person.

Then Betsy pushed and the head emerged fully. It faced to my left, eyes tightly shut, mouth closed in a grimace, nose flattened, covered with vernix.

A wax image, not yet real.

"Put one hand under the shoulder," Jan said, as she felt to see if the umbilical cord was around the neck. It wasn't. Betsy pushed again, and a beautiful, glistening wet infant girl shot into my hands.

No longer an "it," my daughter Rachel opened her mouth and cried loudly.

I straightened up, holding that long, perfect body in my hands. Tears welled up in my eyes and made the room a haze. I handed Rachel to Betsy.

Betsy looked weightless, floating, laughing and sobbing as she took the baby from me. Rachel's umbilical cord trailed down, still attached to the placenta in Betsy's body. Betsy lifted her gently and pressed her wet body against her breast.

Nothing. . . . No one interfered with that moment.

Betsy passed the placenta a few seconds later. Jan handed me a pair of scissors and I cut the umbilical cord, chuckling as I did. I realized at that moment that I was wearing bib overalls and a blue work shirt. "How corny can you get?" I said. "Somebody call Frank Capra."

Rachel began nursing within minutes. The minor details of weighing, measuring, and silver nitrate were forgotten until Rachel and Betsy could share those first incredible moments together.

Then I went out and brought Noah into the bedroom. He had been waiting for this day too, wondering what was going on and when his brother or sister would arrive. He bounded in with a loud, "Hi Momma!" and leaped for the bed. Betsy helped him up and kissed and hugged him.

Rachel was nestled in the crook of her arm, half asleep. Noah stared at her intently, quizzically. I think he'd expected someone his own size. "She's very little," he said as he patted her head. "When will she be able to play with me?"

By nine that night we were all alone. All the phone calls had been made and received. We had supper and calmed down. "How do you feel?" I asked Betsy.

"Tired," she said, "but completely satisfied and content."

Then she put Noah to bed, read him a story, and stayed with him until he fell asleep. Rachel was already asleep in her cradle next to our bed.

I stood in the doorway watching Noah and Betsy. Noah had dozed off while Betsy sat stroking his hair and looking down at him in the yellow glow of his night-light.

Then I realized how quiet the house was. Betsy noticed it too and turned toward me. "It's odd, isn't it?" she said. "I've given birth to Rachel here in the place I love best, surrounded by the people I love best. It's been the most exciting, momentous day of my life. Yet, at the same time, it all seems quite ordinary and natural."

Everything had changed and nothing had changed. We were as we were that morning when it all began—together, a family, at home.

"You're *not* a farmer!" my friend said to me, almost scolding.

"I never said I was."

"But you call this place a farm."

"Well . . ."

"And you call *that*," he said, pointing to the goat house, "a *barn.*"

"It *is* a barn," I said. "Betsy and I built it ourselves."

"That doesn't make it a barn," he said, sticking out his chin. "A barn is a definite architectural entity . . . "

"I don't believe this!" I laughed. "Is this what happens when you go off to art school?"

"That's a *shed,* not a barn."

"You mean it's supposed to be a big red building with a silo next to it?"

"Yes."

"And Betsy and I should be standing in front, me with wire-rim spectacles and a pitchfork, she with her hair pulled back in a bun?"

"That wouldn't help. You've only got two acres."

"So what?"

"Two acres is *not* a farm," he said. "Besides, this is the suburbs."

"Okay, forgive me my sins," I said. "I called our place a farm. I called a shed a barn. But what *do* you call a place like this? We're growing our own food, we have livestock, we have a big woodpile, we have 200 bales of hay in the bar . . . ah . . . shed. Damned if it doesn't *look* like a farm!"

"Well, let's just say you're about 20 miles and 50 years away from the city. But it's still not a farm."

The word we were looking for was "homestead." And, instead of "farmer," we should have said "homesteader." But the first time I heard that word I visualized a scene in a lot of westerns. It's 1889, the government has passed the Homestead Act, and the new territory is wide open. The buckboards, covered wagons, and cowboys are all lined up waiting for the signal to ride like hell to stake their claim on 160 acres.

A pistol shot! And a thousand extras and horses ride off in a roar of wagon wheels, hoofbeats, and hollering.

Gee, all I did was call a real estate agent. And because nobody, certainly not the government, is giving land away, I had to stake my claim with a 20-year mortgage.

The classic homesteaders had a hard life on their 160 acres. They got to own it only after living on it for five years and improving it with buildings and crops or stock. That was true "sweat equity." They earned the land with payments of years of hard work, misfortune, and loneliness.

But I think the name "homesteader" still fits what we're trying to do with our small piece of land. Our goals right from the start were to enjoy the aesthetic benefits of living in close communion with nature, to raise as much of our own food as possible, and—like the original homesteaders—to acquire skills and experience leading toward self-reliance. Besides, my friend was right about one thing: we're not farmers and we never intended to be.

The professional farmer works the land for a profit (if he or she is lucky). Farming is a means to an end. But the modern homesteader produces food, tends animals, and pursues various traditional activities because they constitute an end in themselves. Of course, there are plenty of farmers who love the land and work it for both an income and for the pleasure of being on the land. And plenty of homesteaders derive some or all of their income from sales of produce or crafts.

But, in general, homesteading means working a relatively small piece of land, practicing subsistence farming or large-scale gardening, while searching for independence, self-reliance, and a sense of harmony with nature.

The new homesteading movement began in the late 1960's (though there were similar movements in the twenties and thirties) with millions of people leaving the cities and suburbs for small farms and rural areas. Not all of these people were homesteaders intent on self-sufficiency; some just wanted to escape from the social problems of urban areas. But many more wanted to live on the land, wresting something from it that modern life no longer offered. Unlike the homesteaders of the 1800's, however, these new "back-to-the-landers" are middle class and well educated.

The old homesteader came to the land with a dream of finding security, of "making it," to use a modern phrase. But the new homesteader has probably already made it, achieved professional or financial success, and then chosen to discard it or reshape it, seeking something more profound. The phenomenon has become a cliché. Who's that slopping the hogs? A Ph.D. in political science. Who's that cutting pulpwood in a Vermont commune? A disaffected aerospace engineer. Who's that cleaning out the chicken house? A burned-out social worker who "had to get away."

There's another difference between back-to-the-landers and the homesteaders and farmers of earlier times: working the farm used to be the only way to acquire the capital necessary to *leave,* to head for the city, the bright lights, and *real* success. This is still happening. You can see it in Washington as well as in any big city. Here they arrive from small towns in West Virginia, from the Carolinas, from the Tennessee hills. Young and old, men and women, tired of rural life, sick of low pay, believing the dream, looking for a government job, anything but the hick towns and the dead ends they left behind.

The new homesteaders may have equally passionate dreams as they leave the pressure-cooker cities (some of them came there from small towns to begin with), for the supposed idylls of rural life, but there is this difference—the new homesteaders have turned away from the standard American definition of success. They have turned their backs on an excess of money, possessions, and power.

Notice I said "excess." Few neohomesteaders, myself included, have any desire to suffer the poverty or primitiveness of the original homesteaders or even the generally depressed economic conditions shared by many modern rural Americans. What we want, if I can act as spokesman for so amorphous a collection of people, is something between privation and excess. Call it "enoughness," for want of a better term. Enough money, food, goods, and shelter to meet our needs, with a small margin of surplus as insurance.

"But isn't this merely a quaint affectation?" asks writer Wendell Berry. "And isn't it a retreat from the 'modern world' and its demands, a way of 'dropping out'?" Berry, in his essay, "On Citizenship and Conscience" (*Stepping Stones,* Schocken Books, 1978), says:

> I don't think so. At the very least, it is a way of dropping *in* to a concern for the health of the earth, which institutional and urban people have had at second hand at best, and mostly have not had at all. But the idea has other far-reaching implications, in terms of both private benefits and public meanings. It is perhaps enough to summarize them here by saying that when one undertakes to live fully on and from the land the prevailing values are inverted: one's home becomes an occupation, a center of interest, not just a place to stay when there is no other place to go; work becomes a pleasure; the most menial task is dignified by its relation to a plan and a desire; one is less dependent on artificial pleasures, less eager to participate in the sterile nervous excitement of movement for its own sake; the elemental realities of seasons and weather affect one directly and become a source of interest in themselves; the relation of one's life to the life of the world is no longer taken for granted or ignored, but becomes an immediate and complex concern. In other words, one begins to stay at home for the same reasons that most people now go away.

When we first moved into what was to become our homestead, a friend noted our plans for a garden and goats and lots of do-it-yourself projects. "But how will you ever get away for a vacation?" she asked. What we wanted, I explained, was a way of life that was its own amusement and recreation, or—as Berry says—a "center of interest."

We've accomplished that, certainly, though I'd be less than honest if I didn't admit that there are times, after the gardening and food preservation are finished, or between the twilight of winter and the first rush of springtime, or when the children's voices approximate a fingernail running down a blackboard, that we wouldn't mind a short trip to the ocean. But making your home your occupation is a sword that cuts both ways. The last time Betsy and I got out of the house together, in fact, was when the smoke detector went off.

We can't go away between May and September, this being the brunt of the garden season. Going away in March or April is also impossible because that's the time goat kids are due and I'm at work starting vegetable seedlings indoors. I couldn't leave my racks of young plants to a novice any more than Betsy could leave her baby goats to an inexperienced neighbor.

We could go away in winter, I suppose, but this is one time of the year we really enjoy. We surely wouldn't want to "escape" winter's briskness and beauty by heading for Florida. Besides, we'd be apprehensive about leaving the maintenance of our wood stove (and the safety of our house) to someone unfamiliar with the subtle demands of wood heating.

Then there are the animals. At this writing we live with two old dogs, five stray cats (who wisely stopped straying when they found us), and of course, the goats, three of whom must be milked twice daily.

How would we find a housesitter to handle all that? I've thought of putting an advertisement in the paper:

> WANTED: Housesitter; mature, nonsmoking vegetarian; experienced goat milker, dog-cat sitter, gardener. Must have experience with wood stoves, frozen pipes, old houses. Prefer retired nun with homesteading experience.

(Why would we want vegetarian housesitters? Only because we do a lot of cooking in cast-iron pots. Anyone living here who cooked a lot of meat would coat those pots with animal fat. Otherwise we don't care what our acquaintances eat. We try to be equal opportunity friends.)

The funny thing is, one of the few times we had to go away we managed to find housesitters who almost matched my imaginary advertisement—except for the part about the nun. Hooper and Hollie, newly married and living with Hooper's parents, welcomed the chance to be alone for the ten days we were going to be gone on our trip. Neither was experienced with a wood stove, but the two were so meticulous and well mannered that I had confidence they'd take no foolish chances. Only one goat was milking then, and Betsy gave Hooper and Hollie a crash course in goat husbandry. She also left them the phone numbers of several veterinarians and goat-knowledgeable people.

Hooper and Hollie were vegetarians and so squeaky clean, wholesome, and solicitous that they made me nervous. Being around them for more than ten minutes was like being trapped in an elevator with Donny and Marie Osmond. But the prospect of having them live in our house gave me peace of mind. They were respectful of other people's feelings and property. They weren't the types for wild parties. Besides, they were both members of a meditation group and their lives were firmly fixed to a routine of twice-daily sittings in a quest for calm, inner peace, and spiritual tranquility.

Just before we left on our trip, Hooper pulled me aside. "Where's the strongest part of your house?" he asked. I must have given him a blank look. It's not a question you get asked every day. "I mean, where is the *floor* the strongest?" he asked.

"Are you bringing over your barbells?" I asked.

"No, no," he said, looking like a furtive Pat Boone.

"You've got a pet hippo?"

"No," he said, "Hollie and I do some . . . uh . . . exercises . . . that are, well, uh sort of . . . strenuous . . . and the floor needs to be . . ."

X-rated pictures flashed through my nasty mind. Naw, they didn't seem the type. Hooper must have seen something flicker across my face and he lurched forward, his hands fluttering as though he could erase my thoughts.

"Oh, God, no! It's nothing like that! Wow, no, um, see . . . our meditation practice involves working toward some higher states leading toward . . . levitation." He stared hard at me, expecting a laugh. I didn't laugh. I was relieved. Better a couple of floating housesitters than the Marquis de Sade loosening my floorboards.

Besides, I'd already heard about some members of Hooper's meditation group pursuing this new direction, so I wasn't surprised. Levitation was supposed to be for the advanced students. They assumed a lotus position and bounced. The idea was to cultivate a serene mind while bouncing. If you got serene enough, you presumably bounced up and stayed there.

I knew then that we had the perfect housesitters. Anybody responsible enough to worry about the structural strength of my house would probably take good care of the rest of the place. But I did laugh about the scene later. Hooper and Hollie were so sweet and innocent. I could imagine them bouncing away on their mats, each encouraging the other:

"Gee, Honey, I think you stayed up a little longer that time."

"Gosh, I think I did!"

We went off on our trip, calling Hooper and Hollie periodically, checking on their welfare, our animals, and home. I came away from one of those phone calls chuckling. "What's so funny?" asked Betsy.

"Oh," I said, "I guess Hooper and Hollie are making progress on their levitation."

"Did they say so?"

"No, but Hollie answered the phone, and when I asked to speak to Hooper, she said, 'He'll be down in a minute.'"

"You're awful," Betsy laughed.

She's right, of course. I have no business making fun of Hooper and Hollie. I'm sure some of the conversations and activities Betsy and I have appear just as ludicrous to other people as Hooper's and Hollie's bouncing does to us.

One evening I was sitting in the living room reading a magazine, when Betsy came in and sat next to me. She pressed her body close to mine and said, in a throaty voice, "I have something to tell you."

"Yes?" I looked into her soft brown eyes. "W-what is it?" She was so close I could feel her breath on my cheek. She slid her arm around my neck and held me closer.

"The potatoes," she said, "aren't mealy. They're really nice."

"Wonderful," I said. "Rural life is so lusty. Women in the city need negligees and perfume. All you need is a bushel of potatoes."

Betsy and I have been married for 14 years, and for the past decade our lives have principally revolved around the changing seasons and their differing demands, the garden, the animals, our children, and the work we do together. We talk about other things, about books and articles we've read, about the state of society, and how the neighborhood is going to hell. But what we have most in common, what we share intimately, is our life as homesteaders and the challenges it presents.

Marriage is hard enough, you might think, without throwing in the tension of snap frosts, steaming kitchen work, or sick livestock. But then, most relationships suffer because the partners are estranged, with few common interests. The classic pattern has always been for the man to go off to work, leaving the woman home to care for the children. She often resented his going "out into the world"; he resented her "easy life at home."

The demands of inflation and the social changes wrought by the women's liberation movement have altered this traditional pattern, however. Now both partners may be working, with the children in school or a day-care center. The typical American family gets together in the evening at dinner or in front of the TV set.

Betsy and I lived like this when we first got married. Our dissatisfaction with the arrangement probably helped lay the groundwork for the way we live now. Betsy was working as a schoolteacher, commuting 25 miles from the city to a semirural area, to a school, ironically, only ten minutes from where we now live.

I was working at a radio station on the 5:00 A.M. to 2:00 P.M. shift. I got home at 3:00 or or 3:30 P.M. Betsy got home at 5:00 P.M. or later. Many times she had to stay late after school to meet with parents or to help students. I had to go to sleep by 7:30 P.M. so I could be on my way to work by 4:30 A.M. If Betsy got home on time we'd have about two hours together before my bedtime.

We were used to spending a lot of time together, as we had in college, so we had trouble adapting to this routine. Of course, there were weekends. And vacations. But we thought the arrangement was terrible. An older friend laughed when we complained. "Welcome," he said, "to the *real* world." Betsy and I have never been good at adjusting to "the way it's supposed to be." All we saw ahead was a lifetime of commuting and waving to each other as we passed. It frightened us to hear older friends and relatives talking about how they'd really have time for this or that once they retired.

I solved part of the problem rather rapidly by quitting the radio station job. The hours were bad enough, but I was also weary of electronic journalism—writing six newscasts a day, all of them cloned from predigested wire copy.

The next job I got, all I could get right away, was a temporary job installing speaker wires in a new university music building. The pay was only $2 an hour, but it beat waiting in line to collect unemployment checks. Besides, I worked alone, unhassled. The work was clear-cut. The wires went in one pipe and came out the other end.

I didn't have to worry about upward mobility, fulfilling my career potential, office politics, or making more money. The salary was fixed and the job was over when the work was done. All I had to worry about was getting another job once the wiring was finished.

I wired very slowly.

Most of all, I enjoyed the rich joke I'd played on myself. Here I am, I thought, a $2-an-hour unskilled laborer with a master's degree in communication, stringing wires through pipes at my alma mater. Wouldn't they love *that* for the alumni magazine!

The change of jobs gave Betsy and me more time together, but we were still on different errands all day, earning our respective paychecks but little else. We found ourselves thinking more and more about what our relationship should be, and about what we should be doing with our lives.

We began getting some answers to those questions only after we left the city several years later. By then, Betsy had left teaching for her first love, training horses. I had gone from the speaker-wire job to another electronic journalism job, a more meaningful one in public radio, and from there to being a college English professor.

Teaching freed me from a strict nine-to-five schedule, allowed me to continue my own education, and gave me the chance to do a lot of work at home—grading papers, doing research, and planning lessons. The academic life also gave Betsy and me the time together to begin our first steps in homesteading.

I left teaching five years later for the glamorous life of a free-lance writer, becoming in effect, self-unemployed. So we came full circle. We went in ten years from being commuters, seeing each other at breakfast and dinner, to being together full time, at home. Add to this the tension of raising children, our lack of vacations or "free" time, and the pressure of unrelenting do-it-yourself homesteading chores, and you might think we'd wish for the good old days of automatic paychecks and the simplicity of urban living.

Never.

Well, almost never. Free-lance writing being what it is, a regular paycheck would be a compensation devoutly to be wished. And I know there are times when Betsy would be happy to have me gone for the day, or to have herself gone, free of the children and the endless chores. I've been told, in fact, that the way we live would destroy some marriages. "I can't stand to have him around since he retired," I've heard a lot of women say of their mates. And "I can't stand being home all the time," is something I've heard both men and women say.

But even after a decade of home-centeredness, Betsy and I still like working together. We're helped, I'm sure, by the fact that neither of us has any overwhelming or unrealistic ambitions. Both of us would simply like to get better at doing what we're doing. That helps keep us on an even keel, so that neither of us is chafing at the bit.

Not that there aren't tensions in our lives or occasional shouting matches, tears, accusations, and slammed doors. But we cool off. We apologize. We discuss what went wrong. And we remain friends.

One of the hardest times we have comes every year when we must struggle with putting up our garden produce in the awful heat of a

Washington summer. Betsy and I get short fuses when the temperature goes much over 75 degrees F. A lot of sniping and grumping and not-so-muffled cursing goes on at canning time.

But at least we know *why* we're angry. And, having endured the heat and mess and anger and overflowing tomatoes, we can embrace at the end of the task like sailors who have weathered a storm on the North Atlantic. Homesteading experiences can help or hurt a relationship. If there's a weakness, the demands of self-reliance will seek it out, inflame it, and create havoc. Or the work may pull a couple together, giving them a common challenge and a sense of unity.

We share the work wherever we can, but we're not afraid to make a division of labor. I split more wood than Betsy because I'm handier with a splitting maul. Betsy handles the goats because she has an affinity for animals that I lack. I manage the planning and organization of the garden, but we both work at seeding, harvesting, and cultivation.

I do most of the household repairs. Betsy, like most women, was, as a child, denied access to tools and handyman (handyperson?) skills. She doesn't have the feel for tools that you develop by being around them all your life. But she's making up for lost time. I remember when we first started heating with wood. She wanted to help with the splitting but she couldn't handle the 8-pound splitting maul. "Why not?" I asked. "Any woman who can load 40-pound bales of hay onto a pickup can lift an 8-pound maul."

I showed her how to handle the maul and she practiced every day. Within a week she was splitting wood by the hour and loving every minute of it. Maybe the couple that splits together sticks together?

Betsy does all the cooking and baking. Not only is she better at this than I could ever be—I wasn't around the kitchen for the same reason she wasn't around a workshop—but she really enjoys cooking. She makes everything from scratch, with fresh ingredients, no convenience foods. Thank goodness we never eat TV dinners, frozen entrées, or canned glop. That has surely helped our relationship endure.

With so much close contact, we have to respect each other's differences. Little things can get to you when everybody is home together all the time. I, for example, tend to be an accumulator. I can't bear to throw anything away. Books, magazines, clippings from magazines and newspapers, letters from friends, even direct mail advertisements promising "$100,000 *a day for life!*" I save it all. It might come in handy.

Betsy is the opposite. She hates clutter. She is a stacker. Sweeping through the house at unpredictable intervals, she gathers up everything indiscriminately—unpaid bills, children's books, my precious odds and ends, coats, shoes, hats, and gloves—and redistributes it or stacks it in neat piles. "I can't find *anything!*" I yell.

"It's all right there in that pile!" she yells back. "And be careful it doesn't fall over and bury you alive!"

This has been a running battle since we met. Once, when we were in college, Betsy and I were sitting in the living room of my apartment. While we were talking, a huge ball of dust escaped from under the couch and slowly rolled across the floor.

"What's *that?*" she shrieked.

"A pet dust ball," I said. "Don't worry, it's friendly."

"A *dust ball?*"

"I'm kidding, really. It's a tumblin' tumbleweed. Part of our American heritage . . ."

"Don't you ever *vacuum* this place?"

"Once a month, whether it needs it or not. Constant vacuuming weakens the blood."

"Well, I'm going to vacuum right now!"

"What? Why?"

"Because this place is *dirty.*"

"It's *dusty.* Dust never hurt anybody."

"Dust is dirt!"

"Dust is dirt? Dust is *dust!*"

"You'll make a great funeral director. Now where's the vacuum?"

"I won't have you vacuuming my apartment. You're not my mother."

"I can't have a relationship with a man who keeps pet dust."

"Love me, love my dust."

"Where's the vacuum? You do have one, don't you?"

"Nature abhors a vacuum and so do I."

So it went. But what more could I expect from a woman with Betsy's background? She comes from a long line of women for whom cleanliness *is* godliness. "She keeps a clean house," is their greatest compliment. And they said that about a woman who shot her husband at breakfast. (She put down newspapers first.)

I remember when most of Betsy's family was in town for a wedding. They all dropped by for a visit with us before the ceremony. Suddenly, I saw Betsy's grandmother disappear into our hallway. I followed and found her on her knees on the stairs. She was rubbing away at the carpeting with a fragment of tissue. "What are you doing?" I asked.

"Dirt," she said, dabbing at the carpeting with a saliva-moistened tissue. (That's another of life's mysteries. How is it grandmothers will dab furiously at the "dirt" on a child's face, leaving great welts where they've abraded the child's skin, all the while inveighing against demon dirt while they scrub away with a spit-soaked tissue?)

I knew better than to argue. The rest of the family was in the living room enjoying coffee and cake, while Grandma was attacking dirt particles only an electron microscope could pick out. This is her mission in life, I guess. She only has vision in one eye, but she can spot dirt at 40 paces. She is to dirt what Joe McCarthy was to commies. Are you now or have you ever been dirt? Grandma will rub you out.

We have made progress, each in his or her own way. I try to confine my hummocks of clips and notes to my office, the upstairs bedroom, and Betsy has stopped trying to make our home look like a layout in *House Beautiful.* Even her family has recognized the change in her. A beloved aunt gave her the kiss of death over the telephone, saying, in passing, "Well, Dear, we all know you're not a very good housekeeper."

"What!" I shouted when Betsy relayed the comment. "They dare say that to you, a woman who can put up 50 quarts of tomatoes in one day, split wood, care for two children, run five miles, cook dinner for four, and live with a crazy writer?"

"I think she means I don't take care to vacuum my rugs in the same direction. It screws up the nap."

"Does your aunt dust the telephone the way you used to do?" Betsy really used to do that, used to run the twisted corner of a rag into each little hole in the dial, reaming them clean. "Cleaning out Mother Bell's orifices," was my unkind way of describing it.

How much nicer to live in a relaxed house. I don't think you can be a homesteader and maintain an overwhelming concern about honest dirt. I don't mean you have to have a messy kitchen or a bathroom the health department would board up. But what with tracking in mud and compost from the garden or hauling in several armloads of firewood, not to mention the mess children can make, you'd do better to keep in mind an old adage: a house should be clean enough to be sanitary and messy enough to be comfortable.

Hear that, Grandma?

I like to work side by side with Besty, especially when we're outdoors and there's a breeze kicking up with the smell of rain in the air. Unless we're hauling in hay. Then I could do without the rain, thank you. We haul in our winter hay supply in late summer. All of us, the children included, pile in the pickup and head for an up-county hay field. We drive through the shrinking countryside, noting with every passing year how the new housing developments and shopping centers keep spreading out. How long will it be before the hay field is no more, is only a memory shared by older residents?

The bales are neatly lined up all over the field where the baler has dropped them. We pull the truck up into one row and begin piling the bales on. We've been doing this for years, ever since we got involved with dairy goats, but our enjoyment of loading hay has yet to fade. There is something fresh and invigorating about hauling in the hay, though not, I suppose, if you have to do it for a living. But I remember saying that to one man who did do it for a living. "Hell," he said, "beats working indoors."

We mark our growth as homesteaders by work like this. When we first started all we could get on a truck was 25 or 30 bales. In time we learned the art of stacking hay, how to interlock the bales on the truck-bed like a giant jigsaw puzzle, each bale tying another in place by friction. Now we load up to 50 bales on the truck, without sides to support the load. Funny how a little thing like that can make you burst with pride.

This is hard, dusty work. The binder twine cuts into your hands even when you wear gloves. If the farmer is baling with wire, the job is less pleasant. Binder twine is always helpful around a place. We always have huge rolls or piles of it hanging from a nail in the goat shed. We use it through the year for tying packages or stringing-up plants in the garden. But baling wire, while it ought to be good for something, is springy and sharp-pointed, a danger to hands and eyes.

After we load the hay, we drive home and unload it, shoe-horning 200 bales into our little storage barn. By the day's end we're weary from the driving, tired and dirty; and our mouths are parched from the dust. Hayseeds and bits of stalk cover all of us and blow into the truck windows as we roll along.

When the last bale is unloaded and stuffed into place in the barn, we always stand there for a moment, letting the full sense of accomplishment sink in. That feeling is special, though it's the same whether we're loading hay or hauling in firewood or harvesting the last of the potatoes. Sometimes I look over at Betsy at the end of a day like this, loading hay, the sun setting in a blaze of red and gold, and I marvel at my partner. Her forearms are streaked with dust and sweat, her hair is flecked with hayseeds. "Lord," I say, "you're a handsome woman."

Cue the violins.

At the best of times, homesteading—whether it's in the suburbs or the back end of nowhere—gives a man and woman the chance to really *work* together, toward concrete goals, to share triumphs and disasters in a way modern society usually denies us. I know in our case working together has cemented our relationship in a way no amount of conversation or socializing could have done. The work has equalized us, yet reinforced our individuality. Betsy and I have become cooperators and cohesive.

But lest I wax too poetic about this, let's have no illusions. There's a delicate balance between work and what can begin to feel like slave labor. Tedium can stalk a homestead the way a fox lurks outside a chicken coop. The constant attention to chores and details can wear you to a nub. Tempers flare, as they must, but without a chance to calm down, to cool off, the anger may be turned into a sharp edge that cuts too many cords.

One key is knowing when to quit, knowing when you're beat, when you're in too deep. Honest work balanced by rest may give you a sense of pride, but there's another kind of pride to watch out for. This is the willful, stubborn pride that makes a man refuse to call a plumber when the water is rising over the lip of his toolbox. "I can fix it!" he screams as one of his children floats by. Stupid pride can make a woman tear a ligament or pop a disc trying to lift a sack of feed too heavy for her frame. City people who rush off to the country looking for the good life are most susceptible to this kind of thing. They're trying to make up for lost time, I guess.

Another key to harmony is knowing what you know and what you don't know. Unless you've grown up on a farm, the details of homesteading can swamp you. Two people swamped just drag each other and the whole project down. The first winter comes and you run out of wood, then out of food, then out of money, and finally out of patience. It's hard to exchange loving glances when the world is crumbling down around your ankles. Homesteading, Betsy and I have learned the hard way, contains an essential truth: don't ever expect to finish anything; just know when it's time to quit.

Homesteading has an effect on children too. Even at their ages, Noah and Rachel realize that we're living differently from most other people they meet. Once, after a day of loading hay, Noah clapped his hands and exulted, "Wow! What fun! We jumped all over the hay bales and ran around the pasture and Rachel fell off the back of the truck—we're just like real farm kids!"

But they're *not* farm kids. That's an important point about homesteading. Commercial farming isn't an easy way to make a living and "real farm kids" are often subjected to a wearying round of chores and responsibilities. Some go into farming themselves, but a lot more see the toll it takes from their parents and they leave, looking for a better life.

So what about the children of homesteaders? Will they head for urban areas, turning their backs on their parents' notions of the simple life? Perhaps. Friends tease us about that, saying that it would be poetic justice if Noah and Rachel ended up living in the city, loving the urban life. They may choose that, but it won't be because they have memories of hardscrabble farming. They know that Betsy and I live as we do by choice, because the alternative—normal urban or suburban life—doesn't fulfill us. And I think Noah and Rachel realize that they have something special. There is a directness to their lives.

They *see* where their food comes from. They *see* animals being born or dying. They *see* their parents working to meet the family's basic needs. And, as they've matured, they've been invited to work along with us. We'd like them to have the knowledge that we've gained, to understand that certain kinds of fundamental labors fit into the rhythm of the seasons, that you can work for something more important than cash, and that caring for yourself can increase your awareness of other people's needs.

I am not glorifying hard labor. There are millions of children around the world who have no choice but to gather firewood and water and bend double all day working in the fields—if there are even fields to work in. A lot of these children will never remember much good about childhood.

But affluence carries its own curse. Suburban and urban children in the United States are typically isolated from the sources of their food, heat, water, clothing, and shelter. Like everything appears on their primary source of entertainment, the TV, "things" just appear, their origins unknown.

We have had children visit us who wouldn't eat Betsy's homemade bread. Too coarse and brown. And unsliced! They were used to cottony white bread. They wouldn't drink the milk we offered because it didn't come out of a carton. It came out of—gasp!—a goat's *body*. And they wouldn't eat the vegetables because they "looked funny" and didn't come out of a can or carton.

I'm not condemning them for their attitudes. They're only children and what they do is largely the result of what they've learned from adults. But how sad it is to see children turning up their noses at the real, the handmade, and the natural, preferring the artificial and accepting it as normal.

Seeing modern children scorn our food reminds me of an article I read some years ago about the growing influence of food technology on our perceptions of reality. The day was coming, said a spokesman for the food industry, when the American public would actually prefer things like "genuine imitation strawberry flavor" to real strawberries. The chemical feast—"more strawberry than strawberries"—would become the standard while the real fruit would become an oddity.

So whether Rachel and Noah eventually wind up living in the city, suburb, or countryside as adults will be up to them. But no matter what they do or where they go, Betsy and I will have one small satisfaction: our children will know what real strawberries taste like.

I like to watch Rachel and Betsy together. Rachel works with Betsy outdoors, splitting wood and feeding the goats. She works with me, too, in the garden; she holds the nails when I'm building something, and asks a million questions. We got a good idea of how this affected Rachel's values (she's four, as I write this) during Christmas 1979, when an aunt sent her some money. She was to buy whatever she wanted. Betsy took both children to a huge toy store and turned them loose. Noah picked out a Star Wars toy. That took a half hour of agonizing. But Rachel picked out what she wanted in a second.

"Are you *sure* this is what you want?" Betsy asked.

"Yes, yes!" she squealed in excitement.

She chose a toy chain saw.

"Just like Daddy's!" she yelled.

And last year, in the spring, Rachel got a box of hand-me-downs. She had a wonderful time trying on the various garments, but one item particularly caught her fancy. This was a long dress, all frilly and lacey, with many bows and ribbons. "My," said Betsy as Rachel primped in front of her mirror, "you look like a princess."

"Yes, I do," said Rachel. "And look, Momma—" she tucked her thumb into a tuck of blue ribbon at her waist, "—it even has a place to put my hammer!"

Noah's taste in activities is almost as eclectic, though he is more subject to peer pressure from his friends at school. His big passion, since he was four (he's now seven), has been space travel, Star Wars, rockets, and satellites. The enthusiasm is fueled not by television, since we don't have one, but by his fertile imagination and by the books we get out of the library.

Yet that same Christmas a friend gave Noah a poinsettia. I didn't think it would get much reaction from him, but he was thrilled. "Look what I got from Susie Duckett!" he said. And five minutes later I heard him talking to the plant. He'd named it "Planto," and was chatting to it with the same devotion he usually reserved for Artoo Detoo.

Obviously, our way of living and interacting with the children demands that we spend a lot of time with them. This is hard work in itself, as any parent knows, and I don't think it makes homesteading chores any easier. Nor do I think, no matter how much pleasure we get from our children, that a homestead is incomplete without children.

I think, in fact, that if self-reliance and self-sufficiency are all-consuming goals for you, a childless homestead might be best. Helen and Scott Nearing, the spark plugs of the American homesteading movement, chose this path, believing that the world was already overpopulated and that they'd be just as happy pursuing their own ends without the responsibilities of parenthood.

We enjoy our children. Their presence often enhances our efforts. Everything from gardening to building a new fence is made more vivid by their innocence and curiosity. And, conversely, everything is also made more difficult. Betsy and I were relieved when we passed beyond the stage of having a cranky toddler under foot at the height of canning season. Even now, it's hard having the children to contend with when a particular task demands our undivided attention.

"Whatcha doing, Daddy?"

"Huh? Oh, I'm trying to get this tiller to work."

"What's wrong with it?"

"I wish I knew."

"Can you read a book to me?"

"Now? I just told you I'm trying to fix . . ."

"It's a short book."

"Look, I can't stop and . . ." At this point I catch my finger between a spring and a hot place. I respond with some choice words.

"Gee, Daddy, those are *all* the words you told me not to say. I didn't know you could make a whole sentence out of them."

No matter how I limn these pages with joy, it isn't all sunshine. There's plenty of screaming and explosive anger. Sometimes I wish Noah and Rachel were transistorized so I could switch them off or at least look forward to when their batteries ran down. Having children is like having a good garden. The joy comes mixed with equal parts of disaster and hard work.

I like Betsy's attitude toward child-rearing. "It's a job," she says, "a horrible, thankless, happy, satisfying job. And like any job, it has a beginning and an end." You work at the job steadily until it's completed, then you and your children go on to new challenges. It sounds so terribly simple on paper, doesn't it?

Homesteading binds us together, a single unit of adults and children with all the tasks the seasons demand. We are bound, as a family, by love, continual learning, and the tangible rewards that come from self-reliance. No doubt it would be easier to homestead without children, but, at the best of times, it wouldn't be as much fun.

There is another element in our family life—or perhaps I should say there is something missing from our family life: we threw out our television set. I don't mean that we put it in a closet and take it out occasionally to watch "the good shows." We got rid of it. I've written throughout this book of our attempts to simplify our lives, to live more directly, but getting rid of "the idiot's lantern," as Frank Lloyd Wright dubbed it, was the best of all we've done.

To be fair, I should explain that my enthusiasm for a TV-free life is akin to the evangelistic fervor of a reformed drunk attacking the happy hour. I was, in fact, a videoholic.

My parents didn't get a TV until I was eight or nine, so I was spared the wall-to-wall TV viewing today's children are subjected to. Besides, my childhood coincided with television's infancy, a time when there just wasn't that much to watch. In the late 1940's, TV stations didn't even sign on until late afternoon or early evening. Beyond a few wonderfully unpretentious (but memorable) programs like "Lucky Pup," "Cecil and Beany," "Howdy Doody," "Kukla, Fran and Ollie," and later, "Mr. I. Magination," there wasn't a lot to entrap children. And there was no such things as "children's advertising," Everybody knew in those days that kids didn't buy anything.

But as TV's programming increased, so did my viewing. By the time I left college in the sixties, I was a fully addicted vidiot. Various studies say Americans watch an average of six hours of TV daily, a figure I exceeded regularly. Not that it's hard to do, either. I'd turn the set on at 6:00 P.M. to watch the news and turn it off at 1:00 A.M. That's seven hours right there. Thank goodness I never got hooked on soaps, game shows, or sports. Otherwise I'd probably still be in front of the set.

Why did I watch so much TV? Because it's easy. The path of least resistance is to turn on the tube and turn off your brain. I made escuses for my behavior just as any addict does. I said it relaxed me, that it eased my tension after a long, hard day (did I really say that with a straight face?), that as a writer and broadcaster and student of popular culture, it was crucial for me to watch TV to stay in touch with the mainstream of . . . but the truth is, it was easy.

I tried to limit my viewing by all the classic methods. I tried marking down only the *good* shows in the TV schedule. "We'll watch these *only,*" I said to Betsy. She was very supportive but her viewing habits were only slightly better than mine. She complained about "all the crap on TV," but she watched her share with me. Many summer nights we'd finish our chores in the garden and come in to collapse in front of the set. "Too tired to do anything else," we said in harmony. We watched just as much in winter, too, using the excuse that we'd "earned a long winter's rest." Watching TV is resting?

Restricting our viewing to only the so-called good shows worked wonderfully. For one week. You know how it goes, don't you? I started out with the best of intentions, watching the opera, a PBS documentary on the Common Market, a Jacques Cousteau special on sea anemones, "Wall Street Week in Review," "60 Minutes," and "M.A.S.H.")

Then while I was twisting the channel selector—innocently on my way to a documentary about gold leaf restoration—I just happened to pause between clicks. "Laverne and Shirley" was on. Ridiculous program. Why was it so popular? I wondered. I'll just watch a few seconds . . . just . . . to see . . . what . . . it's . . . all . . . umm.

Now I know what happens when an alcoholic finds the cooking sherry. "Laverne and Shirley" blended into reruns of "The Munsters," then came "Hogan's Heroes," "Gomer Pyle," and *Casablanca* for the fifth time. (Old movies are the best thing on TV anyway, I congratulated myself.) Before I realized it, in a single evening, I had slipped into the gutter again. Suddenly it was past midnight and I was sitting there watching Johnny Carson ask Zsa Zsa Gabor what she thought about the problem of nuclear proliferation and damned if I wasn't interested in her answer!

Shaken by my fall off the wagon, I tried immediate withdrawal. Put the TV in the closet. Amazing. I lasted six months with no slippage and no side effects. Well, I did suffer from bouts of desperation, anxiety, despair, and loneliness, but only during prime time. I kept reading the TV guide but only to keep up with what the rest of society was looking at. Then I noticed PBS was having a festival of great films. "It's only once a week," I told Betsy. "We'll only watch *this* and nothing else. Really."

Pandora would have understood.

It was Betsy, strong willed as ever, who actually weaned herself first. She could walk out of the room while the set was on and go into another room to read a book. I accused her of doing it to shame me. "I'm going to turn this off in a minute," I'd call out to her as she disappeared down the hall. "I just want to see what happens when. . . . umm . . . when. . . . "

The next thing I knew it was 2:00 A.M. and I was watching "The Mount Bethel Born Again True Light Telethon," live-on-tape from Hopewell, Virginia, with Rev. R. B. Fitzkee ("Buzzy") Wilmot and Family. I'm going to turn this thing off in a minute, I told myself.

It took a bolt of lightning to release me. (Hear that, Rev. Buzzy?)

Well, it was actually a combination of lightning and Noah. We restricted Noah to safe programs—"Sesame Street" and "Mr. Rogers"—but neither Betsy nor I liked the effect TV had on him. He sat there like a little zombie, glassy eyed, slack jawed, glued to the tube. Like father, like son.

"Sesame Street," the propaganda went, was reinforcing our good work in teaching Noah to read and cipher. If anything needed reinforcing, though, it was our bank account. "Sesame Street" was a growth industry.

Every supermarket, drugstore, and dry cleaner seemed to have a rack of "Sesame Street" toys, T-shirts, cups, bowls, records, books, decals, underwear, sheets, pillowcases, wristwatches, and figurines. Kermit the Frog, like an amphibian Big Brother, stared out from wall posters everywhere, smiling warmly as Mom and Dad slapped down another few bucks here and there for Big Bird Coloring Books, Oscar the Grouch Nontoxic Crayons, and Mr. Hooper Bi-Lingual Jigsaw Puzzles.

And the program was actually encouraging children to *watch* TV, to accept it, to wallow in it. Noah was already coming home from friends' houses filled with ideas and concepts he'd picked up watching other kid-vid. What were we supposed to do, say "You can't watch television at Jason's house"?

Noah wasn't watching "shows," he was watching *television.* To a child, it's all one big show. The danger signs were already there. "I saw this really neat toy abbertised on TV," he told me. "It's called 'batteries-notincluded'."

As a tube-nik who didn't want his kids hooked, but who also didn't want to give up his own addiction, I put off making a decision. I handled life like a TV set. I changed channels. I didn't want to see us becoming a household where meals were scheduled around program times, eating was done in front of the set, and people avoided going out on certain nights so as not to miss a favorite show, and shushed each other lest they miss any dialogue. A family can end up alone together in the same room, watching, watching, and waiting. No interaction between them, nothing creative, not even any thinking going on. Just watching.

My salvation came a few weeks later. I was watching something of great intellectual value one summer evening—"Baretta," perhaps, or "Hawaii Five-O" ("A psycho is killing prostitutes in Kona, Chief!")—when a thunderstorm blew up. A clap of thunder boomed over the house and a lightning bolt cracked close outside like a rifle shot. The lights flashed brightly, then dimmed and flickered. The TV screen went dark.

I sat there, dumbly, watching the little white dot fading away like a scream. Betsy came down the hall. "What happened?" she asked. "Lightning," I said. "Power surge blew the set out."

"Can it be repaired?"

"I guess. I don't know. Maybe . . . we should just let it rest in peace."

"Cold turkey again?"

"Well," I said, "it took a lightning bolt to wake Saint Paul up."

"That's what I love about you," Betsy said, "your humbleness."

I did it.

I broke the habit once and for all. I became a nonviewer. Why did I succeed when I had failed so many times before? Intimations of mortality, maybe. It finally dawned on me that my life was passing by, measured out not in teacups but in program segments, in little chunks of time that fit neatly between commercials. I was, like so many people, *killing* time. And it was *my* time. Prime time.

What was I looking for, staring into that phosphorescing tube every night? I, who fancied myself a homesteader, a nonconformist, a man who'd simplified his life, who practiced ecology on a human level, an intellectual who taught Thoreau and Goethe to English students, had been sitting for 30 years waiting and watching for . . . what?

What in heaven's name did I have to show for the 65,700 hours I figured I'd spent in front of a TV set? The lightning bolt was an exclamation point!

Four years without television have passed. Do we ever miss it? Not really. I still get a pang for an old movie from time to time, but that's missing *movies,* not TV itself. I watch it when I'm traveling, trapped in a motel room. I watch it if I'm a houseguest somewhere, politely doing whatever my hosts do. But no, I don't watch at friends' houses. I'm cured, Doctor, really cured.

Do I sound like a snob? Fine. If you want to join me, take this test. Keep a monthly diary of every single TV program you watch. Write down the name of the program, the time elapsed, a synopsis of the content, and then—most importantly—write a brief description of *what you got out of the hour or more you spent viewing.* At the end of the month, read back, out loud, if you dare, your notes.

"But what do you do if you don't watch TV?" I've been asked. What a plaintive question, I think. We read. We talk. We go to bed earlier. We read to or play with Noah and Rachel, and work on various projects. Sometimes it seems we don't do anything. But we do it together, as a family. We pursue individual interests. Noah likes to draw. Rachel likes to look through books. Betsy attends to her spinning or weaving. I disappear into the workshop. A television set would be an intruder.

"But you miss so many good shows," I've been told. How is that "good" defined? A lot of the "good" on TV is good only in comparison to what else is on. TV sets it own standards, defining itself as it defines the world.

I have this recurring dream. I see archaeologists 10,000 years in the future. They are sifting through the dust of what was our civilization. "Who were these people?" they wonder. "What did they believe?" They can come to only one conclusion about America: "These people," they will say, "saw a lot of good shows."

We don't see the Super Bowl, the Academy Awards, the blockbuster movies that were playing in neighborhood theaters last year, the PBS specials, the documentaries. We never see the news, either, but we're hardly out of touch with The Real World. "But how do you manage without the news?" people ask. Just fine. TV news is little more than headlines with pictures. And local TV news is almost always an embarrassment.

The actual amount of verbal material transmitted in a one-hour news show, excluding the commercials, wouldn't fill half the columns on a single page of your newspaper, and since even a slow reader can get through a single page of newsprint in an hour, the truth is that an hour spent watching TV pays back in a lot of pictures and very little hard information.

Most of the issues that face us—inflation, energy, geopolitics—are not explainable in mere pictures. They can be dramatized with pictures, something TV is good at (generally to the point of distortion), but complex issues can only be illuminated by verbal material. Which means that if you're really interested in an issue or subject, you'd do better to read about it than to watch the subject explored on TV. (There are exceptions, of course, and one can argue that the best plan would be to see the TV pictures *and* read. That's great if you have the time.)

Cable TV, satellites, cassettes, and disc TV will surely create revolutionary changes in video programming and viewing habits. The revolution may actually kill the networks, freeing individual viewers to pick from a wide variety of commercial-free instructional programs and entertainment packages. How would I feel about having a TV if I could watch *only* a quality production that interested me? Would I then have a "home entertainment center"?

I doubt it. Maybe it has something to do with my having just turned 40, but life seems too short and too precious to spend it being a spectator. If it means not reading to the children or reading to myself or talking to Betsy or working with my hands when I have the chance—it wouldn't be worth it.

I think even Noah, who complains, in predictable cycles, about our lack of TV (usually after viewing at a friend's house), understands that to have a TV would mean a profound change in our family life and his relationship with us.

I remember once when we were having a particularly difficult time with Noah's behavior. He was being horrible, though normal for a five-year-old. Finally, sick of his refusal to listen to anything we said, and tired of making useless threats and meting out punishment, I put him in Coventry.

"Since you won't listen to me or your Mom," I told him, "I won't listen to what *you* have to say anymore." For the next three days I refused to pay any attention to him at all. I spoke to him only if absolutely necessary, ignored him otherwise, and pretended he didn't exist. I gave no hugs or good night kisses.

Betsy carried on as usual, though. So drastic a treatment by both parents would have been too much punishment. But losing my attention alone made the point. The first day passed and Noah thought it was a novelty, his Dad remaining silent. The second day passed and it started to hurt, seeing me read to Rachel only, behind a closed door so he couldn't hear the story. By the third day he was in tears. Then I took him by the hand and we went into his room and sat on the bed and had a long talk about respect for other people and what it feels like to be ignored. I held him in my arms for a long time as we talked.

Now what if watching television was a regular routine in our lives? I probably would have reacted to his bad behavior by cutting off his viewing time, restricting him or barring him from seeing his favorite programs. That would have shifted the focus, however, from Noah's behavior to *my* behavior. Or, if I hadn't reacted by withdrawing the TV, if I had allowed him to go on watching, then he would have channeled his frustration about my not talking to him into TV viewing. In either case, the presence of a TV as part of the family would have robbed us of an opportunity to learn something about living together.

Writer Phyllis Theroux, in telling of her own decision to junk the TV, made an incisive observation on what regular television viewing does to a family. "How will we be remembered by our children?" she asks. "What memories will they have of day-to-day family life centered around TV viewing?"

Ms. Theroux continued:

> Will these passive moments be the sum total of a family scrapbook? It is a real possibility. Those silent evenings when everyone curled up and watched TV show after TV show will gather themselves together into a large, formless time chunk and when we try to recall how it was, we won't be able to remember a thing.

Nathan Major sold his farm last year. He was kind enough to stop at our house the day he signed the contract. "I know how much the land means to you," he said, "and I wanted to tell you about the sale myself." We were touched that he came to break the news, but we weren't surprised or shocked that he'd finally sold his land.

"Nathan," Betsy said, "we've been fortunate you held on to the farm as long as you did."

"Well," he said, "all the old places are being cut up now. Mine was one of the last, wasn't it? Anyway, I've bought another farm up-county. Why don't you come out and see it this weekend?"

We said we would. Nathan sat down and had a cup of coffee and a slice of Betsy's apple cake. Hell, I thought, Nathan could have waltzed in and announced the sale of his grandmother and we'd still all be friends. But it hurt, thinking of the farm being sold to a developer.

"When will they start building houses?" I asked.

"I don't know," he said. "Six months. Maybe next year."

"Two-acre lots?"

"Yes. They'll put up $300,000 houses, big lawns, tennis courts—all the things you love, Vic," he chuckled. "That's what people moving out here seem to want."

"Beverly Hills East," I snorted.

"Now, now," Nathan laughed, "that's your 'last-one-in' mentality speaking. You've got your little homestead and you don't want anyone else moving in to spoil things."

"Come on, Nathan," I said, "I wouldn't be upset if people wanted to move here to build sensible homesteads with vegetable gardens and orchards, or if they came to live *with* the land instead of *on* it, like feudal lords. But you see what kind of overblown housing is going up. It might as well be 1957 around here for all anyone seems to care about energy or land use or . . ."

"People have to live somewhere," Nathan said.

"But nobody says they have to live in *ugliness,*" I shot back, "or cut off from nature, or that good farmland has to be turned into manicured lawns." I ranted on for a while, but Nathan and I had been over the topic many times. Neither of us ever convinced the other. Nathan saw the area's rapid development as progress. I called it uncontrolled growth. He championed business. I condemned it as greed.

"Maybe the truth lies somewhere in between," I said.

"It usually does," Nathan said.

"Okay," I said, "then let's compromise and call what's happening to the land an example of uncontrolled progress and greedy business."

"Some compromise," Nathan laughed.

The other day I took a walk across what had been Nathan's farm. I saw nothing to laugh about. Even Nathan admitted that he hated to drive past the place, that it hurt to see what was happening. I read once that it's hard for a man to fully understand the meaning of rape—the violence, the shame, the helplessness of being abused and violated. But walking the land that day left me with some understanding of assault, at least on a symbolic level.

I watched the huge, blank-faced earth-moving machines gutting the meadows, ripping into them for roads and houses. I watched land I've walked over and loved for ten years torn into by people who knew it only as dirt to be rearranged. Every gouge taken out of a hillside was money in the bank, nothing more.

I watched the workers taming the springs. They laid culverts and forced the water to run into them. Too unmanageable, these springs. Too wild and free. Bottle them up. Put them underground and out of sight.

Once I shared the knowledge of these crystalline springs with Betsy and the children. Now I saw only muddy water sloshing through a concrete pipe.

Am I too harsh in my judgments? Am I, as Nathan says, an elitist? I know the developers and their employees aren't necessarily evil people. I'm sure they see their work as *progress.* They regard their transformation of the countryside as a good and important project, vital to the community. And I'm sure they see me as antigrowth. Another one of those "ecology nuts." But if evil doesn't loom here, ignorance surely does; ignorance of the land's value and of our links to the earth.

Standing there, I knew how the Indians must have felt, seeing the land they called their mother attacked. I saw wounds and scars everywhere; huge rents in the earth. The bulldozers moved with ferocious speed, rupturing the knolls and dells, overturning trees, scraping away the brushlines of honeysuckle and wild rose.

There, where the red clay spilled away from the cold edge of the bulldozer blade, was where Betsy and I walked in summer and winter. There, where another earth mover was leveling a hill, was where I hiked across an ice-blue meadow, snow devils whirling around me, their tiny chips skittering across the moonlit pasture.

I remembered how beautiful these hills were in early summer. The vivid green would shame a color slide. All the words we use to describe nature's beauty—lush, verdant, luxuriant—came to mind. Watching the horses strung out on the hillsides, cropping at the rich grass, I wanted to kneel down and eat those succulent greens myself, so delectable did the horses make the eating seem.

But the bulldozers ate everything. The lacerations they made quickly turned from red to yellow as the soil dried like clotting blood. The wind blew and the dust clouds twisted like tormented spirits, the spirits of the land, racing about in agony, looking for their scattered parts, wanting to be whole again.

I know there is a reason for all this. I know about change and real estate and that, as Nathan Major explained, people have to live somewhere. But I also know about planning and land-use and values that go beyond the considerations of profit and the fine lines on a zoning map.

Watching the machines scraping the topsoil away was like seeing the house where I was born being torn down. Helpful friends might stand with me, patting my shoulder and telling me about changing times. But I only knew that the rooms I'd lived in were being ripped open and turned into rubble.

The walls on which I'd seen faces as I fell asleep were being pushed over. The windows I'd pressed my tongue against in winter, or drawn pictures on in the moisture, were being shattered.

This was Nathan's farm. His investment. But it was also my shelter. Part of me was born or reborn here. I walked these fields as though they were the rooms of a large house. I looked through windows into other rooms and into worlds whose existence was a secret until the land called my name. I saw faces in those fields. I heard voices in whispers. I was told things.

Now, Betsy and I lie awake at night and talk of the spring rains and our potatoes and of the great blue heron who no longer comes to the pond. Perhaps it was frightened off by the surveyors who circled the pond one day and pounded wooden stakes into the ground, leaving them behind like dragon's teeth, a warning to intruders.

Or perhaps the heron heard what we hear all the time now—that ominous rumbling that vibrates in the earth itself: the deep breathing of bulldozers.

Postscript

AN OPEN LETTER TO STEVE McQUEEN:

Dear Steve:

Back in the fifties, you starred in a classic movie called *The Blob.* This science fiction delight, aimed at teenage audiences, showed us what happens when a thing from outer space—a protoplasmic lump of homicidal Silly Putty—lands in a small town.

The Blob oozes along, absorbing everything in its path, digesting all with hardly an urp! It grows larger with each new meal. Toward the end of the movie, having eaten an overweight policeman (who foolishly doubted The Blob's existence), a bespectacled schoolteacher, two local hoods and their customized '51 Ford convertible, and the town drunk, The Blob becomes, in earnest, THE BLOB!

Steve, we were on the edges of our chairs waiting for you to save that town. You did it, too! Forgive me, but I don't remember exactly how you did it, the sequence of the movie having been repressed with the rest of my adolescent memories. But you saved the town and maybe the world. That's why I'm writing.

Steve, The Blob is back!

It never really went away. It goes by another name now. It's even a respected member of the community and is welcomed by civic leaders, construction companies, real estate agents, and other pillars of society. Nobody believes me, Steve, but The Blob is out there! I can hear it snuffling and puckering, trying to ooze its way through the cracks of my life and my home.

They call it by its new name: SUBURBANIZATION. But I know what it really is.

THE BLOB!

Steve, this new incarnation is far deadlier than The Blob you fought. Yours ate a cheerleader or two, or maybe a pet dog. But this Blob swallows farmland, absorbs traditional values, digests whole families.

The Blob you knew ate and ate and never passed any waste. (Maybe that's why it was so mean, tortured by a case of cosmic constipation.) But this Blob leaves an awful mess behind it: fast-food joints; buildings that look like air conditioners; houses that not even the most architecturally inept of the Three Little Pigs would have built; vapid teenagers who can't put a coherent sentence together; blonde women with charm bracelets and capped teeth and rubber shoes from L. L. Bean; and grown men who wear acrylic jogging suits and running shoes all day long whether they jog or not.

Nobody's seen The Blob, that's true. It's gotten terribly crafty since you did battle with it. Now it strikes silently and so quickly that, like a scalpel cut, you never feel a thing. One day you drive past a section of woodland, a little glen with a trickling brook and mote-filled light filtering through a lattice of tree branches. The next day it's gone, gobbled by The Blob; a 7-11, a dry cleaners, a unisex hair emporium, and Nan-Lou's Craft Boutique left in its place.

The damned thing is, back in the 1950's when you kids were trying to wake the town up to the monster in their midst, nobody believed you. Dumb, crazy kids, they called you. Practical jokers. Been drinking Coke and aspirin again, they said.

Well, nothing's changed. People haven't learned a thing, though your movie has been shown on TV hundreds of times. The Blob is here right now, clearing off hillsides and leveling once-productive farms and sucking up streams and wildlife and leaving patios and hot tubs in their place.

That's what I mean, Steve. This Blob has gotten smart. Instead of the slimy path it left behind in your day, now it leaves ruts that look deceptively like bulldozer tracks. Or it leaves asphalt and driveways and sidewalks and shopping centers. Everybody accepts those as normal, so there's no outcry.

And the worst of it is, some people actually welcome the advance of The Blob. Progress, they call it: Growth and Prosperity and The Future. Has The Blob joined forces with The Body Snatchers? I'm meeting more and more pods these days, Steve.

In the old days, in the simpler times of the fifties, you finally convinced the Army to come in and blast The Blob. We can't do that now. Too many retired military and CIA men live in Potomac. And they don't believe in The Blob.

I guess there's no hope. The other day I met a woman who had moved "way out here" to have some open spaces and a garden. She was tired of the city's congestion and the old suburbs' tackiness, she said. She wanted a little country living, she said. "But the only thing I don't like," she said, "is that the nearest store is *three miles away.* I wish they'd build some stores closer. What we need is a little shopping center."

She didn't hear anything, Steve, but I did, right there on the spot.

I heard The Blob chuckling.

Yes. A low rumbling laugh that sent chills up my spine.

The Blob has gotten so crafty, Steve.

I don't think we can stop it anymore.

Bibliography

Here's a list of books we've found especially helpful over the years:

Bubel, Mike and Nancy. *Root Cellaring.*
Rodale Press, 1979

The best collection of material on the subject to date. Step-by-step directions and clear explanations for a variety of vegetable and fruit storage setups.

Bubel, Nancy. *The Seed-Starter's Handbook.*
Rodale Press, 1978

Filled with shortcuts, imaginative techniques, and useful data, this is a joy for the experienced or first-time gardener.

Gibbons, Euell. *Stalking the Wild Asparagus.*
David McKay, 1962

Still the best book for starting out as a forager. Gibbons leads us from one eating adventure to another like an old friend.

Green, Martin I. *A Sigh of Relief.*
Bantam, 1977

This is one we've never had to use, thank goodness, and we hope it will always stay on the shelf. But this "First Aid Handbook for Childhood Emergencies" is a must book for homesteaders. Or anyone else.

Hall, Walter. *Barnacle Parp's Chain Saw Guide.*
Rodale Press, 1977

Absolutely the best book on the subject, one that will help you keep all your kneecaps while you're buzzing away with the saw. I reread parts of this book every year before I go off to cut wood.

Jeavons, John. *How to Grow More Vegetables.*
Ten Speed Press, 1979

This gives detailed information on raised-bed vegetable production, including charts showing yield, spacing, soil analysis, and much more. Invaluable.

Katzen, Mollie. *Moosewood Cookbook.*
Ten Speed Press, 1977

The author doesn't tell us how to cook a moose, you'll be happy to know (the title comes from a restaurant), but does supply a treasure trove of vegetarian recipes, all imaginative and healthful.

London, Mel. *Bread Winners*.
Rodale Press, 1979

This is Betsy's favorite bread recipe book, a marvelous collection of edibles: everything from bagels and tortillas to sourdough and sprouted wheat bread.

Mackenzie, David. *Goat Husbandry*.
Transatlantic Arts, 1970

One of the best books on keeping goats, a solid text based on facts and experience. Not another "oh-aren't-goats-fun" book.

Nearing, Helen and Scott. *Living the Good Life*.
Shocken, 1970
———. *Continuing the Good Life*.
Shocken, 1979

The Nearings are the great-grandparents of the homesteading movement in the United States and their advice is sound, spare, and always to the point. I reread *Living the Good Life* regularly, taking it like a tonic to clear my suburbanized brain.

Ogden, Samuel R. *Step-by-Step to Organic Vegetable Growing*.
Rodale Press, 1971

This was one of the first books I turned to as a gardener and it's as valuable today as a decade ago. Nothing in here about raised beds, but plenty on sensible gardening techniques, compost making, and cultivation.

Pegler, H. S. Holmes. *The Book of the Goat*, 9th ed.
The Bazaar, Exchange and Mart, Ltd., 1965

You may have to search old bookstores and dairy supply houses for this British work, but the effort will be worth it.

Reader's Digest Complete Do-It-Yourself Manual.
Reader's Digest Association, 1973

Leaf through this one *before* pipes burst, sparks fly, and wood crumbles. A great introduction to all the things that can go wrong and how to put them right.

Rodale, J. I. and Staff. *How to Grow Fruits and Vegetables by the Organic Method*.
Rodale Press, 1961

Now in its umpteenth edition, this is the *magnum opus* for all organic gardeners. It was our first book on the subject and we use it still.

Seymour, John. *The Self Sufficient Gardener.*
Doubleday/Dolphin, 1978

A beautifully illustrated and well-written book that almost drags you into the garden. Seymour is witty, knowledgeable in the extreme, and eminently practical. He concentrates here on the raised-bed method but covers other homestead skills.

Shurtleff, William and Aoyagi, Abiko. *The Book of Tofu.*
Autumn Press, 1975
Ballantine, 1979 (revised edition)

A fascinating and thoroughly useful introduction to tofu making and cookery. The 1975 edition is the best, I think, covering every facet of tofu, including data on commercial production. The 1979 edition is slanted more toward home use of this marvelous food.

Thomas, Anna. *The Vegetarian Epicure.*
Vintage, 1972
———. *The Vegetarian Epicure, Book Two.*
Knopf, 1978

Her recipes are rich, sometimes exotic, and always delicious. Just the books to plunge into when company's coming—the folks who think vegetarians eat "bland food."

Thoreau, Henry David. *Walden.*

What list of books on simplifying your life (or making the attempt) would be complete without this classic? Just as a good organic garden deepens in time, so *Walden* gets richer with every reading. And so do we.

Vivian, John. *Wood Heat.*
Rodale Press, 1979

A thorough, detailed handbook on wood heat and safety.

Winn, Marie. *The Plug In Drug.*
Bantam, 1977

This may save you or your children from getting a fried brain, if you're still addicted to the boob tube. A scary, factual, carefully written and researched study of the effects of TV watching (not simply content) on children, particularly. Get rid of that "rotten box" (as Frank Zappa called it) and get out in the garden!